CONVERSATIONS WITH ANNE RICE

CONVERSATIONS WITH

ANNE RICE

Michael Riley

BALLANTINE BOOKS • NEW YORK

Grateful acknowledgment is made to
Simon & Schuster and A. P. Watt Ltd. for
permission to reprint an excerpt from "The Circus
Animals' Desertion" from THE POEMS OF W. B. YEATS:
A NEW EDITION edited by Richard J. Finneran. Copyright © 1940
by Macmillan Publishing Company, Renewed 1968 by Bertha
Georgie Yeats, Michael Butler Yeats, and Anne Yeats.
Reprinted by permission of Simon & Schuster and
A. P. Watt Limited, on behalf of Michael Yeats.

 Published
in the United States by Ballantine Books, a division of Random
House, Inc., New York, and simultaneously in Canada
by Random House of Canada Limited, Toronto.

Library of Congress Catalog Card Number: 96-96011

ISBN: 0-345-39636-7

Text design by Holly Johnson
Cover design by Carlos Beltran
Cover photograph by Neil Alexander

Manufactured in the United States of America

First Edition: April 1996

10 9 8 7 6 5 4 3 2 1

To the memory of my mother and father,
Eula Martin Riley and William Edward Riley

CONTENTS

Acknowledgments ix
Introduction xi
Chronology xv

Part One

1. "A great trust in the imagination" 5
2. "The big furious brainstorm . . . of writing" 37
3. "Roquelaure and Rampling" 69

Part Two

4. "Family voices" 111
5. "The savage garden" 143
6. "A place where Ezra Pound and Mickey Spillane touch" 168

Part Three

7. "Nobody's going to make this movie" 205
8. "The things I loved . . . the things I didn't" 233
9. "From teenagers to housewives to brain surgeons to manicurists to truck drivers" 260
10. "A quest for meaning" 279

ACKNOWLEDGMENTS

A number of people made contributions to this book that I want to acknowledge here. My primary debt, of course, is to Anne Rice for giving of herself so generously. Stan Rice bore the intrusions with patience and good humor. Karen O'Brien, Anne's sister, was always delightful company during my visits to New Orleans. On Anne's staff, Nancy Diamond, Sue Quiroz, and Linda Westfeldt handled a variety of arrangements, patiently gathered materials for me to review, and were wonderfully kind and attentive.

I am indebted to Bryan Bach, whose computer expertise and ingenuity were indispensable to the process of moving from audiotapes to transcripts, from one word processing program to another, and from an old computer to a new one. Barbara Laun Bart carefully transcribed the original tapes, and Polly Baker was extremely helpful in setting up the computer files. Katherine Ramsland generously transcribed the tapes of the final conversation.

I owe a special debt to my friend and colleague Langdon Elsbree, who first suggested a book based on these conversations. I also thank Mark Hassan for providing encouragement and support that made a great difference. So, too, I am grateful to the Dean of Faculty of Claremont McKenna College, Anthony Fucaloro, for providing time that made it possible for me to complete the manuscript on schedule.

I owe a special debt to my editor Clare Ferraro and to Nate Penn at Ballantine, who provided good advice and welcome support.

INTRODUCTION

On Saturday evening, October 14, 1961, I drove with the parents of my friend Stan Rice from Dallas, Texas, to the nearby college town of Denton to attend Stan's wedding to Anne O'Brien. I had never met Anne, who had been living in San Francisco, but I had heard Stan talk about her a great deal. I no longer remember just what impressions of Anne I'd formed in advance, but I do remember the moment we met. I remember being struck by how pretty she was and by her slightly shy and endearing smile. I liked her at once, but even so I couldn't have supposed that moment marked the beginning of one of the most rewarding friendships of my life.

Within a few months Stan and Anne had moved to San Francisco, where they were going to school and working, and a few months after that I moved to southern California to attend graduate school. Airfares were much cheaper in those days (only twenty-four dollars round-trip between Los Angeles and San Francisco!), so not long after my arrival I visited them in their apartment on Ashbury only a few yards from the intersection with Haight, which was to become so familiar a landmark just a few years later. Soon I was visiting regularly, and it was as if Anne and I had known each other for years. No matter what the interval between them, our conversations seemed continuous—always lively talks filled with the enthusiasm, the passionate commitments, the humor and intensity, the urgent engagement with life that define Anne to anyone who knows her.

We had been friends having such conversations for almost fifteen years when Anne's first novel, *Interview with the Vampire*, was published, and her life and Stan's were changed forever. In the years since then I've watched as she has become not simply a successful novelist but one of the most widely read and admired writers in contemporary American literature. I have many times seen Anne interviewed on television, profiled in magazines and newspapers, greeted by throngs at book signings. I've listened to people who have read her books talk about her with the kind of immediacy and familiarity typically reserved for those we know best. In an important sense, I have often thought, they do know Anne well, for her novels are deeply informed by her character and personality. To read them is indeed to have a kind of "conversation" with Anne. But of course there are other kinds of conversations too, and I've seen and heard for myself how many people there are who would like to talk to her.

I should confess that I've found it a curious experience seeing someone I've known so well for so long being embraced by crowds who claim a quite different but certainly potent intimacy. And so perhaps inevitably I have reflected on the relationship between my Anne and the public's. Gradually I've concluded that while the fascination with her is rooted in her work, it also goes beyond that to something in Anne herself, something that is both compellingly attractive and slightly mysterious, and it was with such thoughts in mind that I first spoke to her about taping the series of conversations on which this book is based. I knew quite simply how much fun she is to talk to, how interesting and thoughtful, how candid, how honest and even brave, and I knew that I had rarely if ever seen an interview or profile that I thought did justice to her. Too often the interviewer got in the way. Too often Anne's own voice had to contend with the journalist's impressions of her. Let her speak for herself, I thought. She's wonderfully good at it. And so on four occasions—three spread over a week in late August 1993 and a fourth in early January 1995—we sat in a sun-filled room looking out on the garden of her beautiful Greek Revival house in New Orleans's Garden District and talked as we had so many times before.

If these occasions were necessarily more self-conscious than our usual encounters, I nevertheless wanted to capture as much as possible the tone and texture that have characterized our conversations during these almost thirty-five years. I did make some notes to remind myself of things I wanted to bring up, but I hardly needed them. With an opening question or comment, we were off, and the conversation quickly acquired a life of its own. There was no critical or biographical agenda. Rather, I simply cast the net wide and let Anne's energy and presence, her intelligence, her forthrightness and humor have full sway. Indeed, I might say a word about Anne's humor. Although some people expect her to be quite exotic, if not eccentric, she has a lively sense of humor both about herself and about the world at large, and her ready laughter is one of her most characteristic and appealing traits. It is also, of course, one that isn't readily apparent in print. For this reason, I have sometimes indicated in brackets where her laughter seemed indivisible from the tone and mood of her remarks.

Preparing this book has reminded me again of how much I've enjoyed talking with Anne Rice over the years, and I take pleasure now in sharing these conversations with her readers who want to hear her speak in her own voice and to know her for themselves.

Claremont, California
October 8, 1995

CHRONOLOGY

1941 Born October 4 in New Orleans
1956 Her mother, Katherine O'Brien, dies
1957 Her father, Howard O'Brien, remarries and moves the family to Richardson, Texas, a suburb of Dallas
Meets Stan Rice at Richardson High School
1959 Graduates from high school and enters Texas Women's University in Denton
1960 Moves to San Francisco
1961 Returns to Texas and marries Stan Rice on October 14
1962 Returns to San Francisco with Stan
1964 Graduates from San Francisco State University with a B.A. in Political Science
1966 Daughter Michele is born on September 21
1969 Moves to Berkeley
Writes a short story called "Interview with the Vampire"

1970 Michele is diagnosed with leukemia
1972 Michele dies on August 5
1973 Writes *Interview with the Vampire* as a novel
1974 Attends Squaw Valley writers' conference where she meets agent Phyllis Seidel, who agrees to represent *Interview with the Vampire* and sells it to editor Vicky Wilson at Knopf
1976 *Interview* is published
1978 Son Christopher born on March 11
1979 *The Feast of All Saints* is published by Simon & Schuster
1980 Moves back to San Francisco to a Victorian in the Castro District
1982 *Cry to Heaven* is published by Knopf
1983 *The Claiming of Sleeping Beauty* by "A. N. Roquelaure" is published by Dutton
1984 *Beauty's Punishment*, the second Roquelaure, is published by Dutton
1985 *Exit to Eden* by "Anne Rampling" is published by Arbor House under editor John Dodds's Belvedere Books imprint
Beauty's Release, the third Roquelaure, is published by Dutton
The Vampire Lestat is published by Knopf
1986 *Belinda*, the second Rampling, is published by John Dodds at Arbor House
John Dodds dies of cancer
1988 *The Queen of the Damned* is published by Knopf
Returns to New Orleans and buys a house on Philip St.

1989 Moves back to New Orleans permanently and buys a house in the Garden District
The Mummy: Or Ramses the Damned is published by Ballantine Books
1990 *The Witching Hour* is published by Knopf
1991 Her father, Howard O'Brien, dies at age seventy-four
1992 *The Tale of the Body Thief* is published by Knopf
1993 *Lasher* is published by Knopf
Writes screenplay for *Interview with the Vampire* under a contract with David Geffen
1994 *Taltos* is published by Knopf
Film of *Interview with the Vampire* is released
1995 *Memnoch the Devil* is published by Knopf
Writes screenplay for *The Witching Hour* for David Geffen
1996 *Servant of the Bones* is published by Knopf

CONVERSATIONS WITH

ANNE RICE

PART ONE

1

"A great trust in the imagination"

RILEY: Although *Interview with the Vampire* was your first published novel, it wasn't actually the first novel you wrote, was it?

RICE: No, I worked for a long time on a novel entitled *Katherine and Jean* that I thought was not uniformly successful. I had gotten a great deal of encouragement from a number of people, but I never got that novel to the point where I was a hundred percent behind it. That didn't happen until I wrote *Interview with the Vampire*. When I finished the first draft of *Interview*, I decided to send it out. I thought it would be my first accepted work. I felt that very emotionally, so for about nine months I mailed it to agents and to editors.

RILEY: How did you decide where to send it?

RICE: I sent it to people I knew about. If an editor had dropped me a line and said, we are interested in writers on the West Coast, keep us in mind, I responded. I sent it to a Houghton Mifflin editor because he had made a general query. He rejected it in a very simple letter saying, we cannot successfully publish it for you. I sent it to the West Coast representative of Doubleday because he lived in Berkeley. He sent back a rejection that by all rights should have been devastating, but was just the opposite. He said that it lacked plot, character, writing finesse, and any other qualities that would make it a hardcover novel, but that with a sexy, lurid cover it ought to do well as a paperback! His letter was so critical that it had no sting whatsoever. When Knopf accepted the book two months later, I received a very nice letter from the man saying, try us again, we're not always so stupid. In the meantime it went to an agent I knew of, and she said she didn't understand it. It didn't seem to be black comedy, and it didn't seem to be satire, and if it wasn't either of those two things, she didn't know what it was, so she wasn't the agent. It was then shown to an agent in New York by a friend of mine, and at practically the same time I met another agent at the Squaw Valley Community of Writers. Both of those agents accepted it and agreed to handle it on the same day. So I was in the extraordinary position of suddenly having two people who wanted to represent me, and I had to tell somebody I didn't want to go with her. I went with the agent I'd met at Squaw Valley, and I wrote to the other woman and just explained the embarrassing situation and asked for the return of the novel. It turned out she'd already submitted it to Simon & Schuster, and a very famous editor there turned it down with a letter I never forgot. And this was the letter: *Dear Dorothea, Alas, I cannot see this at all. Lunch soon? Michael.* That was Michael Korda, and I thought it was hilarious. When the agent returned the novel, she included the letter with it. I presume if she'd gotten an acceptance, she would have argued to maintain it. But anyway, the agent I met at Squaw Valley then showed it to two editors who'd also been there at the same time, Vicky Wilson from Knopf and Cass Canfield, Jr., from Harper & Row. Vicky Wilson had sat in on a workshop where we worked together, but we were never formally introduced. As it turned out, Cass Canfield, Jr., whom I had met and talked to, turned down the novel with a very interesting letter. He said, "It seems like much of what Anne does; it seems an exercise for something larger. Keep me posted on what she does, but I do not see this as ready for publication." It was a very kind letter. He'd spoken to me about some short stories, and he had said essentially the same thing: Weave these together into a big narrative; work toward something bigger. But Vicky Wilson got it and, as I understand it, immediately flipped over it, just absolutely went nuts, and took it to the president of Knopf, Bob Gottlieb, who had the same response. They were both incredibly enthusiastic and immediately accepted it and offered a hefty advance.

I remember it was October fourth, which was my birthday. I'd been hanging around all day with Stan at school, at San Francisco State, just to be out of the house, really. To get out. To do things. To not brood over my daughter Michele's death. To not drink or whatever. When the phone rang, it was eleven o'clock in the evening and a woman said, "May I speak with Anne Rice?" I almost never received phone calls. When the phone rang, it was always for Stan Rice, so I just gave him the phone. He said, "No, she's saying Anne Rice," so I took the phone back, and she said, "Would you believe Alfred A. Knopf has flipped over your novel? Would you believe twelve Gs?" Well, it was quite unbelievable! I didn't know what to think. It turned out that they had criticisms of it, and wanted to know if I would attack some of those problems. Of course, it was a foregone conclusion that I would. And from that moment on my life was radically changed. I was a writer with a publisher. I then went back to reattack the novel, and I not only addressed the questions they had talked about, but wrote another entirely new two hundred pages in addition. And then with heart thumping, sent it back to them, fully aware that it was no longer the novel they had accepted. I'd created an entirely different ending and all kinds of things had happened. And they were delighted.

In the years before that, I really had sent out very little material to anybody. I worked continuously, but there was obviously a lack of confidence on my part. I knew *Katherine and Jean* wasn't ready. I remember a friend said to me, "Do you really want to get published, because you're not pursuing all these leads." Well, I wasn't pursuing them because things weren't together yet in that book. There was still something very uneven and wrong about it. I never did go back to that book. I just cannibalized it into other material. Almost everything in it was used in some other book. Basically, that was my history. It had been a long apprenticeship.

RILEY: *Interview* had been a short story earlier, hadn't it?

RICE: Yes, but it was never published anywhere. I had written it over a couple of times and shown it to friends, and I was in the process of doing that again when it grew into the book. There was an Iowa short story contest to which I was going to submit a collection. I had taken out all of my short fiction, and I was in the midst of rewriting that story when it began to take off, so I abandoned the idea of the short story collection and just went with it. I can remember very distinctly the morning I finished *Interview with the Vampire* as a novel, going to the living room, taking out my diary and writing, "I think this will be my first published work." There was a sense of having done something I hadn't done before. And this was the early draft, which was mainly the novel up until they get to Paris. Very little was ever changed in that. I hate to confess it, but I never went back and reread that part when I wrote the rest of it a year later. There was something in me then that couldn't read the whole book. I couldn't go through the beginning, but that's really very sloppy. I mean, you should go through and read your own book! [*laughter*] In the middle of the book, they leave New Orleans, and in the second draft they go to Eastern Europe and they wind up in Paris, and there's a very sad ending. All of that was new material, Eastern Europe and that version of Paris. I remember feeling almost maniacally confident of it. A great trust in the imagination, the weirdness of it, the strangeness. I certainly had doubts at times that they would ever accept it. I remember talking to my father right before it was accepted. We were talking on the phone, and I said, "I'm afraid I've put my heart and soul into a novel that people are not going to accept because everyone in it is a vampire." And he said, "Well, be careful what you wish for, you may get it." I was wishing for success and I got it. He was absolutely right.

RILEY: What were the things Knopf wanted you to revise that led to the substantial addition?

RICE: As I recall, it was basically the ending. In her letter to me, Vicky said, "I think you were tired at the end. The end sort of peters out." I can't remember if you ever read the first draft, but essentially Louis goes to Paris where he and Claudia find the vampires living in a large mansion, and they make contact with them, and they live happily ever after. He has left Claudia with a group of vampire children, and he and Armand have been wandering the world. As Louis concludes his interview in San Francisco, he's still with Armand and still living happily. Vicky said that just didn't seem to be the end, that it was like I was tired at that point. There were some people who read that draft who thought it was completely resolved in that way, but Vicky was right. It calls for a tragic ending, and I had given out before I could write it. When I went back, that's what I did.

For what it's worth, I think that moment in a person's career is tremendously influential. If they'd said they thought the ending was perfect—if they had looked me in the eye and said, we, the editors at Knopf, think it should be published exactly the way it is—I would have believed them. I didn't sense anything. It's interesting how much influence they have. Later, when I went to New York and I met the editor-in-chief, Bob Gottlieb, very briefly—I only met him for a few minutes and never really knew the man at all—but I was talking to him and Vicky and they mentioned that most of the time when they accept a novel and ask for revisions, they get very little back. There isn't much more an author can do, and they know that. They get back some of what they ask for, and it was very surprising to have someone who actually wrote all this new material. But I've heard of other authors doing this. I remember reading somewhere that Walker Percy did the same thing. When they would give him criticism and send back his novel, he would do so much more they were almost tempted to keep doing it just to see how incredible he was going to get. [*laughter*] It's very hard for me to rewrite. If a scene doesn't work, I don't actually rewrite it. I just give them something new. That's almost always what happens.

RILEY: *Interview with the Vampire* has sold millions of copies and been translated into eleven languages, and it's still going strong, yet it wasn't a big popular success originally.

RICE: Not in terms of the initial expectations. In terms of my career as a whole, though, for a first novel what happened with that book was a great success. I was established and known from then on. It was like stardom.

RILEY: American publishers don't seem to have a very effective system for launching first novels.

RICE: I'd say there's no system. Basically, what happens is that they accept a manuscript, and the manuscript is then finished and goes through various stages where they're always hoping for a big breakthrough. It's circulated to the book clubs, then to the paperback houses, and then the very early reviews come through. The biggest break they can get is a book club sale. *Interview* got that right away. The next-biggest break is a big paperback sale, and *Interview* got that right away. Then *Interview* got the movie sale. That was three big breaks, but *Interview* was still a flop. It sold 25,000 copies in hardcover, and it didn't make it. It had tons of advertising, two-page ads, everything, but it was basically ignored by the public. Then, in paperback it was made into a bestseller by virtue of printing something like a million and a half copies, and making it the list leader, and shipping it to stores all over America. Again, though, it didn't catch on through word of mouth, and it died after about eight weeks. One of the things that most concerned me at the time was whether it was going to make the backlist. After about a year and a half a book can vanish, or it can make the backlist. You can walk into bookstores everywhere, and there are certain books on the fiction shelf that are years old, while others aren't there. But *Interview* made it. After two or three years it was clear that it had not only made the backlist, but had become something of a cult book. All of those copies all over the U.S., sometimes hanging on in the Gothic section, sometimes hanging on in the science fiction section. Not hanging on for the right reasons; just hanging on because it was a vampire book.

RILEY: You waited for nine years, though, until 1985, to publish the second *Vampire* novel, *The Vampire Lestat*. Was it the initial reaction to *Interview* that led you to turn to different kinds of material?

RICE: Absolutely. I was deeply hurt by people calling me a Gothic or horror writer. The fact that the *Vampire* books were sold as escapist fiction in the beginning was one of the obstacles they had to overcome. They make more of a demand than escapist fiction. Frequently, when the *Vampire* novels were presented as merely escapist fiction, there could be tremendous resentment on the part of critics. I have many reviews of that kind. But during the years when I wrote *The Feast of All Saints* and *Cry to Heaven*, it was gradually coming home to me that *Interview* had found its audience and they knew what it was about. All the noise made by the critics was not important. It didn't really indicate how people perceived the book.

RILEY: That audience has continued to expand—almost exponentially, it seems—and now with the publication of your new book, *Memnoch the Devil*, there are five novels in *The Vampire Chronicles*. How do you account for their enormous popularity and appeal?

RICE: The people who read the books know better what it is than I do. The first thing I'd say, though, is that it's not what you are likely to think. It's something else, but what that is is not entirely clear to me. The common denominator that does run through everybody's response, from all sides, all classes, all genders, is an identification with the characters. That's what I hear over and over again. Whether they say they like vampire novels or they don't, or they read Gothic fiction or they never have, or they're science fiction readers, or romance readers, or just general readers of literature, or whatever, that's what they say: "I cared so much for Lestat and what was happening to him. I didn't care about anything else."

RILEY: It's ironic that despite their being supernatural beings who prey on humans, the vampires are actually perceived as extraordinarily human. Is that what interests you about them?

RICE: For me the trick is that the fantasy frame allows me to get to my reality. I'm telling all I know about everybody and everything in those books. It's an irony that as I step into this almost cartoon world, I'm able to touch what I consider to be real, whereas when I attempted realism, I never really could. My writing sounded fantastic. For some reason this gave me a doorway—a vampire who's able to talk about life and death, and love and loss, and sorrow and misery, and viciousness and grief, and everything a novelist wants to talk about in any worthwhile book.

RILEY: Lestat is something of a villain in *Interview*. Why did you switch from Louis to Lestat as the central character when you decided to continue the *Chronicles*?

RICE: Louis was certainly me when I wrote *Interview*, and then later Lestat was more me, in a fantasy way. Obviously, neither of these characters is related to my real life. Maybe in creating the character of Louis I exhausted everything I knew about that type of person. I couldn't go any further with a passive, disappointed character. I wanted, consciously, to get into the mind of somebody who always *acted* no matter what happened, somebody who was very strong and who tended to move forward and to make a decision of some kind under any circumstances. With Lestat I was fascinated by the idea of the person who refuses to be bad at being bad. It was a completely different type of exploration for me. I wanted a hero. I wanted to write an epic book. I didn't want to write a book about disappointment and bitterness and grief. I wanted to write a book about exploration and adventure and risk. I saw it as almost a comic adventure.

RILEY: By the time *The Vampire Lestat* appeared, *Interview* had acquired a large readership. What was the reaction to such a pronounced change in tone and emphasis?

RICE: For several years before I finished *Lestat*, readers had let me know they really wanted the sequel. I would run into them on the street. I'd run into them in bookstores. And they would say, "Where is the second vampire novel? What's happening? We really want to know." Then occasionally somebody would say, "I'm surprised you've chosen Lestat because I thought he was really the worst character in the first book to choose to go on with the adventure." But I always felt Lestat's side of it was what I wanted to tell. I knew two days after finishing *Interview* that I wanted to tell Lestat's point of view on everything that had happened as a contrast to Louis's point of view, but I certainly didn't want to limit myself to repeating the same plot over again, just from another perspective. That's how *The Vampire Lestat* was born in my mind—wanting to give the strong, independent, atheistic, child-of-nobody point of view in comparison to Louis's, the sort of aggrieved apprentice or student who feels the teacher has failed him. I wanted to give this teacherless brat his chance to talk about everything. So when the book came out and the response was very strong, that was really all I cared about. I'd felt it was going to be hard to follow *Interview with the Vampire*. It was a dare. It was a risk. Some people even suggested that it would be better to leave the book alone. They felt it was just going to get invidious comparisons, so I shouldn't do a sequel. But I felt driven to do it.

RILEY: Beyond a changed perception of yourself when you wrote *The Vampire Lestat*, was there also a change in your perception of Lestat as a character?

RICE: Shortly after *Interview* was finished, a friend suggested that Lestat was really the star of the show and that if you read between the lines of what Louis said, you saw that Lestat was a strong and powerful and appealing character. Another friend, who was listening to that discussion, said, "You drew Louis in pencil and you did Lestat in oils." It wasn't so much that Lestat changed as that in writing the second book I tried to get very close to the character who was already there, to find out what the world looked like from his perspective and how he would present himself in a sympathetic way. Now, from the first day, the character was always based on Stan, a person who'd become a self-made artist, a self-made intellectual, a self-made poet. It's Stan the atheist saying to me, Louis the Catholic, what do you need all that crap for? Live, look at life around you, reach for it, you've got it all! Don't mourn for a system that may never have existed, or a religion that's dead, or go looking for God and the Devil to justify things. Look at what's right before you. That was very much what I was working with, making the leap into that character. I had not been that character. I'd been Louis if I was anybody, and I fell in love with that as a sort of opposite to me. Lestat grew, certainly, and he enlarged, but I saw it as a deepening and a greater exploration of the very same character. I didn't have any idea until about three years later to what extent it had worked. I didn't realize it had reached so many more people and had actually changed my reputation in some way. Now when I write about Lestat, it's extremely spontaneous. I don't have to sit down and think, what would Lestat do? We just get together and we do it! I know the character so well that I know exactly what he would do and say in all instances. I can walk into places and say, "Ah, boy, Lestat would love this. This is his kind of bar, this is his kind of restaurant, this is a movie he would adore, these are clothes he would wear." Stan's car, the new Porsche? Absolutely Lestat's car. I'll give it to Lestat in every detail.

RILEY: So Lestat is still Stan?

RICE: Yes, in some ways he still is, although Stan is not still Lestat. You could even say, in some respects, that the depression Stan suffered—Lestat suffered a kind of hideous depression at the end of the nineteenth century. Did I ever tell you the film producer Julia Phillips's comment when people would say they didn't want the sequel because Lestat was such a rat? She'd say, "He's just having a bad century." [*laughter*]

RILEY: When you were writing *The Vampire Lestat*, did you already intend that there would be another book about the vampires?

RICE: Not really. I didn't know what was going to happen next. There was a lot of material written at the time that I threw out, stacks and stacks of pages. The world of the vampires was enormous to me, so it was obvious I could write many other books based on those characters. That was very clear, but I didn't have a clear intention of what *The Queen of the Damned* would be. That took a while—for me to collect my thoughts.

RILEY: In *Queen of the Damned* you move away from the voice of Lestat and from centering the story on him.

RICE: Totally, another outrageous risk, but I felt compelled to do that and to try that large-scale plot and bring all those people together. That was the first book, I think, where the actual plot I dreamed up was fully attempted. Almost every other book I'd written fell short of the imagined plot. The plot of *The Feast of All Saints* really should have gone through the Civil War into the annihilation of the colored battalion. That's what was planned, but I was nowhere near able to take the novel that far. Even in *Interview with the Vampire*, there were many things I wanted to make happen but couldn't. I just didn't know enough yet. In *Cry to Heaven* I barely scratched the surface of the darkness and the sinister stuff I wanted to get into. But I really tried with *Queen of the Damned* to write this incredibly fantastic plot that came to me almost like a vision. I was darkly depressed after finishing that novel, though, thinking it was just an outrageous failure. I usually feel that way after I finish a book. But when *Queen of the Damned* came out, it became a gigantic bestseller. That's when I realized what had happened.

STAN RICE

RILEY: Stan has obviously been a profound influence in your life. What difference has it made that he too is a writer? Has his poetry been an influence on your work?

RICE: I've spent many hours listening to his poems, and his lines run through my head all the time. There are so many parts of my books where I'm directly influenced by his rhythm. I wouldn't expect anyone to see it, but I sometimes feel so uncomfortable about it that I actually ask his permission. There have also been really pivotal moments. I remember the time he described to me the whole theory of "the right word," Ezra Pound and *le mot juste*. He described what it meant and how he felt he had to move away from what the poet Yeats called "players and painted stage." He read Yeats's circus animals poem, and he said, "This is what's happening to me as an artist. I've relied on all these 'painted players,' and I have to go back to the 'rag-and-bone shop.'" The day he read me that poem, that must have been in 1965, that had as much impact as any lecture I ever heard in school or anything I've ever witnessed in life when he gave me that phrase: "I must lie down where all ladders start, / In the foul rag-and-bone shop of the heart." I never forgot that. I must think of that three or four times a week. I think of it all the time when I'm writing. My writing is so florid nobody would think of me as related to that school, but when I'm typing away hotly in the middle of a scene, I don't just grab the words and throw them at the page. There's always this drama going on with me of reading Eudora Welty and Faulkner and Nabokov, people who are particularly rich in language, to loosen up my own. I'm always seeking to do that, and a lot of that's been influenced by Stan. That's something a writer has to think about every minute. Those phrases run through my mind all the time, and there are many phrases in his own poetry that do that too—like his phrase in "Some Lamb," "Oh, it is later forever." I just never forgot that. Many times when Lestat is talking, he uses the kind of language I think of as Stan's kind of language, Stan's kind of statement. It isn't any accident I like to quote him and Yeats. They are the poets who have given me the most, phrase by phrase.

RILEY: A conflict that comes up in your work repeatedly is the opposition between substance and abstraction. In *Queen of the Damned* Maharet says that in the flesh all wisdom begins, beware the thing that has no flesh, beware the gods, beware the idea, beware the devil. Was Stan saying that to you?

RICE: Absolutely. That was Stan. From the very beginning, that was exactly his viewpoint, and he was the first intellectual I met who presented that point of view to me.

I had grown up under a tradition that said exactly the opposite. It said that not only does all wisdom exist only when you conquer the flesh, but that virgins and people who have never known physical passion can attain levels of wisdom the rest of us can't.

RILEY: Was that something you had great doubts about before Stan?

RICE: Just before. Not more than five minutes before. At one point I actually thought I had to give up Stan because kissing him had been a mortal sin. I was deeply conflicted about it. I was eighteen years old, and I was deeply conflicted about the fact that when I was with him I found him irresistible, and I committed mortal sins. And Stan was in many ways a very proper and cautious young man. We didn't drag each other into the bushes, you know. [*laughter*] When we finally went to bed, it was actually my doing. I set it all up and got us to the flat in San Francisco, and saw to it nobody was there, and virtually seduced him. It was a wonderful moment. [*laughter*] I can still remember it vividly. Miles Davis's *Sketches of Spain* was on the record player, and the ocean was right across the street, the smell of salt air. The whole thing was my idea. But even kissing him was supposed to be a mortal sin. That was one of my first, most horrible Catholic conflicts: How can this person, whom I consider to be one of the most brilliant, intriguing, and wonderful young people my age I've ever met, somebody I don't want to lose no matter what happens in life, how can he really be all bad and damned and going to hell? How can kissing him be a sin? That's what the Cardinal says in *Cry to Heaven* when he's in bed with Tonio: "How can one be damned for this ecstasy? How can one go to hell for something like this? I don't understand it. What's the idea of all this?" I felt that very strongly, and Stan was very much involved in all that. He was a bombastic little atheist, you know. He'd sit there in class and say, "All the Bible has to be a lie because Adam and Eve's children would have been completely incestuous, and anyone can see that." I thought, wow, what an opinionated little guy. I say little—he was young, he was actually quite tall, but he was fifteen or sixteen when that conversation took place, and I was enchanted by him.

Another thing that fascinates me in my work and always will is when each of us hits a moment of ruthlessness in our lives. When we see something we want so badly that we know we're going to do whatever we have to do to get it. It doesn't matter what. I've had moments like that in my own life. I think almost everybody has. I think those who don't have such moments, if there are such people, are missing something. Stan was one of those things to me, and I was not going to let it get away. I didn't care what the Church said. It was too strong a belief that if I didn't connect with this person, I was going to make a mistake I would regret for the rest of my life. But if you're really a believing Catholic, you're risking going to hell for all eternity, and that was a very serious conflict to me at eighteen. I believe we have a profound moral sense and that for most of us this ruthlessness I'm talking about has to be for something very, very important. There are gradations. But I know its power, and I can imagine what it's like for people when they come to it. There must be moments in the lives of actors and actresses when they see an opportunity and they know they're going to have to do something very unpleasant to get it. Maybe to their friends or their spouses or someone else, but they just can't pass this up. Do you know what I mean? With me it was more romantic and in a sense more innocent. It involved the ideals and beliefs of a young girl brought up in a very strict religion, as opposed to the feelings she had when she was with a young man, and I trusted those feelings. We experience it all the time. In a sense, I know it the way a criminal knows it. I know what it must be like to commit a criminal act in the name of that emotion. I've described it over and over again in *Lestat*: "I just had to do it. I had to see what would happen if a little girl, *this* little, was a vampire. I just had to do it. She was going to die anyway if I didn't, and I just couldn't not do it." He's always trying to describe that, a kind of trust in that really ruthless, thrill-seeking, stimulus-seeking belief in action. You have to be terribly optimistic to be that kind of person.

RILEY: In terms of the themes or vision of the books, that seems to me the deepest change that occurs. When you move from *Interview* to *Vampire Lestat*, the shift is to optimism. Was writing *Interview* an attempt to set aside an aspect of yourself, not just to go beyond the grief and torment of Michele's death, but to complete a whole phase of your life?

RICE: Yes, I think that was true.

RILEY: In talking about these two novels, you've expressed ambivalence about the character of Louis and his relationship to you. You've said you have difficulty writing about him now. Could that be because there is a part of you that's still Louis?

RICE: I'm not him now. When I write those books, I'm

Lestat. If any character speaks what I believe and feel, it's Lestat. Take the ruthlessness we've been discussing, and my understanding of that, and compare it to Lestat's ruthlessness in *The Tale of the Body Thief* when he makes David Talbot a vampire. That's a perfect example: "I'm going to do this and I'm not going to pass it up." That's what I'm talking about, that moment of ruthless ambition and decision and choice. I don't think you can take the vision in *Interview with the Vampire* any further than I did in that book. At least, I can't take it any further. There was nothing to do but grow beyond that because it's a book about disappointment, disillusionment, and bitterness. Every single question that comes up has a disappointing answer. Everything Louis looks for, everywhere he goes, doors close, or darkness is revealed to be at the core, or death results, or things burn down, or they crumble. In *The Vampire Lestat* I deliberately set out to do the exact opposite. I thought, what if his mother doesn't die? What if she becomes a really powerful vampire and they jump out the window together? What if he does find Marius, and what if Marius tells him an incredible story? And what if, at the end, he's just bopping along and becomes a rock star? What if each thing leads to more doors opening and more questions? That's why that book was comic for me, because it celebrated procreation, and it had a great deal of humor and it was about possibility and renewal. Resurrection and renewal. *Interview with the Vampire* was a tragic, lyric book about nothing being possible.

RILEY: Everything since then, in one way or another, is about awakenings.

RICE: And the transcendence of death. In other words,

you could say, here's this woman and basically these experiences should have destroyed her. Her mother's death from alcoholism when she was still a young girl should have done her in. Marrying young, having difficulties, should have done her in. Her child's death should have so crippled her that she wouldn't have been able to go on. She should have drunk herself to death. Everything that happened to her should have done her in, or could have. Now, if she's going to go on, there has to be some radical transformation. Up to a certain point, the books were so much about the awakening that it always happened at the age of either fourteen or twenty-four. Louis at twenty-four, Marcel in *Feast of All Saints* at fourteen, Tonio in *Cry to Heaven* at fourteen—my own age when my mother died, the age at which I found out I was a woman and that women were different from men and that there were different expectations. But the books, thank God, changed after that. They became about other awakenings and other passages, and by the time I got to *Tale of the Body Thief*, there is no fourteen-year-old learning about life. It's really about older people, older minds. It's about coming to terms with all the experiences that come to you later in life. It's very much trying to lay claim to that, and to say that it's not true a novelist only writes about his or her adolescence. It's not true you only write about a very few years of your life. I'm going to write about what I'm finding out now. My life . . . I have lived many lives. I keep living one life after another. Life keeps taking me places where I never thought I would go, and I'm going to be able to do that. And the fiction's very much trying to do that.

TRANSCENDING DEATH

RILEY: When you speak about transcending death, I'm reminded that you've said that to watch death changes you forever.

RICE: Yes, that's true. That's a tremendously valuable experience. It's not something people should turn away from. I was fortunate to be there when my uncle Teddy died, and there when my father died, and I'll never forgive myself for being asleep when Michele died. I don't actively suffer over that anymore, but I'll never feel any differently about it.

We have these notions about Americans wanting to deny death, but I'm not sure that's true. What's true is that all over the nation people are seeing other people die, and sometimes they don't want to deny it. They want to talk about it. One of the things I've been grateful for over the years is that the books are popular with people who have AIDS. And I'm a little bit puzzled by that. I don't know whether, if I were terminally ill, I would read my books. People come up to me and say, "The last book my lover had was *Interview with the Vampire*. He died with that book." A woman called me and told me her son had AIDS and asked if I would I autograph a book for him, and I did and sent it to him. After he died she called me and said, "You have no idea what it meant. He cherished it." That's incredibly moving. I've asked friends, "What is it all about?" One of my friends said, "The books are a marvelous bridge over." I'm not sure I know what that means. But they are dealing with death at a symbolic and metaphorical remove. They're making a coherent world, which obviously isn't the literal world right here, but it's still all about death. My theory is that you don't have to run away from what you're suffering when you read these books. You can experience your thoughts and feelings about it, one step removed. That's what I think literature should do for everybody. I think people want this desperately. I think they want even more literal treatments of death.

RILEY: Death defines the ultimate opposition between mystery and knowing, which is at the heart of *Interview* and is perhaps a key to the book's appeal. Louis is driven by his need to know what it means to be immortal, thus also what it means to be mortal. It's the great mystery he seeks to solve. Later, in *Body Thief*, David Talbot will say that maybe it's supposed to remain a mystery.

RICE: Yes, the idea that maybe if there is a God and a Devil, they do things to keep tripping us up so we can't figure it out.

RILEY: And not just Louis, of course, but Lestat, too. One of the traits that carry over from *Interview* to *The Vampire Lestat* is the questioning. It's very different in tone, but mystery persists and so does the search for meaning.

RICE: Yes, although it's mostly abandoned in *The Tale of the Body Thief*. Lestat's abandoned it. It's a totally different explanation. He says in the very beginning, "You're not going to hear any ancients telling secrets. You're not going to hear any more of that." But then he encounters David, who confesses that he's dying without knowing any more about these things than he knew in the beginning, which is just what my father said. Even at the moment of his death he didn't know any better what it was all about.

RADICAL DEPARTURES

RILEY: In terms of the *Chronicles* overall, *The Vampire Lestat* and *Tale of the Body Thief* both make a break from what has gone before. The most decisive shift, of course, is from *Interview* to *Vampire Lestat*. But I'm thinking also of a moment in the introduction of *Tale of the Body Thief* when Lestat says, in effect, "This is my book, from start to finish." That seems to constitute a kind of clearing of the deck, not only on Lestat's part but on yours as well, a kind of declaration of independence.

RICE: That was literally true in that I was not going to deal with all that cast of characters from *The Queen of the Damned*. I was not going to write about what had happened to all those people. I was only going to mention them, that they exist in this world and this is what's happening with them. But it also meant what I think you're saying. It meant I was going to write that book the way I wanted to write it, from start to finish.

I'm very aware that each novel I write is in some ways a radical departure from the novel before it. And I'm also aware that I have a varied audience and that readers approach the books with a variety of expectations. Many times over the years readers have told me how they expected this or that to happen on the basis of what had happened in the prior book. I wanted to make it absolutely clear to the reader what *not* to expect, so that what was going to happen would have its maximum impact. Otherwise the reader's experience of the work can be undermined. Let me give you a personal example. I watched a movie last night, *Scent of a Woman*, and for some reason I had a preconceived notion that it concerned a murder trial. So I actually spent about three-fourths of the movie wondering when the murder trial was going to come up [*laughter*], and that's no way to watch a movie. In *Tale of the Body Thief* I didn't want someone skipping page after page of Lestat's story waiting for a juicy episode with Armand or Gabrielle, so I said in the very beginning what you were going to get so it could have its own impact.

RILEY: Apart from the change in tone and the shifts in point of view, have the *Chronicles* changed for you in other ways?

RICE: Right now there are all kinds of possibilities. I can pick it up at any time and do any number of things with it. There were a couple of times when it closed up, though, mainly at the end of *The Queen of the Damned.* I felt I'd sort of backed myself to the edge of the cliff with all those characters and their grand scheme. I wanted to get out of that, to get with Lestat and declare that *The Vampire Chronicles* as a forum could be used to tell tales by various characters without necessarily dragging all the other characters through time in each book. I conceived of it then as, say, twelve books that could be read in any order. The number doesn't really mean anything, but I see it as potentially twelve books. I can take Lestat and do *The Tale of the Body Thief* with him, and then if I want I can go to Armand and do a book with him, and Gabrielle, and Marius. Now, I'm not doing that next. I'm going with Lestat again, and that feels very comfortable to me. They may all end up being adventures of Lestat, but there's a wonderful feeling of being able to bring in the others when I want and in whatever way I choose.

RILEY: The new book didn't start out to be about Lestat, though, did it?

RICE: Actually, it did. The original title was *A Dark and Secret Grace*, and it was about Lestat. It tied in directly with the scene in *Tale of the Body Thief* in which David Talbot describes once overhearing God and the Devil talking in a Paris café. Then I made an attempt to move it away from *The Vampire Chronicles*, to have it be the very same novel but to do it with a mortal man as a hero. At the time I wanted the freedom of being out of the *Chronicles*. I wanted to be with a new set of characters, and yet to deal with all the same things and the same questions. I spent an enormous amount of time trying to give birth to the novel with a mortal hero, and it didn't work. It simply didn't work with a mortal character. I couldn't get the voice right. As soon as I entertained the idea of going back to Lestat, everything fell into place. So I went back to doing the very novel for which I'd done tons of research and mapped it all out. It was really meant to be with Lestat.

VAMPIRES AND ARTISTS

RILEY: Beyond the themes we've been talking about—the transcendence of death, renewal, a life-affirming optimism—there is something else I think the *Vampire* novels are about, and this may strike you as an excessively literary or academic observation.

RICE: Oh, I doubt it. I love it.

RILEY: They are about being an artist.

RICE: That's true, although I'm least in touch with that.

RILEY: It's not something you'd necessarily think about, but there are interesting parallels. An artist watches people, uses people, "bleeds" them of their experience in ways that are metaphorically reflected in the vampires.

RICE: There's no doubt about it. It's about trying to be redeemed through creativity.

RILEY: Is there a sense, then, in which an aspect of Lestat's experience is like your own? Could one, in tracing Lestat's journey, discover something like your own autobiography?

RICE: Nobody ever does, but they could. But you have to remember also that there's a statement being made all through the books that true art can only be made by human beings. The vampires can't do it themselves.

RILEY: Let me pursue this further, then. An overt conflict in *The Vampire Lestat*—there's also considerable mention of it in *Queen of the Damned*—involves the idea of Lestat's transgression in making public the history of the vampires. He rejects that view and insists he wants to be seen and known. Perhaps there's a temptation to see that as simple narcissism on his part, but at a deeper level it's about refusing to be invisible, about insisting on his existence: *I am here!* We were talking earlier about how the painful experience in your own life might have destroyed you. It might, in other words, have made you invisible. Perhaps this is a necessary part of every artist's journey, the implicit declaration that *I am here and this is what I have seen.*

RICE: Lestat is sterile. His one attempt to make a child was Claudia, and it was a disaster. And the other vampires he has made, strictly speaking those were disasters too—

Gabrielle and Louis and the terrible things that happened as a result. In *Vampire Lestat*, when he made Nicholas a vampire, his mother stood in the doorway and said, "Disaster, my son." After Michele's death that's how I felt, sterile. Art is the opposite of that. Art is about making something. I think the way Lestat feels is the way I feel about art. When he says he wants to be seen, he's saying, "I want to do something. I want to make something. I don't want to be an anonymous predatory shadow doomed to be misunderstood and only destroy. That's horrible! I want to make something positive."

RILEY: There's another quality I'm thinking of too, one that's different from the desire to make something but also related to it. It's as if you were saying *behold!* to the reader: Look at life! Look at this! However simple or prosaic it might seem at first glance, go back and look again! That, too, has been part of your journey.

RICE: There is a poem of Stan's where he's talking about Michele—I can't quote the line exactly—in which he exclaims, "Look!" and then he describes what he sees. Many times now I've used that in my novels, that "behold!" quality, as you call it. At the beginning of *Belinda* I quoted his poem "Excess Is Ease," which is about really looking at what's right in front of you. That book was about a man who was trying to do that. He was trying finally to paint what was right in front of his face. You can say, of course, he is also trying to paint the thing he cared about most, the thing that had most meaning. But it is also what's right in front of him, not some imagined rats running around the attic of a house that doesn't exist, but Belinda herself.

RILEY: Would you agree, then, that in a very personal sense the novels are your means of "looking"—and telling the reader what you have seen?

RICE: They are—and about the terrible dilemma that what may seem like rats in an attic that doesn't exist are, in fact, things that are right in front of me.

RILEY: Yes, for all that's mysterious, exotic, and even supernatural in your novels, they're filled with the immediacy of the world you've discovered right in front of you. Art, music, even the cities you have visited—they are all there, portrayed with a kind of naïveté, an aesthetic naïveté. Does that seem insulting, to speak of it that way?

RICE: No, I agree with you. I think it's true.

RILEY: There are countless allusions to works of art. I'm thinking of scenes such as the one when Louis and Armand walk through the Louvre amid all the paintings and sculpture, but there are many other instances.

RICE: Yes, there are. People don't mention it, but the allusions are there, I think to painting more than anything else. It's a very rich source of inspiration. Going to Amsterdam to see the paintings of Rembrandt, that was an incredible experience for me—to sit there on the bench, just where I put David Talbot and Lestat later in *Tale of the Body Thief*, and look at the painting *Members of the Drapers' Guild*. Sometimes I think my ignorance makes these things more intense for me. Perhaps if I'd gone there on a school tour when I was fifteen, I wouldn't feel the same way, but because I didn't get there till I was in my forties, it was a wonderful experience. Going to the Metropolitan in New York is the same way. I have never of my own free will left that museum. It's always been that it's time to go back to the hotel because we have to catch a plane, or there's no choice for some other reason. Maybe ignorance and isolation and cultural deprivation in some ways made me more vulnerable to that, because certainly there have been a million kids who grew up in New York who tell how they used to play hide-and-seek in that museum or try to get locked in at night, and they don't talk about going to pieces in front of this or that Rembrandt. It obviously works for different people in different ways. That happens to be very strong with me—seeing a visual image, whether it's a movie or a painting, and being struck by it and wanting, in an almost clumsy way, to speak of it specifically in a novel.

RILEY: I'd also suggest that having once discovered a great work of art, you not only want to include it in a novel, you also want to capture the very experience of discovery. You create something like an analog of your own experience, the emotions you felt, what it meant to you, to try to give the reader the same thrill of discovery.

RICE: Oh yes, absolutely, and I no longer worry about seeming naïve or foolish. I have never been a sophisticated writer. There's something very naïve and almost awkward about a character standing in a novel in 1976 and saying, "What am I and who made me?" From one point of view that's absurd. Most of the writers I knew in Berkeley were far too guarded and sophisticated to write anything like *Interview with the Vampire*. They wouldn't have been caught dead with it. Their writing was much more—I don't want to say cynical or ironic—it was just about completely sophisticated people dealing with things they considered to be way beyond questions like that. When you see my books in that light, they are written in huge chalk letters, and I don't mind that now. Knowing this may be the first time one of my readers has heard of that Rembrandt painting is thrilling to me. I'm not an alienated artist sitting there thinking, well, four out of five of them won't know what I'm talking about. They'll understand that experience, and they'll know what I'm talking about. I'll tell them exactly, no matter how naïve it sounds. The thrill of discovery, the revelation, that's important to me.

I remember being crushed when I saw *A Chorus Line* and they all started to sing about the movie *The Red Shoes*. One of the experiences I'd wanted to describe in a novel was what it meant to me as a teenager to see *The Red Shoes*. I'd had no idea there was an American musical that had about sixteen characters singing about *The Red Shoes* [*laughter*] because that movie had been an incredible experience for them. In dealing with Michael Curry in *Witching Hour* I was trying to describe that very kind of moment of illumination when you walk into a theater and you're just blown away by something you see, and nothing is ever the same. That's how *The Red Shoes* was for me. I love to describe those kinds of things, and if my readers identify with that and then write and tell me they have had a similar moment, that's wonderful. You can't worry about not sounding sophisticated; you can't worry about its being naïve.

RILEY: Is there one of your books that you consider your best?

RICE: That's a difficult question because every time somebody says one is my best book, I get defensive about the others. [*laughter*] No, I don't think any one is my best because I think all of them both succeed and fail at different levels. Take *Interview with the Vampire*, for example: It's an achievement I'm proud of, but I also think it's a heavily flawed book with many clumsy things and cumbersome mistakes in plotting and narrative and language.

RILEY: Was your growth as a writer essentially a matter of learning from experience?

RICE: Yes, I learned to do much better. I think *The Vampire Lestat* has some of the most satisfying writing I've ever been able to do, but structurally the book is a mess. I think *Cry to Heaven* failed for me because it took too long to get to Tonio. It became history bound, and the same was true with *Feast of All Saints*. The history became too important in those books. I wasn't able to get to the real thing I like to write about, whether it's people fighting each other, people seeking to be good, perversity, incest, the feelings of the damned, whatever. I couldn't get close enough in *Cry to Heaven* or *Feast of All Saints*, and that's why I decided never to write another book like those. I consciously chose not to.

RILEY: Do you consciously set yourself dares in different novels?

RICE: Oh yes, whether I can pull something off. Particularly now. I would say *The Tale of the Body Thief* was a huge dare. I don't think I would have attempted it ten years ago. I could have thought of such a plot, somebody sliding into someone else's body and walking all around, but I would never have been able to pull it off, to make a texture strong enough that all of that would be acceptable and you would feel sympathy for the character. Now I really take on those dares, and they're very scary because the plots I want to do, the novels, the ideas, the characters, all of that sort of comes to me almost as it would to an autistic person. It leaps out of me before there is real thought, and what then comes is whether or not I think I can get that thing. You know, I'll see a novel in a burst—for example, that Lestat was going to change bodies with a mortal man and discover it was horrible—I'll see that as if it came from somewhere else and into my brain, and I'll think, could I pull that off? . . . I don't know. More and more I work that way, but that's not the way I wrote *Interview*. That was much more unconscious. That was really a young writer who didn't know from moment to moment what was happening. *Cry to Heaven* is a much more calculated book where the author says, "I want to write about this theme. I want to make my book move in this way, and I want to write it in such a way that this is what I'm going to achieve." There's not very much that's spontaneous in that book. Afterwards there was a real effort to get back to the spontaneity, to trust the work would mean something if I just let it go and pointed my abilities like a fire hose in a certain direction.

2

"The big furious brainstorm . . . of writing"

RILEY: The real breakthrough in readership came with *The Vampire Lestat*, which was published in the midst of a remarkably productive period for you. After publishing your first three novels at approximately three-year intervals, you suddenly published six novels in the next three years alone, five of them under two different pseudonyms—the *Beauty* trilogy* as A. N. Roquelaure and *Exit to Eden* and *Belinda* as Anne Rampling. What brought about such a significant change in the way you worked?

RICE: I saw it as me sitting there frustrated and burning with ambition to do a whole variety of things and finding it very constricting to be working with the cumbersome machinery of American publishing. In batting out the *Beauty* books very rapidly and doing *Exit to Eden* in five weeks, I

***The Sleeping Beauty Novels: The Claiming of Sleeping Beauty; Beauty's Punishment; Beauty's Release*

got back to the kind of spontaneity and fury with which I'd written *Interview with the Vampire*. I got away from the slowness with which I'd written *Feast of All Saints* and *Cry to Heaven*, and back to a trust in the big furious brainstorm session of writing. It was a very turbulent period for me. I remember I wanted very much to write that pornography. I had a great desire to do it. At the same time I was also having trouble with *Vampire Lestat*, with getting the voice of Lestat to be the intimate voice I wanted it to be. I actually had a contract for *Vampire Lestat* when I wrote the *Beauty* novels and *Exit to Eden*. I don't really remember the exact order of how it went, but I remember that Knopf was very patient and waited while I did these other crazy things. At one point the manuscript of *The Vampire Lestat* sat there for a year. I was just stuck. I couldn't get close to the character. I think I was trying to get much, much closer to my own emotions. There's a section at the beginning of *Exit to Eden* where the character Lisa talks about the fact that sadomasochistic play at its greatest should bring you close to another human being the way it would if you were touching the person's beating heart. I was trying to do that with my work. I was trying to get really deep into what I cared about. I was trying to free myself from writing pages and pages of introduction to things. In *Cry to Heaven* I wound up writing two hundred pages I didn't want to write, the whole beginning, just to get the book started. I really wanted to get to when the character Tonio was castrated and pitched into the world of opera and what that was like. I'd written this long section about Venice and his childhood that I felt was necessary in order to compare supposedly normal life to abnormal life and show that the reverse was true—that his normal life had been a nightmare and his abnormal life really became normal. I wanted to get away from that kind of thing and to develop a style where I could go right to what counted. I didn't want to write a word I didn't want to read. I did a lot of reading of mystery writers at that time, James M. Cain and Raymond Chandler and others, trying to get that intimate voice detective fiction often has. I did a lot of loosening up as I wrote the pornography and *Exit to Eden*. And the character of Elliott in *Exit to Eden* was really Lestat. It's as if Lestat was playing Elliott in that novel.

After I finished *Eden*, I was able to go back to *Vampire Lestat* with a great deal more spontaneity and emotion and feeling and playfulness. The fiction is much looser than in *Interview*. There's a more deliberate use of the vernacular and a deliberate use of humor, things I would never have risked in *Interview*. But when *Lestat* was finished, I was blackly depressed. I thought it was a real failure of a book, and in some ways I still think it's a failure. It just ends. Never was I so clearly aware that a book had a bad form. I mean, it really has almost no form. [*laughter*] He tells all his adventures and comes up to this point and just stops the story because there were a thousand pages piled up there, and I had to quit. I knew that if that book was going to succeed, it was going to be in spite of the bad form. It would succeed because of what was really in it of the person and heart and soul of Lestat, and how much I put myself into that, and I loved the book for that reason. I felt I'd gotten a lot deeper into his anguish and my anguish than I had ever gotten in *Interview with the Vampire*. I love the reckless things that happen in *Vampire Lestat*, just mad digressions and experiments, but it's a much sloppier book than, say, *Cry to Heaven*.

There was something else that happened at the time that had a profound influence on me. We went to New York to see a Picasso exhibit at the Museum of Modern Art. It was Stan's idea that we go, which was unusual. Stan seldom suggests a trip, but he really wanted to see this Picasso exhibit. This was right after *Feast of All Saints* was published, and it was before *Cry to Heaven* was actually finished. I knew that my present publisher did not want *Cry to Heaven*. They didn't consider the castrati to be a commercial subject, and they were not interested in publishing it. It was a dark period for me because I wanted very much to write that book and I was struggling with all the questions that any writer faces—how to deal with my obsessions and come to terms with the reality of what publishers would be open to. At one point I remember sitting down on a bench at the Picasso exhibit and looking at all these paintings. I hadn't known much about Picasso's early work, so I didn't realize he'd gone through a period of realism before he got to his abstract work. And I remember thinking, go home and just write, just produce, write, produce, because if you don't do that, everything is lost. The reason we can sit in this museum now is because this man just kept painting. It didn't matter to him if he made a radical departure and went completely out of one style and into another and people said that's not the consistency of genius or whatever. He just went right ahead, and by the end of his life there was no question about his accomplishment. I remember that moment vividly, and I remember going home and actually following that advice. Just pounding out things like *Exit to Eden* and *Beauty's Punishment*, not really analyzing what they were about or where they were coming from so much as just trying to get in touch with that voice that was more intimate and, to me, more daring. I love things that I think are really daring and exciting and that break up everything.

RILEY: You have talked about freeing yourself as a writer. What would you say you've been seeking to free yourself from?

RICE: Convention. I see it as bricks. I see it like starting to build something and hating these bricks and trying to get away from them. I know that sounds crazy, but over and over again I fall into writing what I consider to be well-made sentences and well-made paragraphs to set up scenes. I struggle to free myself from the setups and get right to the scenes. You know, "They threw me off the hay truck at noon." That type of thing. Just to get right into the story, to what I think is important. I think in my early books there are many paragraphs and even chapters that are not important. The voice of the fiction writer was saying, you need to build up to this. You need to slow down here. You need to take your time. I didn't know how to create a shock or revelation without building up to it slowly. I needed some time to move away from the scene and do something else. I would say that when I'm in the first-person voice telling a tale I'm right on the money. There isn't any waste, there aren't any bricks cluttering it up. That's my favorite voice, but I don't find that voice flexible enough to tell all the stories I want to tell. I have to move away from it sometimes. I really work in a personal way. It's just what I want to know at that moment. I think of that all the time. What would I want to know if I were here at this point?

STORIES WITHIN STORIES

RILEY: In your novels there are often one or more sections, sometimes of considerable length, that are stories within stories. In fact one of the major plot events in *The Vampire Lestat* and *Queen of the Damned* is the stories that get told within the main story. Or even more dramatically in *The Witching Hour*, when you suspend the story of Rowan and Michael and have several hundred pages that tell the history of the Mayfair family. Was delaying the Mayfair history a way of getting instantly to the main story and then returning later to what you needed by way of background?

RICE: Of the recent novels *The Tale of the Body Thief* is the only one that's a complete tale in the first-person voice. And in that one—I don't know if you noticed—I moved away from the tale within the tale by not telling David Talbot's diary, by just saying Lestat read it and this is what it was. I wasn't interested in it, not at that point. I wanted to go forward.

RILEY: But you do use that narrative device again in *Taltos*, your third novel in the *Mayfair* series*, where you have Ash's story.

RICE: Yes, that was very important to me, to get to Ash's story. But those things are all struggling; all those elements are struggling. There's a desire to tell a huge story with a

**Lives of the Mayfair Witches: The Witching Hour; Lasher; Taltos*

great many details, and it's very difficult to pin down with one point of view. There's a terrific constraint. So I move away from it in the main story, and I move back into it in those tales, which always bring me closest to the characters. I'd say the very closest. I think the best part of *Lasher*, the second of the *Mayfair* books, is in the tales. Other chapters of *Lasher*, to some extent, really are building, laying the scene. Some of the chapters where the Mayfairs come together and sit around a table and make a decision are more conventional building blocks than in most novels I've written. But I wanted very much to have the reader satisfied on all those story points.

RILEY: In thinking about your novels overall and reflecting on our conversations about them, I get the impression that you're intuitively writing toward some kind of goal.

RICE: I think that's really true. There are times when I feel right on track with it, and the writing is very intense, but there are also times when I feel very removed from it. I think my entire career has been a process of getting more on track. When I wrote *Taltos*, I felt I'd actually eliminated anything I didn't want to hear and know. My sister read the manuscript, and she said, "You had a lot more fun writing this book than you did writing *Lasher*. There's a great deal more energy in this book. There are better descriptions."

"THE UNDERDOGS": *BELINDA* AND *EXIT TO EDEN*

RILEY: You mentioned that you usually feel depressed after finishing a novel. Given the change in approach and attitude you've described, did you feel that way after the Anne Rampling books?

RICE: No, I felt so high writing *Exit to Eden*. It was like being high on a drug. That book just poured out of me, and I was convinced at the end that something had really been accomplished. I only remember that book with happiness and warm feelings even though I knew it wasn't necessarily going to be well received, and in fact it wasn't. The first editor turned it down; the second editor accepted it but it sold hardly at all. People weren't particularly interested in it, but I didn't feel depressed after it. I felt very good. There had been a real burning dissatisfaction in me after *Cry to Heaven* that that book didn't have the impact on people I wanted it to have because it was simply too removed from everything going on around us. I could see that it didn't have the impact, and although one or two reviewers got it and said this is about now, this is about gender, this is about the characters' psychology, most people didn't. I didn't want to be in that position anymore.

RILEY: Do you get many readers responding now to *The Feast of All Saints* and *Cry to Heaven*, who have turned to them because they liked *The Vampire Chronicles* or *The Witching Hour*?

RICE: Actually, I do get a lot of response to them now. Especially here in New Orleans, people tend to be very fond of *Feast of All Saints*; it's not uncommon for them to say it's their favorite book. *Cry to Heaven* has a special kind of following, frequently men, who go out of their way to say they liked it. Those are perceived as underdog novels. When people mention them, they're always saying, "I like the one that no one talks about." They're aware those books never sold like the others, but they have a definite following. The real underdogs, though, are *Belinda* and *Exit to Eden*. Some people don't even know they exist. But I don't have any regrets. To write a book like *Eden* or *Belinda* was very much trying to revolt.

RILEY: I take that to mean not only a revolt against the limits of mainstream commercial publishing, but also an artistic self-assertion, an insistence on writing what was important to you regardless of what others thought. Was that why you dedicated *Belinda* to yourself?

RICE: I felt *Belinda* was about me. It was as if I said, okay, here's Jeremy Walker, who's a writer of children's books, and his paintings of the creepy house and the bats, and he's putting that aside now and painting this naked young girl, and it doesn't matter anymore whether she's naked. Jeremy and the children's literature were basically me with the *Vampire* novels, and the paintings of Belinda were the pornography in an attempt to break out of the European-American voice and actually touch realism. When Jeremy finished his paintings, I felt he had broken through and so had I. The pornography had helped me get away from the Gothic darkness and distance and really write about anything. When he says at the end, "I could write about anything now," I felt I could write about anything too, and I've felt that in *Queen of the Damned* and in *The Witching Hour* and all the subsequent books. *Belinda* was a complete allegory, and it was very much fun to write. I got a lot of flak on it, though, a lot of resistance, and to this day I'm not sure I should have listened to anything that was said about it. I made Belinda a little older at other people's behest.

When the book was published, it was completely ignored. I think it got two reviews in the whole country. It was a book that people simply didn't want. They didn't even go into the bookstores to buy it. I called and said, "Well, how's it doing?" And they said, "It's not. They're waiting for your third *Vampire* novel." I remember one boy wrote me a postcard and said, "I know you have written this book *Belinda*. That is not the book I want. I want more of Lestat." I remember thinking, you said it, kid. People just didn't want that book.

RILEY: There's a scene in the novel where Jeremy makes a statement that seems virtually your own credo: "American life is like a dream. It frightens you. You feel you have to make fun of it no matter how much you secretly love it. I want the freedom of the primitive painters to focus, with love, on what I find inherently beautiful. And I want it to be hot, disturbing and generous always."

RICE: Good. I'd forgotten that passage, but I'm glad I wrote it. That's really true in that novel on every level. It's about the values with which I work and the things I believe in. The characters do these things that are supposed to bring them down, and instead they become nationally famous and successful. That's exactly what was happening to me. I wrote the pornographic novels, and I was told they were going to ruin my reputation. I was asked by my editor at Knopf not to publish them, but they have only added to my reputation and earnings. I was writing about what was happening to me in that novel. You know, it's really what you told me at the time. You astonished me when you described *Cry to Heaven*. You said it was an audacious statement: that in art and sexuality lie liberation. That really is what I was saying in *Belinda* too. I was compelled by the story of those two people getting liberated from these awful constraints, both of which came from their mothers for reasons I'm not sure about. They may be purely literary. Belinda's mother, Bonnie, had done these terrible things to her, and Jeremy's mother had convinced him that he had to write his own novels under her name. I was fascinated with the idea that those characters liberated themselves by this purely illicit relationship that threatened everything, and then they came out on top. That actually was the quality of my life, and it continued to be. I moved back here to New Orleans and into my old neighborhood just as Jeremy does. And my pornography now is known everywhere. It's even been translated into German, for instance, and people with translators seriously interview me in German about the meaning of it. I can't tell you how much *Belinda* was about my own life and how prophetic it proved to be. That's why I dedicated it to myself.

In its first draft, it was even more flamingly outrageous. It got diluted a little when people said it wasn't believable that Belinda could have done all of these things. Actually, I believe totally in Belinda. I know people like Belinda, and I know what I was like at that age, and I know what I would have been like if I'd been Belinda. But I'll tell you a curious thing. She's the only character I've ever created who's been criticized for not being normal. I've had people look me right in the eye and say, "I didn't believe your novel *Belinda* because she just wasn't a typical teenager." The two reviews that appeared at the time said that: You can't take the novel seriously because she isn't a typical teenager. Now, who in the hell would say they don't take *Cry to Heaven* seriously because Tonio was not a typical teenager? But because she was a girl and because she was a teenager, there were expectations with which that character was met. The reviews actually said that the novel betrays its subject matter because she's not typical. Now think about that for a minute. What does that mean? I'll tell you, it's a lot easier to write about gay men than it is to write about women. You meet a lot less prejudice. [*laughter*] People really do take the male characters more seriously. If Belinda had been a boy, that novel might have done very well. I mean that seriously. I know that may sound strange, but that's been my experience.

WRITING ABOUT THE SEXES

RILEY: How do you account for the male characters in your work, including gays, being taken more seriously than the female characters?

RICE: Well, I'm referring principally to the critical response. When I write about men, even if they are gay men, the critical response has tended to be better than to relationships with women. I can present a highly romantic relationship between two men, and the book isn't perceived as just a romance, but that's exactly what happens if one of the people is a woman. They're spoken of pejoratively as "just a romance." When I first started writing, I was very conscious of this. I remember being conscious with Louis and Lestat that if one of them had been a woman, the novel would have received harsh criticism. A scene like the one where Lestat makes Louis a vampire would have been put down as a cheap Gothic romantic scene. But because it was two men, I was able to deal with the real essence of dominance and submission. I was able to remove it from the gender clichés and to talk about what it really is, whether it's with a person of your own sex or your father or mother or whoever. That's really what the scene was about, dominance and submission. To me it was very important when Louis said, "Had there been time, I might have changed my mind. But with Lestat there was no time." I was trying to describe that very decisive, all-powerful aura the dominant take on for the submissive. They always seem to know what they want, and where they're going, and what to do. They can force the issue. I remember being conscious of that at the time and knowing later that it wouldn't have worked with a woman. I think if I were to go back and look at the reviews, I'd find that generally it was taken seriously because it was two men. In later novels when I did put women characters in, I found dismissive remarks would be made right away. I remember *The Mummy*, for example. A reviewer said something like, it's just a cheap romance, she just gooped it all up with this junk with the woman.

I find it's harder for me to deal with women because women have so many limitations that I hit up against the minute I start to write. I don't mean limitations I put in their character; I mean limitations in the world that are imposed upon them. There's a feeling of freedom from all those constraints when I'm writing about men, and I think even the most heterosexual critics tend to treat their relationships more seriously. *Belinda* was the most outstanding example, where the few reviews it got actually said that if she's not a stereotypical teenager, what is the book about?

I thought the book made very clear what it was about: a prisoner of childhood. Both the man and the woman were prisoners of childhood. I've run into the same thing with Rowan and Michael, too. It's as if critics and sometimes even readers don't want to deal with the details of that relationship. They don't want to deal with the intricacy, the fine points, the lessons. They simply dismiss it. It's just another romance at that point, whereas if it's men, I can go very far with it physically, even right into oral sex or anything else, and they'll take it seriously as a relationship. So for me it's functioned well to use two male characters as a way to draw attention to their psychology.

Critics and my readers have been kinder to my male characters than to my female characters. They say my female characters are not as good as my male characters, that they're not as real, that I don't bring the female characters to life as much. I don't agree with that. To me, a character like Rowan is just as important as a character like Ash. When I'm writing about Rowan, I care just as much as I do when I'm writing about Ash or Michael or any male. I remember when I was writing *The Feast of All Saints*. There's a scene in the very beginning when I was writing from a woman's point of view, the scene where Marie Ste. Marie takes a walk from her home to the office of a lawyer. I was perhaps more deeply involved in that scene than any in the book, describing that woman's feelings, everything that surrounded her, the tight web of respectability.

RILEY: What's your own perception of the differences between your female and male characters?

RICE: I don't think about it too consciously when I'm working, but obviously there's a huge difference. In *Taltos* I don't think I could have made Ash a woman. I couldn't have made the novel revolve around a female in that way. It was something about that person being a male and being able to slip in and out of life and have certain problems resolved from the very beginning that gave the character its momentum. It is much easier to describe a wanderer like Ash because the figure is a male. However, I have Gabrielle to get to, you know. I haven't gotten to her yet. I really want to write more about Gabrielle, and she would be the nearest thing to the female equivalent of Ash, a sort of roaming, independent immortal. You know, when you're dealing with a character like Gabrielle, you're dealing with somebody who's a virtual political prisoner in the eighteenth century because she's a woman and has no rights, no hope, no way to get out of her life. Her bursting into this transvestite role as a vampire is really claiming freedom. Those dramatic times are realistic, that's what I'm saying. Eighteenth-century literature, as you know, is filled with transvestite figures. It's filled with images of women dressing up as men to get by and to do things. Casanova mentions it, Defoe's *Moll Flanders* does, it's all over the place. It must have happened a lot more than we think because the status of women was so politically and legally different. Now, with Mona in the *Mayfair* novels I don't have to deal with any of that. I'm able to get in touch with somebody who has the complete freedom to make different choices, to do what she wants, and is sort of encouraged to. She doesn't care too much about feminine identity. So it's complicated for me, and as a writer I think you have to tune in to it, you have to cooperate with it. You have to not politicize it, and yet at the same time recognize the limitations.

RILEY: Is this a challenge to you, to write more about women, to push that part of your imagination harder to see where it takes you?

RICE: Not really. I believe you have to follow your instinct, and I don't believe you can push yourself to write about women simply because you think you should. I've been asked that: "When are you going to write more about women, when are you going to have strong women characters?" I think you tune in to what's in you when you write, and if it turns out they're all men, then they're all men. Now the truth is, I'm finding out a lot about myself and about women by writing about Mona. She is maybe the first woman with whom I've been able to achieve the complete freedom I can with a male character. She can do anything I want her to do without lapsing into a rigid female role. I love writing about Mona. She's probably my most successful female character.

RILEY: Mona seems a direct descendant of Belinda.

RICE: Yes, she is. There's a lot of what I believe and feel passionately about in those girls, a lot of what I know and what I've seen. And a lot of what I didn't do. I feel very strongly about the right of a girl Belinda's or Mona's age to desire an older man like Jeremy Walker or Michael Curry. You know, I think the person who writes most eloquently about that is Edmund White. He has described so beautifully how as a boy he wanted desperately to have sex with an older person, and he felt cruelly shut out from the adult world. In *A Boy's Own Story* he gave one of the most vicious and heartrending descriptions of that sense of exclusion I've ever read when at the end the boy turned in the teacher and said, "It was my revenge against the whole cruel adult world." Well, that's what I'm writing about with Belinda and Mona, the way the adult world shuts out that kind of young person and how strong that person's desires are and how random the wisdom can be. I feel powerfully about that, although at fourteen I certainly never had the nerve to go seducing somebody like Michael Curry. I wish I had. It's about something very deep for me, very unresolved, and it's just beginning. I could write many more books in which I explore that very thing.

RILEY: Do you think that dilemma is likelier for a girl than for a boy?

RICE: No, that's what I meant about Edmund White's work. He describes so clearly how he wanted an intimate relationship with an older man, and he couldn't get it. He didn't know where to go. He didn't know how to find a male with whom to have that relationship. Being gay and being where he was, he just didn't know. If I remember correctly, at one point he finally went to a hustler. White also gets into that in *States of Desire*. He describes how Philippe Aries in his book *Centuries of Childhood* talks about a time when children were not segregated sexually from adults. I realize, of course, this is a very powder-keg subject we're talking about, but I really wanted to deal with that in *Belinda*, the right of a girl that age to be with somebody she wanted to be with. I was very much concerned with that, and in a way maybe it was also my right as a writer to write about that regardless of whether the character is a female or a male.

RILEY: So it's not a matter of your understanding either women or men better?

RICE: It could be. Perhaps I mark my own frustration

about certain aspects of the whole thing. I do believe there are profound differences between men and women that people just aren't ready to acknowledge on any level. What it means to be a woman is something we've barely begun to scratch the surface of. It's a very difficult thing to be. This may sound like a ridiculous statement, but I think most men hate women, and I think most women hate women too. Still, most of the time we go around with the illusion that's not really happening. But it is, and it's happening on just about every level. I've never known anybody in my life who I felt treated the sexes equally. Everybody I know either gets along a little better with women than they do with men, or they get along with men very well but they dismiss women. I know women who dismiss women completely. Women just don't exist for them. Their whole psychological life is with men. And I know others for whom the reverse is true. I think one of the skills of life is to find out very early how you differ on that score. In publishing, for example, I can be made angry by men, but I was never hurt by them. But I can be hurt by women. I found that out a long time ago about myself, that I could get very angry at a male editor and very hurt by a female editor. It's a feeling of betrayal.

RILEY: Given what you've said about the difficulty of being a woman, about hostility toward women not only from men but even from other women, was there a struggle for you to like being a woman, or perhaps a dislike of what you understood being a woman to mean?

RICE: I remember perceiving very early, in almost a raw way, that if people didn't find women almost seductive, they generally regarded them with disgust. I remember seeing that and knowing there wasn't a neutral feeling toward women, whereas people mainly felt toward men in a neutral way. They didn't go out of their way to make fun of an older man walking down the street, whereas with a woman there were countless ways to describe her, as a cow or a dragon lady, all those contemptuous terms. Unless she's up-front seductive, generally the terms are contemptuous. I remember realizing that as a kid. I remember even discussing it with people, trying to figure out why it was so. I was absolutely baffled by it because I perceived myself mainly as neutral and invisible, and I didn't particularly want to be perceived either way, either with disgust or as seductive. So obviously that must influence my writing. I don't like to deal with that aspect of life. I don't like going around in a book being somebody who has to either be seductive or face people's disgust. I haven't resolved all my feelings about it, so it's easier to write from the male point of view. I do find it easier to write about gay men for that reason and others. I feel like I'm removed from everything, that I can really have a fresh perspective.

"THE GAY AESTHETIC"

RILEY: You say that it's easier to write about gay men than about women. Given the fairly high degree of homoeroticism in the *Vampire* novels, and the considerable homophobia in a good deal of American society, how is it this has been so acceptable?

RICE: That's a central question to my life and success right there. Why didn't it put readers off, and why did it become mainstream? How could things this transgressive become mainstream? And they did. We're living in a very unusual time. The mainstream, as we call it, is more open than it's ever been before to all kinds of experiments and forms and fashions, to different ways of looking at things and doing things. We've been through many periods of both exploration and repression, but we're really in a time now when all of the different transgressive ways of doing things have merged into the mainstream. It's wide open. That's the nature of our mainstream right now, and very much influencing it, very much part of it, is the fact that we're finding out the gay aesthetic, insofar as it ever existed, is in fact everyone's aesthetic. There's no difference. Many people have tried to say the gay aesthetic is something else, but it's not at all. It's just a more heightened and intense expression of what we all want. It's been working for us in America for years and years, and there's never been a time when the public was more open to it than right now. I mean, what goes on in movies today . . . what goes on in rock music . . . what goes on in rap music . . . what goes on all around me is so transgressive as to be shocking to me continually, and yet it's all happening. The society is tempered as a result, much less easy to shock, and much less easy to mislead. Kids today sit through nude scenes we never conceived would be on the screen in any way, shape, or form. They sit through violence we never dreamed of in our worst nightmares. These kids are tough. They've seen imagination used in all kinds of ways, and they're not quick to condemn. They're not terribly vulnerable. I think that's a wonderful thing. I think there's a sophistication now in

America that never existed before in my time. Curiously, it followed upon a sort of temporary recrudescence of a puritanism that I thought was going to be the wave of the future.

I think it was in 1980 that I saw *Kramer vs. Kramer* and *The Great Santini*, and I felt at that point we were headed for a backslide into puritanism, into a repudiation of everything we had achieved in the sixties and seventies. The fact that people would stand in line to see a movie like *The Great Santini* was very interesting to me. I remember standing in San Francisco, looking at the line in front of the theater, thinking, the times are changing. I liked the movie. I thought Robert Duvall was very good in it. But it was like a TV drama with that kind of wholesomeness, that kind of childlike simplicity to it, that kind of stereotypes. Yet people ate this up. *Kramer vs. Kramer*, the same thing. When it beat *Apocalypse Now* for the Academy Award, that was an astonishing moment. But the strange thing was that this neopuritanism or whatever it was didn't last very long. Almost as soon as it started to gain momentum, you had movies like *Dirty Dancing* cropping up. When I saw *Dirty Dancing*, my first comment was, "We didn't dance like that in the fifties! Nobody did!" The dancing in that movie is shockingly erotic. Yet obviously the American people wanted that movie, and they wanted X-rated videos, and they wanted them in the corner store. They wanted to take them home and play them on their VCR. They simply didn't settle for the new puritanism, whether it was being packaged for them by the Republican administration or by the feminist movement. They didn't put up with it, and so, very quickly, we reached the point where I think we are now, where the mainstream is the flood of all these different transgressive streams that before have been "other."

RILEY: Your novels have been very popular with gay men. Do you have a sense of what kind of reaction they generate from other men?

RICE: When you reach the point where you're selling so many books, you can't do that in America unless you have a large readership of both men and women. It's just not numerically possible. Even if you're Tom Clancy, you have to have a large women's readership. You can't do it on men alone. You also have to have a very large male readership, and I do have that. I have, for the first time, been getting a little flak about Lestat's homosexuality. One young kid at a signing said, "I have trouble with that . . . that's he's gay. I have trouble with it." And I of course said something like, "He can do anything. He can do anything he wants. If he wants a man, if he wants a woman—you know, he's completely powerful, he can do whatever he wants." But I have many heterosexual readers who don't notice it. Either they don't notice it, or they don't understand what it means, or they're enjoying the novel on other levels so they just don't think about it. They don't seem to know it's there. I mean, picture this: Richardson, Texas, Taylor's Books, huge suburban bookstore, huge signing, hundreds of people lined up. Many Texas voices coming through the line which I as someone who lived in Texas know. Dallas voices, country voices, voices from around North Dallas. Picture a man coming up, in a Billy cap, with a narrow head and eyes that are a little too close together and one of those beautiful country faces, very deeply lined, and saying, "When's Lestat coming back?" I really am as baffled by that as anybody else would be. I felt like saying, do you really like that character? How do you feel about this, that, and the other thing? That happens to me all the time. They say, "We want Lestat." How do they deal with it? I don't know how they deal with it. In some ways you can say that if you pull off certain things in fiction you can get away with an amazing amount of other things. But it may be nothing that devious. It could be that they like the freedom. They like the power. To tell you the truth, I don't have the answer, and I don't look too deeply for it because I've never really understood why my characters are androgynous or why they are gay. I've never totally understood it, so I sort of let it go. It feels so natural to me and so normal. At any point in *Taltos* I could have veered off and had an affair between Yuri and Ash, and I would have loved it, absolutely loved it. If I didn't do it, it was only because the momentum of the plot was moving me toward things I had a greater interest in. But I could have easily done it. That's so simple for me. There's something unexplored there I just can't get into.

I do believe it, though, when I say the gay aesthetic is our aesthetic. When a movie like *Bride of Frankenstein* works perfectly as a gay allegory and then works also for millions of other people as perhaps no other horror movie in American history has ever worked, there's something really meaningful. It sounds like a cliché, I know, but to me that's the greatest example. *Bride of Frankenstein* is a gay allegory at the very highest pitch. People have written eloquent essays on how it works as a gay allegory and that James Whale, the director, was gay and that other people connected with the production were gay. It's true, but that movie is about all of us. It's about every outsider who's ever lived. It's about every person who tried to give birth and failed. It's about everybody who ever attempted something huge and lost control of it. It's about all of those things, and it's a masterpiece.

A COMMUNITY OF OUTSIDERS

RILEY: Your characters are typically outsiders, but what I find especially interesting is that in your work those outsiders are almost always connected by their very nature to some larger community in the world, whether they like it or not.

RICE: You pointed that out to me once, and I never forgot it. You're the only person I know who's ever said that, but you're right. Each has his own group. I think that's obviously one reason the gay allegory is so immediately available, because that would be true of many gay people: perhaps feeling terribly alienated from your family and your community but then being connected to a great many other gay people and their political concerns and their way of living. I think it's very similar, and I don't really know the reason. Maybe it's because all my life, as I write about outsiders, I see other outsiders who are part of the same thing. My readers, for instance, the ones who come to the signings, they dress in very similar ways. All the way from Boston to Portland, Oregon, they wear the same clothes. In fact, those clothes are now in fashion. The catalogs are filled with the kinds of clothes my readers have been wearing for years, and I'm kind of eager to see what they're going to wear this fall since Donna Karan and Calvin Klein and Ralph Lauren are now making the very clothes they have worn. Crushed and distressed velvet, antique lace, tall leather boots and tight little skirts, and extremely white face makeup with very red lipstick, huge red nails—all of this is in fashion now. Perhaps all of these people are in some way rebels in their community and see themselves as dressing differently, so sometimes they're surprised to discover they look similar to the people in Los Angeles or other places. Also sometimes they're very happy to discover that. That's part of what started the fan club—people who said, basically we all share the fact that we like her books and we like crystals and we like velvet and we like leather jackets; so they made this huge network where they all write to each other and to me.

RILEY: How did they find each other at the outset?

RICE: At the signings. That's where the fan club formed, a signing where a group of them came together in their velvet clothes and spike heels. They didn't really start to show up until *The Vampire Lestat*. I remember the first signing for *The Vampire Lestat* in San Francisco, and people coming in vintage Victorian clothes—the genuine article they'd found in antique clothing stores—layered with lace, their faces painted white, and presenting me with dead flowers. That's where it began, but now it's happened everywhere. Fashion is right on this for a hundred different reasons. Madonna's popularized it, too, and rock music has always loved those images. There've been a number of rock figures who've worn eighteenth-century coats and were drenched in lace and who used a lot of S & M imagery. Someday somebody will analyze it and figure it all out right down to the last gene. All I know is that I'm the dullest-looking person at any signing of mine. [*laughter*] They'll say, "You don't look anything like I expected. I thought you'd look more erotic." And I tell them, "No, I leave that to you."

THE EROTIC: "JUST A DANGEROUS AND BEAUTIFUL GAME"

RILEY: One of the things I hear repeatedly as we talk—a kind of subtext, if you will—is that there's a part of you that wants to write that which is dangerous.

RICE: Absolutely. Dangerous and transgressive, to use that overworked term. There's something in me that spontaneously writes what is transgressive, that is drawn to transgressive imagery—for reasons that have to do with *why* it's transgressive rather than merely the fact that it is. For example, I find something absolutely mesmerizing and terribly, crucially important in the image of a transsexual or a transvestite. That image keeps appearing in my work over and over again in characters. When I consider them truly wise, and truly powerful, and truly possessed of many options, those characters are almost always androgynous. They're almost never fully stereotypical males or stereotypical females. I don't see the perfection of gender as a route to superiority or to capability or to power. On the contrary, I see surrendering to a kind of blending of the sexes as extremely important for characters to discover their vulnerability and to go with it. Fiction is just a luscious game of exploring all of that and tumbling around in it and setting characters into motion and exploring what's going to happen. And it is transgressive material, over and over again.

Another thing that fascinates me for reasons I don't know is incest. It's the love between a brother and sister, the love between a mother and son, the love between people who are so close that the world really should stand back with a little respect for the way that closeness can sometimes become erotic. That fascinates me, the way anything can become erotic.

RILEY: The relationship between parents and children is one of the most persistent themes in your novels, and it's almost always highly eroticized.

RICE: I think I go through the world seeing everything as highly sensuous and erotic. I sometimes perceive the world so much in that way I'm not even aware of it. I'm not even particularly aware I'm eroticizing what I see when I write about it, or that the feelings are bordering on the erotic. The world is that way to me. To deny it is false, it really is. Clothes are about sexuality, dress is about sexuality, photographs are. *Vogue* magazine is about it. When *Vogue* presents photographs of naked children, which it often does, those pictures are erotic. They're beautiful, they're fabulous, they're uplifting, they are gorgeous to behold, but they are very erotic. The erotic and the wholesome are not mutually exclusive. They exist in everything beautiful, and that's the way I see them.

RILEY: Has being a mother, having children and watching Chris grow into his adolescence and mature, has that influenced this perception?

RICE: With both my children, the principal thing I felt

was utterly abandoned to the pure, sensuous enjoyment of kissing them and hugging them and how sweet and cuddly and soft and silky they were. There's never been anything genitally arousing or disturbing about it. There's never been any conflict in my mind. What we have to remember when we're talking about things like this, of course, is that I'm a woman. When I say something is erotic, it's very different from a man saying it. Now, if I were to hug my child and feel a hard-on, that might be very disturbing, but I don't feel things like that. I think that's one of the reasons it doesn't disturb me. Someone else could say, I'm very disturbed by Louis's relationship with Claudia in *Interview*, but it doesn't disturb me because I never had any feelings toward my sisters or toward my daughter that I thought were forbidden or dark or unwholesome. I remember loving them and their beauty so much it made me want to cry—the beauty of a child, its little cheeks, its mouth, its lips, its glistening eyes, all of this. I could just look at people for hours, and they look beautiful to me. Almost anywhere I go, they look beautiful to me. I really see people the way I describe them in the books. Perhaps I'm using the wrong word; perhaps what seems erotic to other people is not erotic to me. Perhaps it's just sensuous, truly sensuous. I loved describing Claudia's bonnets and her ribbons and her hair and her dresses, and of course doing that from Louis's point of view. Maybe for someone else that does have a terribly transgressive overtone, but it doesn't for me. I meant exactly what I said. I loved the ring of her little voice like a bell, loved it when she'd put her little arms up and stretch. That's the way I see life. Possibly if it were more erotic for me, I would have backed away from it, because certainly with my own son I don't feel any erotic desire. I just feel a great delicious love of him growing big and strong. I don't feel anything that threatens my peace of mind in any way.

FEMINISM AND PORNOGRAPHY

RILEY: When you spoke of a potential return to puritanism, you mentioned the feminist movement as one source. Do you think the feminist movement is essentially puritan?

RICE: First of all, I don't think there's one feminist movement. It isn't monolithic. There are many different people who call themselves feminists and many different groups that unite under that banner, and many spokespersons and writers who claim to be. But I would say one segment in the feminist movement is very much puritanical, and that segment is fascist and tyrannical. It has a whole slew of biases that are essentially puritanical and antisexual and, I think, antiwoman. Deeply antiwoman. And they don't know it. I'm talking about the segment of the feminist community that says nobody should pose for *Playboy*. Nobody should buy a magazine that presents women in that light. Nobody should even ride in an automobile that's owned by a limo service called Playboy Limo Service. There are people who won't do that, who actually will stand in front of the Beverly Wilshire hotel and say, "I refuse to get in this car because it's a Playboy Limo and I'm a feminist." I know of an actress who did that. As a matter of fact, I'm very much an admirer of the actress, but that's what she chose to do. That kind of thinking is very shortsighted. I think it's shallow and conformist, and I think it's often very aggressive.

RILEY: Have you gotten much criticism from feminists?

RICE: I get almost no negative feedback from feminists. This is not a whitewash. It's really true. I've gotten perhaps two letters in my life that I know of that were negative letters from women, and one was an absolute lulu. It was just a raving screed. There were statements in it like "While I and my friends are out breaking our asses trying to write rational fiction, you are writing foolishness about vampires and nipple clips. How dare you!" It was just incredible. And I did get a letter not long ago from a woman who sent my books back to me and asked me to send her the money for them because she didn't want to support anybody who wrote pornography. I wrote a really furious letter to her and said, "How dare you! I've donated those books to the local high school," and I invited her to send a copy of the entire correspondence to *The New York Times*. I said I would go to the Supreme Court of the land for the right of women or men to read what they want to read and write what they want to write. But, in general, what I see and what I'm grateful for are a tremendous number of women readers of all different kinds who show up at the signings, at any kind of event, and are very supportive of the books. Women have gone out of their way to tell me how much they like the pornography and how glad they are I did it and that they would love to have more dirty books, as they put it. They're very outspoken. I also have had many visible lesbian readers. I have had since *The Vampire Lestat*, and I'm talking about visible. I'm talking about people who want to be perceived that way and are dressed to be so perceived. I sign hundreds of books all the time for women-and-women and men-and-men. I love my female audience. I'm more aware of what's going on in feminism not so much from what people tell me, but from reading about the actions of people like Andrea Dworkin and Catharine MacKinnon and hearing the kind of legislation they want to push through and the frightening stories about how close it comes. That to me is very scary. But I really don't get much flak. Women do not walk up to me on the street and say, "How could you write pornography?" They're very supportive. I think my books are in most women's bookstores that I know of.

ON BEING A SUCCESSFUL WOMAN

RILEY: Has your success, which has transformed your life in so many ways, changed your own sense of being a woman?

RICE: No, not really. If anything, it's pointed up the maddening things a little more. For example, it's fairly common for people to ask me if I ever cook for my family. Now, I don't think they ask James Michener that. I doubt they would ask John Grisham. It's even common for there to be jokes about the fact that I don't cook. *You* cook a meal?! There's always a little implication that I've somehow failed in that regard, that a true woman makes a couple million a year and cooks for her family. So I do get that sort of thing. Actually, it's true I don't cook anymore. [*laughter*] I don't have time, and I don't want to do it anymore. I'm doing other things. There's another thing, too. Throughout the years of this success, many people have asked me how I deal with my husband, how I protect him from my success, and how I take care of his needs. As a woman who's well known, I think you confront an enormous amount of sexist prejudice. The margin of privilege, or whatever it is, that surrounds a man simply never surrounds a woman. It just doesn't happen.

RILEY: That's an ironic double standard, isn't it, because people rarely presume a wife is denied any kind of personal identity just because her husband is a great success.

RICE: *Denied* is the key word. But if the wife is a great success, there's an automatic suspicion: What must that do to the man? I suppose I've learned to live with it. I'm more at peace with it now than ever in my life, but a lot of that comes your way. There's a perception that you're denying your son and your husband things they deserve. You're perceived as having done something to them that must be awfully hard on them. People suppose you must have to make a lot up to them for what they have to go through, seeing you on tour or on television. You're never perceived as taking care of your family. You never get that reward.

3

"Roquelaure and Rampling"

RILEY: It's not uncommon for an author to move at some point from one publishing house and editor to another, but your experience is unusual. You've actually worked with several different editors and houses simultaneously.

RICE: After *Interview* was published, I desperately wanted to work on a sprawling novel about the Free People of Color in New Orleans, which was a subject I'd been researching for years. I was in love with the idea of the octaroons and the quadroons making up a class of their own, free but not equal—a caste, so to speak—in New Orleans before the Civil War. I wanted to write not only about the beautiful quadroon women who so often became mistresses of white planters, but also about the quadroon men who had published the first literary magazine in Louisiana, of which there were three issues. I was intrigued by the fact that the men had left us their names but the women had not. Yet it was the women that history perceived as having had power in white society, while the men were confined to the shadows, or sent to France. When I presented the idea to Vicky Wilson at Knopf, I received an excellent advance of $150,000. Part of that was to be paid on signing, and the rest in increments. When I handed in the first hundred or so pages for the second payment, I didn't feel Vicky was enthusiastic about the book, and I didn't feel Bob Gottlieb was either. I had direct dealings only with Vicky, but I knew of Bob's feelings, and Bob was the man who ran Knopf.

The lack of enthusiasm instantly frightened me right into the arms of another publisher. Simon & Schuster's Joni Evans liked the pages very much and was enthusiastic about the change in direction in my work, so she picked up the contract—that is, she matched the advance. Working on the novel, I had much enthusiastic input not only from Joni, who was based in New York, but also from John Dodds, who was then a Simon & Schuster editor working on the West Coast. He lived in Belvedere just across the bay with his wife, the actress Vivian Vance, who had co-starred in the *I Love Lucy* show. By that time Vivian, who later died of cancer, was already quite ill. Meeting John, working with him, was wonderful. Joni was also a joy. When the novel, which was *The Feast of All Saints*, was finished, the house was extremely enthusiastic, and so was my agent. But *Feast* did not do well. It didn't become a bestseller, and it did not earn back its advance. And Hollywood was not interested in it either. All of this was very painful to me. But I had already been struck lightning-bolt style by the idea of a novel about the Italian castrati. I'd come across a paragraph in a book describing them—boys who were taken from poor families, and castrated, and then trained to be singers, some of whom went on to become great celebrities all over Europe. I was intrigued with the idea of following one such boy through tragedy and triumph.

RILEY: What was the response at Simon & Schuster?

RICE: Joni was not interested in the material. She was quite frank about it. The subject matter—Italian castrati, the eighteenth century—did not work for her. But she was kind enough to give me a small advance against a future contract, which under the circumstances was a wonderful thing to do. She knew by then that *Feast* was not going to work with the public, but she remained loyal to me and good to me. It's my opinion Joni just couldn't figure out why *Feast* hadn't been a huge bestseller. She loved the storytelling in it and the characters, but it ended up selling only modestly. I don't even remember the figures now. In the meantime I pursued the castrati book, knowing full well Joni wasn't going to want it. During this period Vicky Wilson, who'd been my editor at Knopf, paid a visit to the West Coast. She was in San Francisco and then she headed down to Los Angeles, seeing her West Coast writers. She and I had remained in friendly contact after I left Knopf, and of course she had witnessed the failure of *Feast* to become a bestseller. We visited and she told me she was very interested in seeing what I did with the castrati novel, which was *Cry to Heaven*. In other words she graciously made the gesture that meant, if we like this book, we'll take you back to Knopf.

RILEY: So you continued to work on *Cry to Heaven* without knowing where it was going to end up?

RICE: I was essentially still a Simon & Schuster author,

but I was not really. I was sort of up for grabs. At the time I met an editor from another house who was also interested in *Cry to Heaven* on the basis of what he had heard. By the time the novel was ready for a publisher to look at, it was almost finished. Although I would do one more revision, it was all done except the last chapter; so I decided to go for a contract at that time. Eventually I sent manuscripts to Joni Evans, to this other editor, and to Vicky. I didn't know who, if anyone, would want this book. Joni at once declined, but she was most kind. She said that *Cry* had some of the best work I'd ever done, but the world of the castrati simply didn't exist for her.

RILEY: Were you very disappointed?

RICE: As I told her, I'd been expecting this. Meanwhile, at Knopf, Vicky Wilson received the novel with open arms. Both she and Bob Gottlieb—and his word was law in those days—were enthusiastic about it and willing to publish it.

RILEY: What about the other editor you referred to?

RICE: I had met the other editor, who didn't want his name mentioned, in the midst of all this, and he was willing to pay more for *Cry to Heaven*, but I knew that I wanted to return to Knopf. There was also interest from someone else. If memory serves me, John Dodds had moved from Simon & Schuster, and he was also interested. I decided against an auction. I wanted to go home to Knopf. I accepted their terms, an advance of $75,000. John was extremely understanding, and so was the other editor.

RILEY: What made Knopf so attractive to you?

RICE: Having come to appreciate the uniqueness of Knopf as an imprint, the physical beauty of their books, and the incorruptible nature of Vicky Wilson, I was very happy to return. And I have never regretted going back. I did revise and finish *Cry to Heaven* with Vicky's input and blessing. But it was not a big seller. It didn't even sell as much as *Feast*, but it received a glowing review in *The New York Times* from the writer Alice Hoffman—the first positive review I'd ever had there—and this proved an enormous critical asset. Thereafter, I remained a Knopf author. I never severed the tie again. When I did my pornography and Vicky did not want to publish it, we agreed I would go elsewhere for it but remain at Knopf for my Anne Rice books. And it worked.

RILEY: You published the pornography at another house under the pseudonym of A. N. Roquelaure. Was a similar decision made when you later wrote *Exit to Eden* and *Belinda* under the Anne Rampling pseudonym?

RICE: Similar but also different. Let me say first that Vicky never saw *Exit to Eden*. That book grew out of my Roquelaure—*Beauty* books—identity, and was presented to the editor of the Roquelaure books as an erotic novel. But he didn't like it. I didn't think there was a prayer Vicky would like it, so I went to John Dodds, who was now at Arbor House. He loved it, and that launched Anne Rampling. When I wrote *Belinda*, it was with a contract from Knopf for a new novel. Once again, Vicky and Bob Gottlieb were not enthusiastic about it. I don't know the whole behind-the-scenes story. My impression is that Vicky was more optimistic, but Bob didn't care for the book at all. There were many complaints about it. So I said, "Look, let me take this to John Dodds and see if he'll publish it, and then you stick with me until I get *Queen of the Damned* done." And they agreed. There was an advance from Knopf against *Belinda*, and they actually agreed to put that against the third *Vampire* novel and to wait. I don't even remember exactly how it worked out contractually, but they were very patient. Vicky and I talked it over and we agreed. You know, you make those decisions on the basis of what people are saying to you second- and thirdhand. It's a question of gauging the temperature of enthusiasm at the house, and in terms of Bob Gottlieb there was no enthusiasm for *Belinda*. I felt that I wanted to go with the novel, and I believed that John Dodds would get excited about it and would publish it. I thought it over and decided to publish *Belinda* not as Anne Rice but as Anne Rampling, the author of *Exit to Eden*. John had published *Eden*, and he took *Belinda* at once. If he had turned it down, I don't know what would have happened with it. So Vicky let me go to John with *Belinda* and remain a Knopf author for everything else. This was a unique path to take, but it worked for both of us. I think we shocked the publishing world a bit by these understandings—that I could be Roquelaure and Rampling at other houses, but be at Knopf for my other work—but it was all very amicable.

THE *BEAUTY* BOOKS

RILEY: I gather that the *Beauty* trilogy continues to sell at a tremendous rate.

RICE: The *Beauty* books outsell almost everything. I mean, they're selling so much that it's almost ludicrous. They even outsell *Interview with the Vampire*.

RILEY: Recently, one of the *Beauty* books was number four or five on the *Los Angeles Times* paperback bestseller list. I found that quite remarkable all these years after they were originally published.

RICE: There were a couple of deejays in Los Angeles who read one of the books over the air, and they caused an enormous run on the bookstores.

RILEY: To say nothing of the FCC!

RICE: No doubt. [*laughter*] It made a huge stir in California, and bookstores even had to send down to San Diego for copies. There was a flurry of publicity about it, and a couple of articles in the paper. That's probably when you saw it. But they are selling like mad. Very sadly their editor, Bill Whitehead of Dutton, died a few years ago, but I wish Bill could have lived to see this. He would have loved it. You know, those books still have the covers Bill put on them. There was a point where the publisher was going to change them. They wanted to put some frontal nudity on the covers, and I said, "No, don't, because the secret of those books is that people don't stare at you when you buy them. The covers are so artistic that really there's no embarrassment. If you put nudity on, then women are going to be embarrassed to throw it into the baby carriage in the grocery." But Bill's covers were just perfect. Those books, what can I say about those books? The three of them together have outearned *Interview with the Vampire* each year. To me that's quite amazing, and they're just backlist books. They're just being shipped out of the house. For years, though, they had a hard time. We couldn't even get the house to ship them. One of the most frequent questions I would get was, "Where can I get your *Beauty* books?" And we would call and call the publisher, but finally it became too big even for the publisher to ignore. [*laughter*]

RILEY: Why wouldn't the publisher ship them?

RICE: Well, publishers are so inefficient, among other things. There's a lot of heartache on that score, and we could talk about that at length—books that don't get shipped and orders that don't get filled. All the word of mouth in the world can't pull the book out if they don't ship it. Also, that particular publishing house has problems that way. But it is so amusing to me now because, when I wrote them, Bill and I took so much flak on those books. I remember having my secret suspicions people would like those books if they knew about them. [*laughter*] I remember that Bill made a little cardboard dump, with boots and a whip, for the bookstore displays, and the people in the chain stores were so outraged by this dump they threw it in the trash. They wouldn't use it. Now the main buyers of the *Beauty* books all over America are women going into the chain stores and buying them. They come up to me with their baby strollers and their children and the groceries, and say, we love your dirty books, and they laugh. That's the main backing for the *Beauty* books, very much mainstream America, very much the secretaries, very much the housewives, very much the mall shoppers.

HER OWN VISION

RILEY: This was not only a period of unconventional arrangements for you. I've heard you say that you also learned a great deal. What exactly did you learn from all this?

RICE: First and foremost, I cannot be deterred. If I believe in a book, if I start on it and pitch into it, I have to and will continue it to the bloody end regardless of editorial criticism. I realized a little more each year how much I had to pursue my own vision. When rejected, I refuse to change a book. I simply move away. There is nothing personal in this. It is simply the way I work. In my own way, I cannot write anything I'm not wholly committed to, and once that commitment is made, only I can reject that work for my own interior reasons. I will shop anything that's rejected until I find a place for it. What I also learned was that Vicky Wilson in her integrity, in her inability to publish something she does not love, was almost unique in publishing. She simply couldn't do the Roquelaure books. She didn't want to, and she couldn't. She did, by the way, recommend Bill Whitehead, the editor who published them. My final estimation of Joni Evans was that she was essentially an extremely nice person but a commercial editor. After the failure of *Feast*, she could not be enthusiastic for anything except something she thought would be a bestseller. That was her nature. She had taken me on as the big bucks author of *Interview with the Vampire*, and I had failed with *The Feast of All Saints*. Vicky Wilson and Knopf were much more responsive to me as an eccentric author who went to weird subject matter with great passion. I remained friends with Joni Evans, with John Dodds, and of course with Vicky. All of this went down, as they say, without harsh words. It was unusual to become three authors and to end up with three publishers, but it worked.

RILEY: Beyond the fate of the individual novels and the varying degrees of enthusiasm, or the lack of it, have your actual working experiences differed significantly with the various editors?

RICE: John Dodds was totally different from the others. He was kind of laid-back, but he was a really fine editor. He didn't mark all over manuscripts or attempt to change all kinds of things. When John presented his criticism of what worked for him and what didn't, or when he had gotten bored, it was very easy for me to take. I would go back fired up to redo a section after talking to John and hearing him say, "By the time we get to this point, we've heard too much about this character." I'd listen to that and go back and redo it. I never felt exactly the same kind of ease with Vicky or with Bill Whitehead, because they were very different kinds of editors. They're both very highly respected—very able and very highly respected—and I wouldn't want to imply that they weren't. But they're much more hands-on and in some ways more dedicated. I believe John was deeply respectful and understanding of writers, but other people might have seen him as simply less dedicated. I'm not sure. He didn't seem to me to have the same emotional investment in the books he published as Bill and Vicky. The book really had to be theirs in every regard for them to publish it. John could publish a wide spectrum of things—he could do a book by Merv Griffin or a book by President Johnson or he could do the Rampling books—and he was very good and very professional about it all. For some reason that coolness on his part, or that distance, allowed me to hear him. I could be too threatened by Vicky and Bill. There's no room on that page for anybody but me, and if somebody else comes along with a lot of intensity and starts to mark things, I can't take it. So I struggled a lot with both of them. Bill would change things, and I wouldn't want them changed. There was some very heavy copyediting done on the *Beauty* books, and I wound up sending the manuscript back and demanding they erase everything off it. It was the same basic misunderstanding I've had a lot of times with other people. But both Vicky and Bill were very understanding, and we worked it out. Bill was particularly understanding when I got so emotionally upset about the copyediting. I said, "I cannot read through these things. I don't even know who this person is, and they've rewritten phrase after phrase." I just exploded, finally. I said, "You're telling me to read these rewrites, but if I met this person on the street and they asked me to help them get published, I wouldn't have time. Yet here I am, having to read their rewrites of every third sentence I've written." I was just in a rage on the phone, and I remember him being totally charming and nice and saying, "I'm sorry and we'll straighten it out."

RILEY: You've had a copy editor literally rewrite your work?

RICE: Oh yes. It happens all the time. Your book goes in and is sent to the copy editor, and the copy editor decides to rephrase all these things. Then you're told, well, you should just read the comments, and if you don't like them, just write "stet" in the margin or erase them. But, you see, you really shouldn't have to read those comments. You have to get to a point where they don't do that to you, but it's happened to many writers. Behind the scenes there are a thousand stories of people who have gone through this. I was talking to an English editor not long ago, and she told me about a very well-known literary author to whom it had happened to such an extent that a copy editor had virtually rewritten her book and just crushed her for years. It's so maddening, and an author doesn't even know who the copy editors are. They're anonymous people who are simply supposed to proofread. I suppose rewriting may be very important if they have an illiterate writer's manuscript on their hands, but it's just an endless nightmare. What has finally happened with me is that I've gotten the clout to mail it back and say, take everything off of it or I will not read it. Now, Vicky takes very good care that these things don't happen. She and I have a wonderful working relationship, and she sees to it that doesn't happen. The copyediting is clean. I send the sheet in, and the sheet says: Add no words; change no words; mark errors in the margin; where a word appears to be left out, do not volunteer the word, simply put a question mark; if something doesn't make sense, put a big note; do not do any rewriting; do not do any cutting. I give these instructions—*proofread only*—and that's what's supposed to happen, but that's the culmination of years and years of tears and screaming and fighting because, yes, that's what they do. They sit there and rewrite your sentences. I think there's a great deal of pride involved in it, and it can be very annoying and very hard for you to get to the real copyediting through all those other things. On *Belinda*, for instance, there was a particularly aggressive copy editor who decided that my definition of AIDS wasn't correct, so he deleted half a page that I had written discussing AIDS—just deleted it. And in another instance I had mentioned the King parties here in New Orleans after Christmas when everyone gets King cakes, and the copy editor had scratched out *King* and written *Rex*, apparently thinking it referred to the Rex parade at Mardi Gras. Anytime he didn't know what something meant, he wrote in some long explanation of his own. Things like that are not only intrusive and inaccurate, they're just maddening. With fiction writers, so far as copyediting goes, there are no rules, and unless you give very strict directions, you can get a very over-copyedited book. I've heard other stories. There was a nonfiction writer who had written her autobiography. She's a sports figure, and I remember being told that when they sent it to the copy editor, to their amazement the copy editor virtually rewrote it. The entire voice that had been achieved by this woman, which her own editor valued, was rewritten, and so the editor had to send it back to say, again, take everything off and start from scratch; that wasn't what we wanted. But they'll do that, they'll actually revoice a book. I think they're creative people who want to do a good job and who want to help you, and they just get carried away.

RILEY: How much autonomy does a Vicky Wilson or a Bill Whitehead have to say yes and make it stick? Does a book typically have to go beyond them to an editorial board or a committee of some sort that has the final power to say yes or no?

RICE: That's a hard question to answer for a variety of reasons. Bill Whitehead had a lot of power, and he would take on anybody in the house to fight for the books he wanted to publish. I think he took on everybody for the *Beauty* books. I don't think anybody wanted them. Everyone thought they were horrendously politically incorrect and just outrageous, and Bill took them all on and got them through. What his actual position was at that time, I don't know. I remember John Dodds turning down a novel a friend of mine had written because he said he couldn't get the support he wanted in the house. So it varies from house to house. Vicky Wilson has tremendous power. She can virtually accept the manuscript for Knopf and say, this is satisfactory and acceptable and here's your check. On the other hand, when it comes to novels like mine, I don't know what would happen if Vicky rejected it. You see, at this point we're dealing with so much money that if Vicky were to call me and say she found a book unacceptable, I would just turn around and call the head of the house and say, is this it? Do you want me to leave? Is this what's going on? It could be very confusing. There's so much money involved, there are such big printings now, there are so many readers that it's very hard to say. But Vicky, I would say, is just as powerful as any editor at Knopf except the president himself, and she always has been. And Bill was always very powerful. With John, it depended. He was at several different houses when I knew him, William Morrow, Putnam, Simon & Schuster, Arbor House, all of them different, so it would vary.

There are many editors who don't have that kind of power, and there are many stories of editors who love books and can't get them through the editorial board. That's particularly true at houses like Simon & Schuster that really do have a board and the whole board wants to rule on the book before it's accepted. To my way of thinking, that's one of the reasons the terrific brouhaha over *American Psycho* was so misconceived. I felt that if the feminists in the NOW organization had succeeded in making Random House drop *American Psycho* they would have been basically stripping the individual editor of the power to just say, I want to publish this book, I don't care if it's politically correct or not. That's a very important power. That's the power by which really eccentric and weird and transgressive books get published. NOW treated the whole thing as if it were a corporate decision by a monolith. They said, Random House thinks that killing women makes money, and we want to boycott Random House because they published this book. Well, that kind of thinking would lead directly to boards of people ruling on every book and to young editors being told, no, we can't do this crazy novel.

RILEY: Once some years ago we were talking about *The Vampire Lestat*, and you told me about a disagreement with your editor. She didn't want you to mention *Interview with the Vampire* explicitly in the sequel, but you felt that, given the shift in focus and tone, readers were owed some explanation or acknowledgment.

RICE: Yes, I remember. I felt I had to do that, and I did include it. It's very understood with Knopf now that I will make no changes. It's really take it or leave it. It's been that way since *The Queen of the Damned*. You know, I'd always had mixed feelings, really tormented feelings, about the whole process of an editor wanting this expanded or that changed, and the vulnerable state in which an author makes those changes, waiting for acceptance from the house, waiting for an advance check. And I finally just said, "This is it. You either publish it or I'll go somewhere else." *The Queen of the Damned* was really the one I went to the barricades on. And even then I still did a few little things because I was encouraged to do them by my editor. There was a section in *The Queen of the Damned* in which she really felt it was best to cut some material out. I'm not sure it was ever better for having been cut, but I did do it. Before that, I would try very hard to accommodate whatever people said, and I was very attentive to them. But now, no. I try to be very polite listening to what they say, but I do not change the novel on the basis of it. Almost never, unless somebody points out an absolute mistake. Frequently, Vicky will feel strongly about something, about whole sections even, and I'll say, no. She didn't want the introduction to *The Tale of the Body Thief*. She wanted just to begin in Miami, and I said, "No, they have to know where we've been and what we're going to do. The readers are entitled to know that, and then we'll go to Miami. You can't have readers going through the Miami section wondering, where are the others, where's Armand, where's Gabrielle, when are they all coming together, what's he doing now, where's he been?" One of the biggest wars I have is to keep Lestat's flippant and vernacular statements, like when he says, "I'm the James Bond of the vampires." They wanted to cut that line, but I said, "No, leave it in there." I'm very glad I leave those things in because I think they're important, that tone is important to his character, but I have to fight for him all the time on that score.

But Vicky and I have a wonderful relationship that isn't just the conventional relationship of an author listening to an editor. What she does now, really, is she discusses these books with me, and she gives me terrific insights into them by virtue of her response. It doesn't have anything to do with changing the book, though. For example, with *Taltos* she said a fascinating thing to me. She said, "This is a fairy tale, and it's hard to pull off a fairy tale." She said that it requires a certain voice and lightness all the way through, but that it was achieved in *Taltos*. And she talked about how when you go home and you deal with your demons, you can sometimes finally come to a place where there's a great deal of light. She felt that after everything had been worked through with *The Witching Hour* and *Lasher*, that *Taltos* was this place of light. So her interpretation was fascinating, and when I look back on it, I realize the novel does move like a fairy tale. It's as if I had said, I'm going to take the conventions of a fairy tale. I'm going to have a dwarf and a giant, and I'm going to have three witches and they're going to go out to the woods, and then it's going to end with the couple going off to the circle. It really seems like an almost deliberate use of the conventions of fairy tales, but it was not. I was just sitting there writing. I just knew who Ash was, and I knew what I wanted to get across about him, and I knew what I was dealing with and what crazy risks I was taking.

LANGUAGE: "AN INTENSE CHOICE"

RILEY: Critics, of course, are a significant part of the book world, too, and one of the things about which they've been extremely uneven in responding to your work is your use of language. It's not a matter of simply liking or disliking it—obviously some do and some don't—but I have rarely read anything in which I thought a critic understood how deliberate your language is.

RICE: What a choice it is, what an intense choice. It's a dedicated choice, that's true.

RILEY: Not long after *The Witching Hour* was published, I was talking to a friend who quoted someone else as saying that it was overwritten. I remember telling him I thought that was a misconception. I wouldn't say the novels are overwritten. Instead, there is what I think of as a kind of overripeness that's characteristic of your style, but that's a conscious artistic choice on your part.

RICE: I get that all the time. It's very common. In fact, as I've mentioned, one of the things I did in the Rampling books was to try to get away from that very thing and to go deliberately to a strict Raymond Chandler type of prose. It always amuses me when somebody calls one of the Rampling books florid. I remember my agent reading one of them and saying, "You know, it's interesting to read these books you write as Rampling because critics accuse you of being bloated and florid and none of that is true here." It was a recognition of what was attempted in that book. There's a curious irony about it. Those who value my other kind of language think the Rampling books are failures. One critic—I was devastated by this statement which was written by, I think, Dorothy Allison in the *Village Voice*, but I could be wrong—but she wrote a really thoughtful article, and she said, "In the Rampling books she's operating at sixty percent of her power." I was crushed. I don't feel that at all. A book like *Exit to Eden* was written in this white-hot passion, and I think it's a completely amazing book by anybody's standards, whether you like it or dislike it. How can anyone say that was at sixty percent of somebody's power? She went on to say that it was worth reading *Exit to Eden* for Lisa's clothes. I thought that was an interesting comment at the time.

RILEY: A New York comment.

RICE: The best-dressed dominatrix in a book this season [*laughter*], the best-dressed bisexual dominatrix. But anyway, the people, some of them my friends, who thought my earlier books were overwritten and impossible, just really overdone and completely misconceived, those friends often had profound reactions to the Rampling novels. They would say, "You've really grown in writing ability in this novel *Belinda*. It's amazing that you could do this. You got away from all that stuff we couldn't figure out, all those drowsing flowers and picket fences and burning skies." But in a way *Belinda* does not get away from all those things.

Every single novel I write, the people nearest me tell me I have given up my florid language and this one's all story. I kid you not. [*laughter*] And then the book is published, and lots of people call it florid and dense and unreadable, and I can't figure out why the people closest to me say that, but they do. They say, "You'll never write us another florid book like *Interview with a Vampire*. *The Witching Hour*'s all story." *The Witching Hour*? [*laughter*] It's just pages and pages of people standing on the corner listening to the crickets and going crazy, or with the light changing and reflecting in the windows. I don't understand what they mean.

RILEY: There is an especially suggestive passage early in *The Witching Hour*, right at the beginning of Petyr's history of the Mayfair family, which explicitly talks about the language that's going to be used in that section of the novel.

RICE: Oh right, I know what you're referring to. I had so much fun with that. It was Aaron Lightner saying that we have to remind ourselves that even in the 1600s phrases like "the coast was clear" and "her pretty nice voice" were common. I love that kind of thing. When I'm reading a memoir or a book from that period, I'm very aware of that. Another common criticism that comes from New York is that the tone is too contemporary, and very often they're talking about a phrase that is in fact very old, that almost goes back to Shakespeare. Of course, I say I want to keep it in, and they say, you may be right technically but it doesn't sound that way. I was using the word *advertise* in *Cry to Heaven* in the way I think Shakespeare uses it: "We are advertising that we are castrated by the way we dress," and everybody objected. But look at Shakespeare; look at what that word really means. Anyway, I'm glad you saw that because nobody else has ever mentioned that and I loved that. That was carefully drawn; that was attempting to be very accurate about the kind of voice that would occur in books in the 1600s—the snideness, the humor, the cynicism, the sarcasm. No, not snideness, but the kind of rapid sophistication that a man like Petyr would have had when he describes that dinner party where everyone is getting drunk and falling in the soup and the spirit possesses the old man. I thought that was a hilarious scene. I was laughing out loud as I was writing it. That's very characteristic of the memoirs of that period, to write like that.

RILEY: Have you read for the explicit purpose of language—that is, done research to see what the pitch and tone and temper of language were in other periods?

RICE: Wallowed in it, just wallowed in it. I have gone back through the memoirs and travel books of the period, the adventures of various people, and I've studied the turns of language and the things they would say. That was one of the great discoveries for me when I moved away from the nineteenth century and began to explore the eighteenth—how much faster the narratives moved and how much fresher the language seemed when you read Casanova's tales or Goldoni's autobiography or the memoir of Lorenzo Da Ponte, the librettist who worked with Mozart. There wasn't that ponderous Victorian quality. There was a very sharp tone, very free, more modern. One of the reasons I was able to do *The Vampire Lestat* was that the research into the eighteenth century for *Cry to Heaven* helped give me the security to attempt Lestat as this very fast-talking, sophisticated aristocrat. Louis's voice in *Interview* is really more in the Victorian, Henry James, Dickens mode: "I went out into the night and my mind was a pool waiting for the moonbeams to strike it." *Interview* is filled with language like that, and some of that doesn't get my respect as much as the things achieved in *The Vampire Lestat*, for instance when he says, "Last night I dreamed the dream of family," and then he tells that incredible dream. That line was borrowed consciously from a poem by James Merrill, who wrote, "Again last night I dreamed the dream called / Laundry." Many times lines from poems will be springboards for me. I'm probably admitting too much. [*laughter*] People will say I imitated it too closely. But no one ever mentions it. I tear my hair out over these things, and no one ever sees the influence or the similarity. They don't even get anywhere near it; they never expect to—critics least of all because they don't think someone writing this type of fiction would read Flaubert or Yeats. That perception exists far more in their minds, though, than in the minds of readers.

BOOK REVIEWING: "IT'S JUST CHAOS"

RILEY: There's a bias created instantly by the subject matter: If a novel is about vampires, it can't possibly be by someone who is widely read or concerned with serious questions and themes. There's a whole set of presumptions such a book is likely to be met with.

RICE: Sometimes a book will be trampled in the name of those presumptions: Popular fiction should be about ordinary people with buckets of tears, but this stupid book is about vampires. That's the most maddening thing about American popular criticism. It really is. It is so slipshod, so uneven, and it's so without any tradition of accuracy or excellence that it doesn't give you an accurate view of the perception of a book either in academia or among readers generally. You cannot read the reviews of any author's work, whether it's Updike's or Stephen King's or Donna Tartt's, and get a coherent picture of what those writers are about, because the reviewing standards are so abysmal. Anybody can review a book, and they can write any stupid thing they want, and they can do it in the L.A. *Times* and *The New York Times*, too, most of the time, if they play their cards right.

RILEY: It seems to me that one of the problems with popular book reviewing is that there are, in fact, too many people doing it.

RICE: Oh yes, freelancers for twenty-five dollars and fifty dollars. For example, *The New York Times* is not supposed to hire you to write more than two or three reviews a year because that's their union agreement. They have to spread the books out among all these freelancers all over the country, so there isn't any coherence. Even when you tell them, "I haven't read the other books by that author," they'll say, "Oh well, give us a fresh perspective." Well, who needs a fresh perspective on someone who's written three novels? Somebody should review the third novel who's read the other two. There are frequently reviews of my work written by people who haven't read the other books. They're not very helpful. They're not going to be very helpful to the reader of the review, and they're not going to be very helpful to the reader of books. Too often the reviews are too ignorant, they're too off the mark. It isn't really even a body of work; it's just chaos. It's reached the point where I don't think publishers should support them anymore. If I were running a publishing house, I would not send out review copies. I'm always telling them, "Don't send any. Don't send the *San Francisco Chronicle* a book. Let them buy it if they want to tear it to pieces and call it the worst book ever published, like they did to *Vampire Lestat*. Fine, let them go buy it." But publishers need the free publicity, whether the review is bad or good. They need it desperately for most of their books, so they send out tons of review copies and they support these newspapers by doing it. Even if it's a small book section, all these books come pouring in. I even know of cases where people have sent a copy of a book to a critic with a letter saying, please read it, and then later found the book in a used-book store with the letter still in it.

RILEY: Nonetheless, you've written book reviews yourself. How do you decide when you will do a review?

RICE: I don't do them much anymore, but I did it for years when I was asked. If I was asked by *The Washington Post* or *The New York Times* or the *San Francisco Chronicle*,

I would do it, but for various reasons I finally stopped reviewing altogether. The last time, I think it was *The New York Times* that sent me a book. I knew there was no way I could do justice to it, given what my schedule is like now, so I sent it back. But generally for years I would try to review whatever the *Times* presented to me. I remember when they called me about Scott Turow's *Presumed Innocent.* They said, "This is a new novel; do you want to take this on?" And I said, "Yes, send it, it sounds like it's up my alley." That was my one review that made the first page. That was my biggest splash as a reviewer. But I didn't do it often enough to be a presence in the *Times* or anything like that. I did it a couple of times a year at most and finally just stopped. Once or twice I've called them and said I was at a point where I'd really love to review something, and they would send something. You can't ask them to send a particular book, of course. They wouldn't do that, but they look around and find something. I reviewed true crime for them. I have a special interest in it, so I reviewed a number of books in that genre for them.

American literary criticism—and here I'm talking about book reviewing rather than scholarly studies—is much more hospitable when it's a foreign writer who's making dramatic experiments in style and form and who's writing something that has nothing to do with the middle class. The critics are much quicker, for example, to latch on to something like John Fowles's *The French Lieutenant's Woman* because it's written by an Englishman. If that had been written by an American, it might not have gotten nearly as much attention. An American should be writing *Rabbit Redux* or Anne Tyler's novels. An American should be writing Alice

Adams's stories in *The New Yorker*. That's one reason I was so thrilled to see the success of a novel like Donna Tartt's *The Secret History*. Fiction like that about educated people is often dismissed as unrealistic. There is also a real prejudice in American literature that if you're writing about someone rich, you're writing fantasy. We have a body of intellectuals who don't consider the life of someone like David Geffen, who produced the film of *Interview* and who's very wealthy, to be a worthy subject for literature. That's a powerful bias. The junk writers are generally the ones who write about the rich and famous. At one point, I decided to find out whether these writers really knew the rich and famous, or whether they were making it all up [*laughter*], whether it was just a fantasy. I actually read a couple of biographies of Jacqueline Susann and all of her books, and I discovered Jackie Susann was writing about her own world. Bad as her stuff was, she was writing about people she knew. She had worked in the theater, and she knew all of those models and actresses. The most dramatic scenes she described were scenes that had to do with her friends. Her books are perceived as trash, just junk, and I think finally they are. She was not intelligent enough or talented enough to pull it all together into great books. But my point is that the subject matter itself has become the mark of the junk writer. The assumption is that a serious writer just wouldn't write such stories. Now, that might have been different before my time, when there were serious American writers, quote unquote, who wrote about the rich.

RILEY: Well, Fitzgerald, obviously, and Henry James, Edith Wharton.

RICE: I think that bias is one of the problems in American literature. This great, materialistic country is always trying to subdue its literature and to make it almost like TV docudrama. If you read the reviews in *Time* and *Newsweek*, the bias is clearly that the more like ordinary life and the more like news the writing is, the more likely it is to be serious. They give a much better shake to nonfiction books than to what they would see as a highly imaginative or fanciful work or an allegorical work. They tend to ridicule those.

RILEY: Don't you think, though, that despite that bias and the assumptions that underlie it, some genuinely significant American literature has been written about the commonplace, the ordinary world?

RICE: Oh absolutely. My argument is that it's not the only thing that can be done well. It's not the only literature that's worthwhile. I think Saul Bellow has written brilliant novels. I suspect Updike has. I think a novel that crossed both popular and intellectual lines was *Ordinary People* by Judith Guest. That was a fine book with wonderful characters, wonderful truth and emotional impact, and beautifully written. What I'm objecting to is the bias. There's always been more than one kind of good literature. For every Jane Austen and Henry James, there's a Herman Melville and a Nathaniel Hawthorne, or there's a Mary Shelley, who I think is a terrifically underrated writer. I realize I've jumped over to England [*laughter*], but you know what I mean. Finally, at this point, we may be easing up a little and giving our writers freedom to make experiments that aren't going to be judged solely by whether their work is about the average American, but it's taken us a while to do that. It seems to me that if you look at the whole century, from 1900 to the present time, this bias took over more strongly in the fifties. There was a shift then where the *Saturday Evening Post* short story truly became the model for the American novel. At least up to that time people expected a little more of the novel. They expected Hemingway, they expected Faulkner, they even expected Carson McCullers. There's an enormous amount of spectacle in a novel like *The Heart Is a Lonely Hunter*. Somehow or other by the sixties, though, they became convinced that *Saturday Evening Post* stories about ordinary Americans and incidents in their lives were the proper subject for the novel. You expand that, you put handsome covers on it, and it deals with, say, a young person in her thirties struggling with a divorce, an abortion, a marriage, a personal conflict, and that really is just about the highest the novel can attain. Anybody who isn't writing about middle-class manners and mores is writing foolish nonsense.

RILEY: So you think there's a greater flexibility now?

RICE: Yes, I think it's more wide-open. More experiments are happening. I think *The Secret History* is a testimony to the new flexibility. I'm not sure what would have happened to that as a first novel in the late sixties and seventies. Now, though, the fact that it could burst on the scene and two hundred thousand people would buy a novel like that is a wonderful thing for American literature. I think part of the enormous success of *The Joy Luck Club* was a direct tribute to the fact that people were tired of reading about ordinary Americans. If Amy Tan had written that about ordinary Americans, it would have fallen in with all the other books about ordinary Americans, but she wrote it about Chinese Americans, and there were new lessons to be learned. She could go back in her characters' imaginations into China, which was totally alien to us, and describe this incredible experience we didn't know about of what women went through who came out of this old and rigid society and then came to America. When she gave us all that, it was as much related to our lives as any other immigrant experience. The fact that she swept up readers as she did, that the book was hugely popular, that was American literature opening up. It was saying, we want other things, we want other voices, we've had enough of Rabbit. The Southern writers have always been a refreshing wind through all of that. They do write about craziness and grotesquerie, and they bring spectacle. I really believe in Aristotle's principles: Give them spectacle, drama, catharsis, pity, fear. That's what readers want. He said it about the drama, of course, but I believe it's true about the novel. I don't think there's any better advice on the novel you could give someone than Aristotle's *Poetics*.

I think this is a good time now because I see things opening up again. I see people looking at gay literature, and I see them looking at literature that had been relegated to the genres and now giving it another chance as something worth their attention. Of course, somebody else who knows more about it can probably annihilate my arguments because he or she could bring up so many writers I don't know anything about, but that's my overview. That's the overview of someone who drifts through bookstores every few days, and does read *The New York Times Book Review*. That's the picture I have of it.

THE "LITERARY SCENE" AND NEW WRITERS

RILEY: I've referred to the American literary scene, but that's probably a misleading term, or at least one that oversimplifies. The literary scene is made up of not just the publishing houses that determine what gets published, but what the reviewers are saying. It's also the bookstores that decide what they'll carry, and what's actually bought in those bookstores. Even film rights are a part of it.

RICE: What's being published and bought is John Grisham and Danielle Steele, overwhelmingly. This may not strike you as relevant, but let me tell you a story. A couple of years ago a woman calling herself "a better fiction writer" wrote a letter to PEN, the writers' organization, saying that she and other "better fiction writers" were depressed and upset by the fact that everywhere they went they saw Stephen King, Danielle Steele, Tom Clancy, and a few other big megasellers, and they felt that they, the writers of better fiction, were being pushed out. Well, this is a common cry. It comes up year after year. This "better fiction writer" defined herself as somebody who doesn't write detective fiction, fantasy, horror, romance, or just about anything else. [*laughter*] What that person basically was arguing for was being allotted some space, almost like being subsidized. The argument is that "better fiction writers" should be subsidized, whether they sell or not. That's a popular idea in academia, that if somebody has worked very hard on his thesis and done a good job, he should be awarded a master's degree and if possible a job. But, you see, that doesn't work in the American book world. Novels are not published simply because somebody has worked hard and done an acceptable job. Those who are rewarded are those who make an impact, and that's all there is to it. If you talk to these "better fiction writers," who write largely American realism, you'll find they feel they're a martyred group, that because of what they've put into it, and because of their intentions and their hard work, they should have earned some recognition, and that there's something radically wrong with a world that gives that recognition to Stephen King instead. That's bullshit in the arts! That wasn't true two thousand years ago, it wasn't ever true in the arts, and it never will be. Whether you took five days or twenty years to write a book doesn't make a damn bit of difference. It's whether the book grabs people by the throat. That's what's going to be rewarded. I wanted to write a response to the letter. PEN called up and invited me to, but I just couldn't get my thoughts together about it. This troubled me for years. Stephen King did write a response, and he went way out on a limb saying, "Who says you're a better fiction writer, what makes your fiction better?" It was a big controversy. But, in a way, that original letter was outrageously arrogant.

Many novels are published in America with the belief that a particular new young voice should be heard because the dues have been paid and it's time to publish that kind of novel, but it's often a terrible disservice to these writers because their works are never truly published. They rarely get more than a few thousand copies, and a few book review copies, and perhaps a mention in *Publishers Weekly*. Maybe a review in *The New York Times* if they're very, very fortunate. And these people go off aggrieved, believing we're nothing but a nation of crude thrill-seeking monsters who have relegated them to the back shelf. Their arguments do imply that they should have a government subsidy.

RILEY: One hears it said that publishing has changed a great deal in recent years as the traditional houses have been purchased by conglomerates, that they're not the same kind of institution now as they were in the past.

RICE: What they were in the past was elitist institutions that published their friends. You know, if you knew Alfred A. Knopf and you could get in there and write your book, he'd publish it. [*laughter*] Is there no justice? There was never any justice. There was never any system where the good always rose to the top, but nevertheless that system was just as good at finding a Raymond Chandler or an F. Scott Fitzgerald or a John Steinbeck as the present system. They're not very different.

RILEY: What I'm thinking of is the perception that the major publishing houses traditionally published the big mass-sellers and then were able to use their success to underwrite the costs of publishing worthwhile books that by their very nature were not likely to reach as large an audience. The same thing was true of the film industry in the heyday of the studio system. They could subsidize an artistically ambitious film by the success of a broad range of popular films.

RICE: That's absolutely alive and well as a concept in New York publishing, and it happens all the time. Every major publisher I can think of does that. They publish big moneymaking bestsellers, and they also publish a few first novels every year that they consider to be by talented people on the way up. I know people all through publishing, and have known them for years, who believe very much in championing a young unknown author and pushing that author through the house, trying to get recognition for his or her novel. It's still a working system. The tragedy of the system, though, is that there are just too many people being published. They cannot effectively publish all those writers. I don't know if I told you this story, but one year I was asked to judge a first-novel contest for a national award. At that time, I was going to bookstores at least four or five times a week, and I read *Publishers Weekly* and *The New York Times Book Review* through and through. I thought I knew what first novels had been published in America that year, but when they began to ship me the novels, I got novels in the mail I'd never heard of, novels I had never seen on any book counter. I'd never known they were ever published anywhere. I discovered there were something like a hundred first novels published in this country, and most of these writers, I'm sure, had never gotten any chance at really winning an audience. Even if you were John Updike trying to keep abreast of literature as a *New Yorker* critic, you couldn't possibly have read all those books with everything else that was going on in literature, the new book by Graham Greene, the new book by Norman Mailer, the new book by Saul Bellow. You couldn't have done it, and there's something wrong when it reaches that point. It's a system in which people are bound to be disappointed. They're bound to be heartbroken. They cannot successfully be debuted to the public. They can't be introduced. I remember one by Tracy Hotchner, a first novel about her family, a wonderful book about their mother, their father, their lives. It was a fairly hefty effort, and it was packaged well.

I'd never even heard of it, and I've never heard of it since, never even seen it in a bookstore. It was just in the box of first novels published that year that was sent to me.

RILEY: Whose failure is it, exactly? On the one hand, the enormously successful bestsellers can subsidize the worthwhile first novel, and they do, but then publishers just seem to push these novels out the door and fail to promote them in a way that's likely to get them the attention they need.

RICE: I would say it's the failure of the system. I think the individual editors want very much to promote those novels, and they try very hard, but the truth is that there isn't any reliable, effective way to market them. A common experience I've heard described by people I know is the young author who calls and says, "I got a rave review in *The New York Times*. Why aren't they going to run an ad for my book?" Well, the reason they're not going to run an ad for the book is that an ad is not going to sell one copy. An ad just doesn't effectively sell a first novel. It's too hit-and-miss, too tiny, so they aren't going to run the ad until the author has already caught on. The ad is the mark of success, the mark that the author's being well treated, that he's really being presented to the American public. Most of the time, editors tell young writers they're counting on the reviews to get the word out, which of course is awful. That's like saying, we're counting on the four or five people who piss on your fence every day to say that your garden is beautiful. [*laughter*] But they do count on that. They count on the reviews to pick up the novel and praise it and talk about it. That's the best way they can get some word of mouth going on a novel. Then, of course, we get into the whole question of the reviewers and how likely they are to attack an unusual first novel and tear it to pieces, and to resent the risks it takes. So it's a very bad system. There's no real system to it.

The thing I would suggest, and it's a ruthless thing, is to publish far less and publish it much more effectively. If I were running a publishing house, that would be my maxim. I wouldn't take on a novel unless I could publish perhaps 25,000 copies and truly launch it. But, you see, that's a huge figure. There are many novels that never get anything like 25,000 copies. They have maybe 6,000 copies published, maybe 7,000. I know young writers who get statements back that say they sold 400. They stand there with that royalty statement they've been handed, and they say, "I don't think they ever shipped it out of the warehouse." And the truth is, maybe they didn't. Except to a very few bookstores. The chains—Waldenbooks and B. Dalton—won't buy a first novel unless the publisher agrees to print so many, because it's just the way they operate. They have to have enough copies on the shelves of all these stores to justify the central office making an order. So that would be my solution, and I also don't believe there are a hundred or a hundred-fifty budding-genius new writers in America in any one calendar year.

BOOKSELLERS AND READERS: "A UTOPIAN VIEW"

RILEY: Have the booksellers, the large chains, fundamentally changed the American literary world?

RICE: I have a utopian, optimistic view of that that may

be self-serving. I think the chains have greatly helped book sales in America. They've brought books to people who never saw or bought new books in their life before. I grew up in a household where I doubt my grandmother had ever been in a bookstore. If she had, I never heard about it. And my mother, who loved books and had them all over the house, never to my knowledge had the opportunity to browse in a bookstore in her life. There was none to be browsed in. Maybe she went in one when she was young, but I don't know where it was. I grew up never setting foot in a bookstore until I was about fourteen or fifteen and I discovered a very stuffy narrow little bookstore downtown. But malls and chains have brought books to all kinds of people, and people love to read. They have responded enthusiastically, and they buy not only the junk novels but the good novels. They buy them by the ton. They're buying them more than ever, and it's the direct result of the chain store and the mall store and the big superstore. I truly believe that. I stand in the mall and I watch what people buy. I stand in the bookstores, and I watch them talking and see them loading books into their baskets. I study them and eavesdrop on them to see what they're thinking. Those same people wouldn't even have known bookstores existed when I was a kid. They would have gone to the library and checked out some books, but they never would have owned them. I think it's a very good thing. Everything is happening rapidly, and it's very exciting. I realize there are dozens of economic conditions that have to be factored in, like the dire predictions we're always hearing that books are going to disappear because the cost of printing is so high. Well, that's ridiculous. Bestsellers now sell hundreds of thousands more than they did even ten years ago. There's no comparison. I can remember because I used to read *Publishers Weekly*. A big printing for Stephen King would have been 200,000. Stephen King now goes out with a million hardcover books, and people buy them. And not only do they buy him, they also buy John le Carré, who's a very skilled, dense, demanding writer. He's writing something that's going to endure. And as Dick Snyder, who used to be the unpopular head of Simon & Schuster, pointed out, they buy more biographies than they ever did before. They go for big hefty, thoughtful biographies of Truman, of Kennedy, and they plunk down twenty-five or thirty dollars for them. So I think making books a consumer product has been a very good thing. I think kids have been turned on by Stephen King and Peter Straub and have gone on to read other stuff. I've told you about the parents who have come through the line at my signings and said, "I got my son to read your books and now he's reading everything. He wants to know all about literature." It's a fabulous thing. I think the people who are angry about the book chains just don't know what they're talking about. Go into a bookstore now and walk back through the fiction section and look at the backlist there. Look at the books you can find. You know, the Brontë sisters share every bookstore in America. There isn't a chain store in America that doesn't have at least *Wuthering Heights* or *Jane Eyre*. Think about that. *Jane Eyre* in malls all over the country, and Dostoevsky's *The Brothers Karamazov*. I remember walking through a Wal-Mart in a town in Texas and seeing *Dubliners* by James Joyce on the counter. It was a new mass-market printing. There are all kinds of books. But my view's very different from a lot of other people's, and I realize my view's more comfortable for me because I am well rewarded for being a writer. I think when you're not, you can look at the dark side of this, but if you're looking at it from the standpoint of somebody watching the economy and watching history and watching politics, it's a terrifically interesting phenomenon. I would say the chains have been great in bringing books to people.

FILM RIGHTS: "AN EXCRUCIATING DILEMMA"

RILEY: So far as the film industry goes, this is an era of sequels, but typically they're generated from material in an earlier film rather than a series of literary works. The film rights to your novels, though, whether it's *The Vampire Chronicles* or the *Mayfair* books, must raise different issues because you've already written sequels yourself. And you're likely to write other novels in both those series in the future. Also, there's the matter of rights to the individual characters as well as to the novels in which they appear.

RICE: Every time I choose to write about the Mayfairs or the vampires, I throw away a lot of money because if I were to write the same book with brand-new characters, I could sell the Hollywood rights to it separately. I do think of that: If I could do *Memnoch the Devil* with a mortal hero and keep the vampires out of it, I could sell the rights without any strings. But these works are all connected contractually. Not only does Warner Bros. own *The Witching Hour*, for instance, but nobody can make *Lasher* and *Taltos* except Warner Bros. and David Geffen until a certain amount of time passes. With the vampires that time almost ran out, but David and Warners got an extension. Overall, it's an excruciating dilemma when I'm writing. Sometimes it becomes a great assertion of will to sit here and write with these characters even though someone else owns the film rights to them. I have to put it out of my head as a contaminating force—and it's not just a question of money. It's the fact that they're my characters. Even when I write about the Talamasca, there's a sixty-day clause in the contract that David and Warners have a right to look at anything that has the Talamasca characters in it. They're held out. There's very complicated language in the contract, and it was a huge legal fight to get it in, working with lawyers and agents who didn't know what I was talking about when I said, "Hold out the Talamasca. Do not sell the rights to the idea of the Talamasca *per se*. Specify that they can only use the Talamasca in conjunction with the vampires or *The Witching Hour*." That battle was won even before the novels were done. I understand why writers like Stephen King write novels none of which is connected to the one before. Not that he necessarily set out to do it that way. It may be that his imagination simply works that way, but the rights to each of his books are entirely separate.

RILEY: John Irving once told me that when he sold *The World According to Garp* he specifically withheld the rights to "The Pension Grillparzer," the marvelous story that Garp writes within the novel.

RICE: Oh really. That's great. Well, you can do it, but you have to know a lot about Hollywood and you have to have a lot of stamina, because the studio lawyers just come back and say, no, we won't go for that. They want the whole thing. Then the agent calls you, and the battle goes back and forth. It's the same with sequel rights. Contractually, David Geffen controls any book in which Lestat appears. Whether he's acquired it yet or not, he controls it. Nobody else can do it. When I write another book with Lestat, that means I'm definitely choosing not to go the Hollywood route. I'm not attempting to set something up somewhere else. I have to make that choice. Technically, they do have to acquire the individual *Vampire Chronicles* or *Lasher* and *Taltos*. They don't just automatically own them. They do have to buy them. They cannot use material from *Lasher* or *Taltos* when they make *The Witching Hour*, and it's the same with *The Vampire Chronicles*. They have to buy those books if they want them. Anyway, it's a path I have to go. There are times when I try to free myself from those entanglements because I don't want the worry and frustration of any connection with the development of those other books, but I really can't do it. I wind up writing again about the same people. They're my world.

PART TWO

4

"Family voices"

RILEY: Since your return to New Orleans, the role of family in your life—Stan and your son, Chris, of course, but also your larger extended family—has been reflected in your work as an increasingly important theme.

RICE: I think the Mayfair family took a quantum leap in development after I returned to New Orleans. I don't think I could have written *The Witching Hour* in California. I'd started it, and I had written the first four or five chapters, but I realized I couldn't do it. I didn't know enough about what I was trying to write about. I didn't know enough about New Orleans anymore to set the novel there. I tried to write the section in the beginning where the priest goes to visit the Mayfair family, and I realized I didn't even know the present state of the parish or what the priest's house was like or what the community was like. When I came back to New Orleans in 1988, I first moved right at the crossroads between the Irish Channel and the Garden District. You saw that house, didn't you? Yes, I remember you came there. I moved into that house where I could actually see the old Catholic churches out the window and where I was just around the corner from my Irish Catholic cousins, the Murphys, a huge clan. In the next two or three years, I heard more family voices, more family stories, and saw more family faces than perhaps ever in my life from the time I was thirteen or fourteen years old and went to a family funeral. I became emboldened to create this big Mayfair clan, to go back into memories that had been totally inaccessible before and to mine them to create the character of Michael Curry, who wasn't in the novel until I moved back here. He wasn't even invented as a character. It was a woman.

RILEY: There's a lot of you in Michael Curry.

RICE: There is and there isn't, but there's a lot of my cousins in Michael. I have aunts and uncles who are a lot like Michael's family. I didn't grow up in the Irish Channel, and my parents weren't proletarian people like his. Parents who were first-generation intellectuals was really more my situation.

RILEY: What's been the response of your family to your novels? Have many of your relatives read them? And if they have, have any of them been shocked or offended?

RICE: Some do read them and mention them, but the vast majority don't do either. I have many Catholic cousins here who I'm sure don't read them, and they would never dream of even looking at the pornographic books. It's just not part of their world to read them. Then I have a lot of cousins who do read my books, and read each one. I send a copy when a new one comes out, and they'll send a note and say, I really liked it for this or that reason. They tend to be the ones who simply like to read, period. That's part of their world, and they read widely in American fiction. I suppose that's what you'd say: If they're readers, they may read it; if they're not, they won't. I have many cousins who are not really readers. They probably don't read anything contemporary very much.

RILEY: How did your father respond?

RICE: My father was one of the most thoughtful and satisfying of all my readers. I can still remember his letter on *Feast of All Saints*, what he thought was good about the novel, what he had liked, and the things that really didn't work for him. He wrote me pages and pages about *The Witching Hour*, his response to it and what he thought. He would give me tremendous feedback. He was terrific. He had the greatest resistance to sex. He had a horrible time with *Cry to Heaven*, and yet he would say, "It draws me in even as it pushes me out or repels me." At the time, of course, I had no idea how pornographic *Cry to Heaven* was. I must have been living on another planet when I wrote that book, because it just never occurred to me that to write those detailed scenes of oral sex would offend anybody. I don't know what I thought I was doing. [*laughter*] I was just writing what happened to Guido, and I really didn't think about it. Later, you know, that's my one book that somebody, to my knowledge, brought back to a bookstore and said, "This is pornography, and I want my money back!" A college professor in Stockton, California, came back to a bookstore which was owned by a good friend of mine and said, "I don't want it. I cannot read this." I understand now why he did it, but at the time I didn't.

RILEY: I suppose you were armed with your innocence.

RICE: I must have been. But in any event, I think my father had the hardest time with that novel and, to the best of my knowledge, never read any of the pornography. He certainly never discussed it with me, and when I told him about it, I asked him specifically not to read it. He did read *Belinda*. I gave him that. I think he enjoyed it, but, again, I think it was just too transgressive for him. He was a wonderful responder or critic of the *Vampire* novels. He and I had a little joke between us, the phrase "one fine blow." I would always use that phrase somewhere in a book, and he would look for it. It first appears, actually, in *Feast of All Saints*, where Rudolphe deals this man "one fine blow" that sends him across the pavement. I didn't even think about it, and my father pointed it out and said, "I thought this was a misprint but you really mean this, 'one fine blow.' " And I said, "Yeah, you know, 'one fine blow.' " So the next time I planted it in there for him. It was in *The Vampire Lestat* when Armand dealt Lestat one fine blow that sent him out of the Cathedral into the Square. My father said, "You know, I don't think a bad person can deal 'one fine blow' to the hero." So we were getting into this whole thing [*laughter*], and I said, "Well, it's Armand, you know, sometimes it's the villain." Then I used it in *The Witching Hour*, where Lasher dealt Michael one fine blow that sent him into the pool. It was in *The Tale of the Body Thief*, too, but he never got to read it. Right at this moment, I can't remember where, but it's in there, and I was going to say, "Dad, 'one fine blow' is in there as always."

But as I was saying, my parents were very different from a lot of other members of my family. My father was the one who brought home the records of Tchaikovsky and introduced us to Dickens and took us to the library. In the novel, Michael learns those things on his own. He doesn't have anybody to teach him. But in my case there was my mother telling me to be a great writer if I wanted to, and telling me all about the Brontë sisters and how they had taken assumed names, and all kinds of things. Michael didn't have that experience. He really is a person who fights the proletarian background. That's the key difference. But many of my longings and frustrations, all of that, I put into him. I was writing about a boy who played football, and it was quite a stretch for the imagination. At the age of fourteen, though, when I went to Redemptress High School in the Irish Channel, we did win the city championship, and the games I describe in the novel really did happen. In California I would never have remembered those things, and if I had I would never have had the courage to try to bring them to life, even just briefly, in Michael's life. When I moved back here, all of that changed. In *The Witching Hour* it was as if my vocabulary doubled or tripled. My access to memory accelerated one hundred or two hundred percent, and a great explosion of the novel resulted in about five months' time. By the time I really sat down to attack the book, I'd been here almost a year. The first four or five chapters had taken five years out in California, and then the entire remainder of the book took five months. As soon as I moved into this house, this became the Mayfair house. Everything began to click, and I wrote it all upstairs here. It was a wonderful experience for me. Earlier I was describing the whole process of someone trying to get closer and closer to what she considered to be the heated reality she had to convey and how the pornography, the Roquelaure books, helped me with that, and how the Rampling books were another step. Well, this was really when Rampling and Roquelaure died, because once I came home, I was able to get in touch with all that as Anne Rice. There was never any need for a pseudonym after that. It's like all the attempts to write in a palsy-walsy voice, and whatever I was doing as Anne Rampling, I was able to bring those voices into *The Witching Hour*. All at once I was able to have lots of different voices. I was able to vary the texture, and so finally all three voices were together for me in that book.

Somehow or other I tied in to things that had a great resonance and a great truth, and I'm still hearing all kinds of things that connect with it. I could tell you such stories. I could go on with them until they became tedious, but they're absolutely astonishing to me. I wrote things that I didn't even know yet! Just a couple of years ago I was over on Magazine Street at the Murphys' on St. Patrick's Day. I was eating and a cousin of mine was sitting next to me. He's about seventy-five or eighty years old, and he was telling me how when he was a boy in school Sister Patrick from Ireland used to tell them stories all day in class, so they would never get anything done. I nearly fell off my chair because in *The Witching Hour* that was the nun I based Sister Bridget Marie on. I had written that Sister Bridget Marie would tell all these stories about there being witches and all sorts of things, but I didn't know that Sister Patrick had actually done that when she was a substitute teacher. It was something I just imagined. By the time of this conversation the book was already written and published, and my cousin had never read it. I do remember Sister Patrick; I remember her very well. I remember her Irish accent, but, again, in California I would never have attempted to write about her. I would never have felt sure enough. I would have had to write about Tonio and the castrati in Venice. I would have had to write about someplace I could research and control, because I didn't have a real place to write about. I was too uprooted and too far away.

RILEY: These two cities, New Orleans and San Francisco, have both had a great impact on your work.

RICE: Less San Francisco, though, because I couldn't connect with it; I couldn't understand it. Because I couldn't get a hold on it, my most far-reaching fantasies were written there.

RILEY: Over the years, whenever we've talked about New Orleans, it's always been obvious that there was much more involved for you than just an attachment to the place where you were born and lived as a young girl. What is it about New Orleans that has made it such a powerful presence for you?

RICE: This is really off the wall, but let me answer in this roundabout way. I think *The Wizard of Oz*, the movie, with Dorothy and Toto and all the others, is basically about Protestant and Catholic values and about realism and fantasy. The lesson of that movie is that the truth is in your own backyard, and it's Kansas. Well, do you remember Dorothy's backyard? Yet that's what the movie says. No fairies and no little people, no trees throwing apples. There's no wizard, there are no lions. Here's reality, Dorothy, with the pigs. Well, that's the message of a lot of contemporary American realism. In this country there's a strong critical bias that the best novel is about the ordinary middle-class person in an ordinary community, facing three or four ordinary choices, however intense they may be, who makes a small choice and has an epiphany about that and comes to terms with life. Now, of course I don't dismiss realism, but I do dismiss that critical bias. Readers also crave spectacle in their literature. They crave the heroic and mythic in serious literature, not just in junk fiction.

I know this can simply sound self-serving because I'm talking about my own work, but my kind of fiction is like the Land of Oz because this is my backyard. It's New Orleans and it's not like any other place. It's the most incredibly different city in the entire United States. It was settled by the French and Spanish and still has a milieu that's Caribbean or Mediterranean or both, and it's a Catholic city. Even San Francisco is really a Protestant city, a city that goes by the Protestant ethic, the Protestant norms and rhythms and values. In New Orleans you will see and experience things you cannot find any other place. A different ethic prevails, and it influences all of life, from the way people keep a garden or drink a cup of coffee or eat a gumbo or walk down the street. It's a way of celebrating life, of experiencing life as a festival and everything that goes along with the Catholic idea of what is important. It has nothing to do with work or getting up early or cleaning up the streets or mowing your grass. Those are not the dominant values. It's much more about getting the best cup of coffee, staying close to your family, going to dinner at your mother's house once a week, seeing your cousins. It's a mellow place and lifestyles are evolved. They are not invented. Most people are here because they want to be. At some point in their lives, they had a choice about going off and they chose not to.

If you talk to almost anybody here who's forty or fifty years old or older, they'll tell you the story of the day they got a chance to go to Chicago or a chance to go to New York, and they came home and realized they didn't want to leave. People here really do have dinner with their mother once a week. There's even a song called "The Yat Christmas" that has a line about that. It's sung to the tune of "The Twelve Days of Christmas" with lyrics as if they were being sung by what's called a Yat, a New Orleans person with a very thick accent. When I was young, one of the expressions we had to use with each other was "Where y'at?" It's almost a Brooklyn kind of English. In the song one of the things you get on the fourth day of Christmas is "dinner by your mama." That means to go to your mother's house for dinner, and I understood it the minute I heard it. It's absolutely a New Orleans thing to hear a grown man say, whatever he's doing: "I'm going to have dinner with my mother Tuesday night"; "I'm going to have dinner with my cousins"; "I'm going to see the family." I love that about New Orleans. That's what New Orleans is about. It is also an absolutely extraordinary place physically. It's tropical and humid and decadent, and because of the incredible laziness here, it is filled with some of the most beautiful architecture in the United States—because nobody has bothered to tear it down. It's because we are a depressed city, a poor city, that all the wonderful old houses have not been torn down. They are still standing, and the people here have come to love and value them. These houses were deeply threatened in the fifties, but there wasn't enough money and momentum or Protestant gumption to really change the city into Atlanta or Dallas. It just couldn't be done.

I think New Orleans is unique, and an honorable recipient of devotion on the part of its native sons. It's given me an enormous amount, and I had to invent a fantasy way to get back to Louisiana, just to get the wisteria creeping through the boards of the house, to get the shutters, to get the way the trees look against the swamp. Even though I was running the risk of being called Gothic and Regency and those other nauseating labels, I was back describing just exactly what I had seen and remembered and what preyed on my mind and what I craved. I've also given up caring how many times I use New Orleans. I've decided I can use it as many times as any New Yorker uses New York. So New Orleans is my backyard, and the crisis of my writing life was finding a way to come back to it when I could not write about Berkeley and Big Sur and Haight-Ashbury.

RILEY: It's also true that, apart from missing New Orleans so profoundly, you eventually came to feel disaffected and deeply alienated from San Francisco.

RICE: Deeply, but still a great love. I have a great respect for San Francisco and for the experience shared by thousands who came there and for what the California experience meant to so many people of my generation. You went there to be free—so that you could be gay, or you could be an intellectual, or you could be a poet, or you could be a hippie, or you could write pornography. You could do whatever you wanted, and I will always be grateful to San Francisco for giving me its particular kind of tolerance. I don't know if I ever told you this, but one day, the last time we were there, the Gay Pride parade was passing by, and there were wonderfully outrageous people in drag and all kinds of crazy things happening. Chris and I were standing on the corner, and I said, "Take a good look at this, because you're not going to see this anywhere else. You'll see a different kind of tolerance in New Orleans, but you will not see this. This is San Francisco, and it's the great thing here that these people can do exactly what they want to do." He watched it and I think he understood. He grew up watching that, and it has given him a great immunity to the biases of others that he grew up in that environment in San Francisco.

But it's true that I hated it in the end, and I wanted to leave. There's also a kind of barbaric California I cannot bear. There are things some people will do and say which nobody here would. I wore out on what I saw as the savagery of California. I became a cringing hermit. More and more often I would go out of my house and hear people say things that just stunned me about how they hadn't spoken to their family in years. How psychiatrists had told them to have nothing further to do with their family. Or how their father was dying but they couldn't deal with it, and their psychiatrist had told them they didn't have to, so they weren't going to go to the hospital room. I thought it was nauseating. I remember one horrible experience—I think I've mentioned this in interviews—of sitting at this big party for a poet and listening to a very old-guard liberal professor friend of mine tell me he was so mad about nuclear power that he was going to kidnap Caspar Weinberger's wife and shoot her. I thought, are you out of your mind? Have you forgotten the meaning of freedom and democracy? Are you crazy? But that's the way it was for me at the end. My friends had turned into fascist feminists or fascist liberals. That's the kind of conversation they had routinely. They spoke of boycotting this and banning that and disrupting something else. It was barbaric, and I encountered it more and more when I went out. I remember one night going to a poetry reading, and this woman we didn't know started talking to us. She told me how distressed she was that one of her grown children was coming home for a visit and she didn't want him back in the house. She had no intention of opening the house to him. Again I felt myself shrinking, the horror that someone would feel that way about her child, about flesh and blood. She was talking in that flippant California style of selfishness I heard everywhere, and I was appalled by it. I couldn't make any connection with it. I had to come back here.

RILEY: Even so, in an ironic way that was still a significant influence on you as a writer. Long before you moved back to New Orleans, you were figuratively pushed out of a place you couldn't get a hold on and into another realm in your imagination.

RICE: Yes, if you look at it that way, you see this writer struggling to write in the seventies. It's the age of realism, and the biases are in favor of the semiautobiographical. Henry Miller is big, and Anaïs Nin's diaries are very hot. All that's going on, and here's this person out here in Berkeley, California, swinging Berkeley, and what does she write? A book about a nineteenth-century vampire in Louisiana. That's really somebody having to create a fantasy to get to reality because the reality is back there in Louisiana, and it's so mixed up and so sordid and so confusing and so intense for this writer that she can't really gain access to it any other way. She can't write about the hippies and the revolution in Berkeley and the Floyd Salas type of thing, so what does she do? She writes a fantasy that allows her to go back home. That's really what happened. It's as simple as that. Of course, I didn't think that's what was happening at the time, but that's exactly what it was. When you asked me earlier what was the explosion that came with the Roquelaure and the Rampling books, it was an attempt to get deeper and deeper into that. You know, I never thought of this before, but I think you could see *Interview with the Vampire* that way. You take a fantasy framework, you step into it, you try to write reality. Then *Feast of All Saints* is a step away from that. It's to gain greater competence and control over the historical framework and to bring the material more into the real world, but it's not entirely successful. *Cry to Heaven* attempts to do that, too, but what that writer's doing with each of those books is getting more remote from reality. By the time of *Cry to Heaven*, the language is very stylized and very removed. It's a language that if translated into foreign tongues, no one could tell the nationality of the writer. It's so European-American that it transcends any locale. So there's this person having done that, who wants to get back to whatever that intensity was in writing *Interview with the Vampire*, and she starts all these crazy experiments. What that really was is hard to define. It's like a fantasy realm where that person feels the most intense reality. Does that make sense? I never saw it that way until now, but I think that's what was going on.

HEATED REALITY

RILEY: You've referred to the "heated reality" a writer has to convey. How would you define yours?

RICE: Certainly whatever it is, it's expressed better in scenes and by characters than in any overt philosophical or moral statement. The author's message is in all of the different scenes and characters, but to step back from them a minute, I can describe it vaguely. There's a feeling in me when I get to a place in a scene where I'm touching what I call "it." That's all, it, in quotes, and it produces a particular feeling of intensity in me. It's the feeling of risk, exposure, a thrilling feeling, but what it's all about, what it boils down to, cannot be summed up in any few words. I could tell you scenes where I think it happens, and my goal as a writer is to make it happen more and more until there's nothing left that isn't like that.

In *Taltos*, for example, for some reason there's a scene in an Italian delicatessen near the end of the book. I can't tell you why. I hope to know why eventually. When those two people, the dwarf and the tall man, are talking, the very gentle man and the very gruff man, their conversation was "it." It was absolutely on some track of intensity for me, and I can't explain it. I fully expect to find out later why that was. I'll be surprised if that scene disappoints me five years from now. I expect that if anything it'll be much clearer to me. Right now, though, I'm not kidding when I say I don't really know why that was. I just know something happened between those two characters that had to do with love and expectation. There was a way when those two characters would get together in the novel that they always took things dangerously further than I had planned to go. In the very beginning there's a scene where they're sitting in a hotel together and they're talking, and the dwarf says, "Yuri's falling in love with you," and Ash, the tall one, gets very angry and says, "Don't start saying stupid things. It's not important." To me, that was a lusciously intense and thrilling scene to write. I felt very in touch with my subconscious and very trusting of what was happening. But I can't draw back like a critic and tell you, okay, I was writing there about the capacity of one human being to spellbind another, and about how dangerous that is, and that's something I've been writing about all my life in some form. Perhaps it's all of those things, but there's something else as well.

There's another scene in *Taltos* that I love. It's also a scene between the very tall man and the dwarf that takes place in the same restaurant. Again I don't know why, but I know that scene is about a lot of things. I know it's very powerful, and I love it. But I really don't know what it's about. I just know that when the dwarf says, "Take care of my dog. He's very easily hurt," and Ash says, "I'll keep that in mind," the whole thing means something to me. I fully expect and trust that a few years down the line some critic or interviewer or some friend or some reader will be telling me what that scene means. Of course, I could be wrong, but that's the kind of dare on which my career rests. If I'm wrong, it could be a bunch of junk. But I got that buzz when I wrote that scene. I got the buzz all through *Taltos* when I wrote various scenes, and I trusted it even though I knew that on the surface the novel was preposterous. It was just utterly preposterous.

RILEY: I remember being told by a teacher years ago that if you apply the test of strict plausibility in literature you have to give up on *King Lear* in scene one. The story premise of a king relinquishing his kingdom and dividing it among his three daughters is so unlikely as to be implausible.

RICE: Absolutely. Shakespeare provides the most wonderful examples. There are ghosts and witches and sprites, just everything, and I go back to him for defense all the time. I suppose I'm most sensitive about *Taltos* right now because only about four people in the whole world have read it. We'll have to see how readers respond when it's published. But in another way I'm not sensitive about it at all. It's done. It's like a boat that's sailed; it's gone into the world. I trust it's going to prove itself to have been something of worth. You know, I do listen to people's responses. I hear between the lines of what they say. I'm now in a position where nobody at the publishing house is really going to tell me the truth unless it's a certain kind of truth, but I know enough to hear when they don't like something, when they don't think it's going to succeed or they don't think I pulled it off. And I know with *Taltos* they think I pulled it off—for better or worse.

PLANNING A NOVEL: "IT STARTS WEAVING"

RILEY: Is my recollection correct that when you wrote *The Witching Hour* you didn't intend a sequel?

RICE: I thought the ending was perfect. I thought it was the best ending I'd ever done. I was so flabbergasted when some of the reviews said it was an obvious setup for a sequel. I just couldn't believe it. To me Rowan had, for all the obvious reasons, left with Lasher, and the climax of the novel came when Michael went down into the swimming pool and was presented with the vision that said, "We've used you." That's what it was all about: The Devil has won. I felt that was it. I remember when Julia Phillips read it. She said, "It's a slam dunk. The Devil wins." That was her description of it as a potential movie.

RILEY: But because of your readers' desire to know what happened to those characters, you did decide to continue the Mayfair story, first in *Lasher* and now in *Taltos*. How far ahead of the actual writing were you planning those books? When did *Taltos* begin?

RICE: I was working on the Lestat novel in the fall and all winter and spring, and when it didn't come together, I set it aside and went to *Taltos*. *Taltos* was a novel that had been brewing all the time I was dealing with *The Witching Hour* and with *Lasher*. First I had to go over the copyedited manuscripts of those books, and then I had to go over the galleys, and by the time I finished with the galleys of *Lasher*, *Taltos* was a full-blown concept in my mind. Often I can't do that. When I'm doing the galleys on a novel and I want to deal with another novel, I know I have to wait, but this time I thought, no, just do this, get *Taltos* out, and do it the way you want to do it.

RILEY: We were talking earlier about the differences between a novel as you envision it and the final form it takes. How fully do you plan a novel in advance?

RICE: It varies, but if I cannot see an ending and a grand theme, I don't begin. With *Taltos* I had the theme and the ending and the whole shape of what was going to happen, but then it changed as I wrote it. Very dramatic changes began to be made. A "what if?" syndrome set in. With the Lestat novel that I'm back to writing now, I know what's supposed to happen right up to the very end. What I often don't know is the middle. [*laughter*] I can see the end; I can see how it's going to begin; I can see a lot of what it's going to involve; but I can't really see how it's all going to get there. The middle is the frightening part. I'm trying not to think about the scenes before I write them, but just to get into them and let things happen. I did that more in *Taltos* than in *Lasher*. *Lasher* was more envisioned scene by scene. Ideally, I'd love to write a novel in which I didn't have any idea who the characters were going to be or what they were going to do from day to day and try to preserve that all the way through.

RILEY: You remarked earlier that *The Queen of the Damned* was the first novel in which you actually fulfilled the vision you originally had, that the other novels had fallen short of your intentions.

RICE: Yes, they were falling way short of the original intentions. In those days I would have a vision, and I just wouldn't be able to realize it completely. With *Feast of All Saints*, as I mentioned, I wanted to take the people from the 1840s right up through the Civil War, and I then wanted to go on into the twentieth century. I wanted the book to end with a descendant coming back and destroying all of the hero's photographs, his daguerreotypes, because white descendants of people of color did do this. They would come back to New Orleans and destroy everything to erase any official indication that they had African blood in their veins. I wanted it to end in that way, saying, "The descendants of Marcel Ste. Marie passed without history into the white race." I had it all planned; I just didn't know how to do it. I didn't know how to make those leaps in time; I didn't know how to handle the Civil War. In that novel I was carefully building scenes that happen within a very short span of time in this boy's life. It's really a novel of adolescence, and I was not able to expand it in the way I intended. Now, I don't think it suffers from that. It's just a different thing, but that was my vision. As I lay there in bed at night during the time I was writing it, I saw many scenes in that novel—as if they were scenes from a movie—that never made it into the book. Certainly I never got to that ending, nowhere near it. I just got to the end of the summer, and it became a novel about a boy finding out that he's black, and finding out that he's human, and finding out that he's mortal. That's really what it's about. I got a lot out of it and was very happy with it, but it fell short of my dreams.

Cry to Heaven was the same way. I felt I'd just barely gotten Tonio launched by the time I was finished. I spent so much time laying the groundwork for what happened to him, his education, getting him out into the world. I never had the feeling of just dancing with Tonio after he was created as a character, and taking him to new challenges and new places. He made his debut, his father tried to kill him, he had to go to Venice, and then that was it. Again, I was very happy and satisfied with that, but it fell short of being something sinister and wicked that I'd wanted to write. I wanted to get into cruelty and how it affects people, but as I said, I got too history-bound in that novel. I took what I could find about what the conservatories were like and what Tonio's life would have been like, and I didn't dare to invent anything spectacularly sinister or cruel and attach it to that. Actually, I think it's a very responsible novel, but way short of what I was envisioning. So it wasn't until *The Queen of the Damned* that I achieved all I'd set out to do.

So far as *Exit to Eden* was concerned, you can't compare it because it was written so spontaneously. I didn't know what was going to happen next. I just set out to write a pornographic novel about this man in this club and was quite amazed when it grew into a full-scale story about two people who were real to me and who fell in love and came back to New Orleans. *Belinda*, I would say, grew into a bigger novel than I'd envisioned, but that novel was such a strange experience. It was so weird I don't quite know how to comment on it. Actually, my vision of *Belinda* when I first presented it to the publishing house and drew an advance for it was very limited. I had originally intended that Jeremy would do all these paintings of Belinda and that he would not hang them for years and years for fear of hurting her or even ruining her. Then finally, after not having heard from her for many years, he would hang the paintings, and Belinda, the older Belinda, would show up at the exhibit and barely be interested. You know that kind of irony which has been done many times: The focus of a man's obsession turns out to be relatively unaffected by the whole thing, and having kept back his best work all these years was a waste. But that just didn't happen. When those characters started to move, a much richer and, I think, much better story emerged, but I think the other story would have been more acceptable to the publishers.

RILEY: Crime doesn't pay?

RICE: That's right. [*laughter*] As I said earlier, I think *Belinda* would have been a roaring success if Belinda had been a boy—or perhaps if Jeremy had murdered her. It might have been a bestseller if he'd killed her. If it's ever made into a film, I'll be surprised if they don't kill her because it moves like a murder mystery anyway. There's a point where he could have killed her and buried her in the yard in New Orleans, but of course he didn't. Remember, the detectives come, the dogs come, everything, all the crimes and things they get into until finally people are saying that somebody's got to produce the body of this girl or there's going to be some sort of court action. I loved playing with that, how she disappeared and there was a suspicion of foul play. Even her mother was in deep trouble: "You either come up with Belinda or we're going to accuse you and Marty of killing her." I had wonderful fun doing all that, just imagining each day as the news got thicker and the newspapers said she was missing, and Jeremy's house was surrounded and detectives were coming. I love to do that kind of writing. I do it all the time now in my novels, but that was the first time I ever really did it.

RILEY: How much are readers' expectations an influence on what you write?

RICE: They're a constant sort of torment, just a terrible fear of failing the readers. With each decision, I'm aware of failing a segment of the audience. As I do this next Lestat book, I will fail those who wish I'd leave him alone and get on with something entirely new, and yet I want to go back to him. If I do a book with the *Witching Hour* characters, I'm conscious of failing the audience that wants only *The Vampire Chronicles*. Commercially, writing from Lestat's point of view in a book about him is apparently the least disappointing path I can take. His books still sell the most. That *The Tale of the Body Thief*, as weird as it was, would sell 510,000 copies in hardcover amazes me. That's why I remember the number. Imagine summarizing that book: This is about a bloodsucking vampire who's actually in love with a seventy-four-year-old man who won't become a vampire, and he switches bodies with a young man and the young man steals the body. [*laughter*]

RILEY: Sounds like a sure bestseller to me. [*laughter*]

RICE: I can imagine trying to pitch it in New York and the editor saying, "You're out of your mind, Anne. Go home and think of something we can publish." [*laughter*] But I'm sure now of one thing. If I get as weird as I want to get, and as crazy as I want to get, readers will go with me.

RILEY: This goes all the way back to the breakthrough period we were discussing, doesn't it? It seems clear that this fierce determination to trust your own instincts has been essential to your growth.

RICE: You know, many novelists peter out. They die with a whimper. They begin to write thin versions of what they wrote when they were young. I don't want that to happen to me. I don't think *Taltos* is a thin version of *Witching Hour*. I think it's another completely bizarre development. It's saying, okay, every time we got close to the monster before, we killed him, but this time we're going to posit that he's alive and well and in New York. What does he do in the morning, and what does he do at night? He reads the paper; he calls his secretary. And then here's the girl, and we're not going to kill her either. She's not only going to be alive, she's going to be hanging around the house driving everybody nuts. That was a big thing with me in *Taltos*, to take imagination much further, to say if you're going to deal with something so far-fetched, let's really see what happens. Now, of course, I can see somebody saying it's a complete failure, you know, the novel's fantastic and ridiculous and silly. But it really is attempting to take the imagination further, to extend it. It's saying that there are a lot of Mayfairs, and we're not going to kill them all off. We're going to mention them and not even bring you up to date totally on characters like Ancient Evelyn and Bea. You just know they're out there and going on with their lives. There are a lot of stories. With Mary Jane, for instance, I just barely scratched the surface of what I wanted to say about California and that kind of kid who's been exposed to those things. There are other novels I want to write about that. So a lot of that was working in *Taltos* and still is, my wanting to have a huge canvas and wanting to tell many stories, wanting to get out everything I know. I want the freedom and flexibility. I didn't feel that when I was jumping between *The Vampire Lestat* and *Exit to Eden* or *Belinda*.

RILEY: Because they were separate worlds?

RICE: Yes, they were separate worlds. Anne Rice and Anne Rampling and A. N. Roquelaure weren't together, and now I feel they are. If there's an absence of an erotic scene in *Taltos*, for example, it's not because I don't feel free to write them. I just didn't do it because something else was interesting. I feel I can write the most erotic things I want to write. Actually, I think there's another kind of sexuality in *Taltos*. There's a terrific focus on Michael's body in my mind, and a similar focus on the young witches, Mona and Mary Jane, and what they are physically like. Those scenes are almost obscene with Mona and Mary Jane. They're presented like succulent little partridges there in the swamp. The scene where Mary Jane first comes in is almost a kiddie-porn scene the way it's described through the eyes of a woman who's watching a man's response to this young girl. Actually, I think it's a very titillating scene to a man who's in any way vulnerable to a young girl like that. They're just different kinds of sexuality.

RILEY: Will there be other stories for the character of Mona?

RICE: Oh, yes, I love Mona too much to do anything bad to her. She'll go through things, but I'll never kill her off, let's put it that way. In fact, one of the things that excite me about the *Mayfairs* is that there are all these possibilities of the Mayfairs themselves, the different cousins. When you set the stage with the family that big, you can bring in a Mona or Mary Jane anytime you want. There are all different kinds of Mayfairs; they're supposed to be all over the United States. There are rich Mayfairs, there are poor Mayfairs. The idea that in that big family there are all kinds of potential stories of witchcraft and psychic ability and hauntings that can be told is thrilling to me. Now there's the possibility the family will never extricate itself from its relationship with the Taltos, from the mystery of the Taltos. Morrigan and Ash can theoretically take over the world within about six months, or they can vanish. But what is it like to know they may come walking through the door ten years from now, twenty years from now, fifty years from now, and they may look very much the same as they did before? The family has a "familiar," it still has a demon, it's still privy to knowledge of a certain kind of immortal, the Taltos, and it can't get away from that. The Mayfair family is still bound up with it, and I love the fact all those doors are open.

RILEY: I find it interesting and suggestive that these two series of novels, *The Vampire Chronicles* and the *Mayfair* books, as separate as their story lines are and as different as they are in other ways, too, are beginning to be connected. The individual instances may be modest, but now the Talamasca and David Talbot and Aaron Lightner have all appeared in both worlds. Are you consciously merging them?

RICE: It's the same texture and the same cosmology. The vampire world and the *Witching Hour* world should be able to mesh completely. I think that's a wonderful thing to discover in a book. It's the power of the imagination at its strongest and its most dazzling when it can contain a world that large. Then there's the possibility of writing the greatest kind of novel. I know it's kind of a bold thing to say, but no matter how outrageous these conceits are, these things I get myself into—like babies who grow to be six feet tall in five minutes—I'm going to make them work in this big texture. It's all going to come together, that's true, but a lot of it's very disorganized with me. I'm not actually thinking of it in an organized way when I'm writing. Also, I trust this is going to have enormous meaning. I trust that. But there was a time when I didn't trust my instincts, and I was terrified it wouldn't. *Cry to Heaven* is that kind of book. I almost always rejected anything that didn't seem to serve the theme in a total way.

RILEY: You told me an anecdote years ago—I think the incident occurred when you were on tour with the paperback publication of *Interview*—about a young journalist who interviewed you. After he finished, he stayed a while just to talk about the book. He laid out a rather elaborate and complex interpretation, and you said to him, "You're absolutely right. Everything you say is there just exactly as you say it is, and I never thought of a single one of those things when I was writing."

RICE: I remember that occasion. That was actually a gay interviewer, and he did that at my house in Berkeley. He said, "This is a gay allegory, the longest extended gay allegory in the English language." He showed me all of these passages he'd marked, and said there were even comparisons between the basement of the Theater of the Vampires and the cellar bars in New York and the baths. He went into all of this, and I said, "You're absolutely right, but I was not aware of any of it."

RILEY: I have used that anecdote, garbled though I've had it, many times over the years in both film and literature classes as a way of trying to get past the resistance students sometimes have when they say, "Aren't we reading too much into this? How do you know that's what Fellini meant?" or, for that matter, "How do you know that's what Anne Rice meant?"

RICE: Yes, I understand. As a reader you have to come to a point where you know that an oak tree, or whatever, means what it means in the work even if the poet didn't fully know it at the time. It's not a matter of someone coming along and saying, "This is the meaning of the oak tree in the poem. Don't you know that oak trees always mean that?" [*laughter*] It's very complicated to explain, though. As a writer I didn't trust it in myself in the beginning and I worried, and then as the spontaneous novels got some coherence, I learned to trust it. And I'm still trusting it.

RILEY: In the Mayfair novels were there plot reasons for making Rowan a neurosurgeon? It's such a specific and even uncommon profession. Did you see possibilities for knitting various strands together?

RICE: I'd like to tell you that she just evolved to be that, but she didn't. I wanted her to be what I call a person of substance. I wanted her to have a real life. You know, what makes *Romeo and Juliet* such a tragedy is that Romeo and Juliet had real lives. They had big families, they were young, they were beautiful, so when all of that was lost, it was something real, it was a lot that was lost. I wanted Rowan to be that kind of character. I wanted to show that she had a genuine alternative to the Mayfair family, that she had a huge life ahead of her doing something very worthwhile. If she had never found out about her family and never gone home, she was still very successful. I also like to write about successful people. I like to write about powerful people. I wanted to talk about a woman faced with those problems who was not a failure for whom the whole thing might have become a redemption, but instead was somebody who had to give up something to take the risk and go back there. I was also fascinated with the real dilemma of her giving that up and changing to the vision of Mayfair Medical, the complicated question of how best to serve. There's a terrible clash between middle-class values with their sort of flippant perception of rich people and the actual ability of somebody with that kind of fortune to influence medical history by creating something much bigger than one operation or two operations, the dilemma of saving one life on the operating table versus building a medical center. Ultimately, I don't have any answer as to which is more important. All of that fascinated me, though, and once it worked for her as a character, it became an organic part of the whole novel. Then to have Petyr Abel's father be a doctor and to find out that witches and cunning women and midwives were all connected—it all just falls into place, it starts weaving. But I can't claim that when I made her a doctor I consciously knew all that, that I was going to be able to draw a thread all the way back to Suzanne, the healing woman in the village. I didn't; it just happened. I love to find all that in the writing. I love to knit it all together. I'm confident now that it will be there because I've so often in the past put it all together. It's been a process of discovery where I've come up with something spontaneous and thrown it out there, and then something else, and something else, and then seen that they are all connected.

OLDER MEN AND HER FATHER'S DEATH

RILEY: Earlier we were talking about your moving beyond a focus on youthful awakening to a growing interest in the experiences that come as one leaves youth behind, an interest in older minds, as you said, even old age itself. I'm thinking now particularly about *The Witching Hour*, *Lasher*, and *The Tale of the Body Thief*, and about the characters of Aaron Lightner and David Talbot. You haven't typically written about older characters. On the one hand there's your obvious delight in a character like Lestat, at least in part because he's outrageous and transgressive, but these two older men, who are anything but flamboyant or outrageous, are among your most sympathetic and appealing characters. There's an appreciation for the dignity of those two men.

RICE: And for their quiet brilliance. They're willing to take a backseat, but they're really very smart. I've known a lot of people like that. John Dodds was like that. John and Vivian had known everyone. He had so many incredible stories he could have told, but he was very circumspect. In his last years, though, he would say very unguarded things to me. At the end he talked about sex and death with no fear, and as a consequence he gave me many rich experiences because he was willing to do that. I remember our last lunches and talks more fondly than anything else because he was so willing to discuss everything. I wish I could remember all the things he told me. He just knew so much. Near the end he invited me to a couple of dinners at his house, and I can remember John telling fabulous stories about writers and people he'd worked with and experiences he'd had. I said, "Why don't you write this down?" And he looked at me and said, "I can't write." I remember thinking that was so funny—not in the sense of being amusing but just a strange irony about a man who knew so much about writing and writers. When he went, he took with him a lot he had seen and known. He was so generous and so good and shared so much with so many people. He was a genuinely good person who would never deliberately hurt anybody.

RILEY: How did John feel about being a character in *Belinda?*

RICE: Oh, he loved it. Especially when he got to the line in *Belinda* where Alex Clementine says, "Let's all go to Trader Vic's while there's time," because that was John's favorite restaurant. He said, "I fell off the couch when I read that." He knew I was putting that in there for him. I think as I move along and I know more and more people who are older and I learn more from them, they are going to appear more frequently in my fiction. A great deal more. I want to open up. I want to expand. I want the repertoire of my characters to be enormous. Was it Gore Vidal who said, "Every writer has a limited number of characters. Shakespeare had maybe forty. Most people have only three or four"? Well, I want to have forty if Shakespeare did. I want to be able to explore people as different as David Talbot and Mona as successfully as I can explore Lestat or Michael Curry or Jeremy Walker. That's my goal. Too much fiction is a failure of imagination. I don't want imagination to fail in my fiction.

RILEY: I'm wondering what role your father's later years and his final illness might have had in your interest in characters who are older. Or was that only a coincidence?

RICE: It was worse than coincidental. I'm going to answer this in what will probably seem a weird way. After I wrote *Tale of the Body Thief*, I was very blackly depressed. I went to the doctor and got Prozac, and I kind of climbed out of the depression. About that time my father came down here to New Orleans for a visit. He was staying in the guest house, and he fell down and broke his hip and went into the hospital and died. For two months, I stayed with him almost night and day. I was there when he died. I was holding his hand. We were all there. During those months *Body Thief* had been lying there. I had been sent the copyedited manuscript in August, and during all the time my father was sick, I had not sent it back. After his death I finally sat down to read the manuscript, and I was terrified it was going to sound like trash, that I was actually going to just throw it out the window. But to my amazement, I not only didn't feel it was trash, I felt it was everything I had wanted it to be. It was exactly as I wanted it, and it was about my father and about his death. I was very glad I had not given it to him in manuscript form in August and that he had not read it. That was a bizarre experience. I didn't even know my father was seventy-four, or if I did know, I didn't know that I knew. And I don't know why I had selected that very age for David Talbot, because when I go back and look at David in the earlier novels, he could have been younger than seventy-four. There were choices as to how old to make David Talbot. But it was definitely about my father. It was almost as if it were a premonition of his death. He died very confused and upset and not feeling he had found what he wanted. He voiced the same kind of dissatisfactions that David Talbot voiced. There in the hospital he said to Stan, "I hope you find what I was searching for." Even on the day of his death he was calling out "you fool, you fool" over and over again to this friend of his who wasn't there. He was seeing things. It was a terrible, anguishing death where he felt bereft of consolation and felt that perhaps he had not spent his life in the wisest way. It was just anguishing. And when I went back to *Tale of the Body Thief*, the whole subject of the novel seemed to be about that. So when you ask if my father's last years and his death were related to my work, the answer is yes. It was related; it was about it all.

5

"The savage garden"

RILEY: One of the most daring aspects of *Taltos* is that Ash's story is not only the history of his character, but at another level it's also a sustained confrontation with the history of Christianity itself.

RICE: I just started with that. It's really the central theme I'm dealing with in the novel I'm writing now [*Memnoch the Devil*], the history of Christianity. I had originally wanted to take it farther with Ash, but what I decided was that once Ash left the Glen I was not interested anymore, at least not in terms of *Taltos*. I had wanted to take Ash on to Glastonbury, to all that controversy between the Church in Rome and St. Columba. I think I alluded to it—that St. Augustine and the Romans were now in a big row with the Celtic Church and St. Columba. They were quarreling over the calendar and the whole nature and form of monastic life, and the Romans were about to win that struggle and cast out everything St. Columba had done. My original intention was to lead Ash right to Rome to Gregory the Great, who was Pope at the end of the sixth century. In fact the reason he's called Gregory the Great is because he extended the power and authority of the papacy and the Roman Church over the Celtic Church and others. Ash was going to see the incredible ruins of Rome, and then even go on through time, through one controversy after another. But I thought, no, I'll do that in the next book. You know, I frequently do that. I'll be thinking about what I want to do in one book, and in another I'll cannibalize it and use it sooner. I'm glad you saw that because it's definitely what I wanted to do, but I decided to leave it at that point in *Taltos*. To me, the thread of that novel is that the moment has come for the Taltos to take over the world, and if they wanted to, they could. For a variety of reasons, Lasher was right and so was Ash, but I played with it as much as I wanted to at the time. All those elements are in there, but they were not my central theme.

RILEY: What strikes me is that you've been working your way toward this for many years now.

RICE: Yes, I have. That's the meaning of the statement by Belinda when she says to Jeremy that his work has to do with the pictures on the ceiling of this church they've seen. And in *Interview with the Vampire* a big theme is what the Church means and how it has let Louis down.

RILEY: Coming out of your Catholic childhood, the role of the Church—its dogma and belief and ritual—has always been there working in your imagination. It's in almost all of your novels in various ways. I don't know if you will agree with me, but it seems as if, when you were still fairly young, you came to a moment when you rejected the Church in its formal, institutionalized sense. And in your books, over and over again, you've been trying to find another explanation. It's as if you saw the Church as wrestling with the right things but coming to the wrong conclusions, and your work seeks to construct its own mythos in response to many of the same matters the mythos of the Church is a response to.

RICE: You're saying something that nobody's ever mentioned to me before about these books, but that's absolutely the truth. My father did once say, "You're rewriting the history of the Catholic Church," although I'm not sure he totally understood. Obviously there's a great effort in the books to go back and reclaim and acknowledge the tremendous power of all that history of the Church and to search for another truth in it, a truth other than that which it presents to the world, which I felt had to be rejected. If I understand you correctly, that's true, and that's what the new novel is all about. Lestat will encounter God and the Devil, and I would never have attempted that ten years ago. I wouldn't have attempted it a year and a half ago. When I first thought of it, I thought, no, you cannot have God as a character in a novel, and then I thought, why not? It's going to be my biggest dare. It will be God and the Devil. Or will it be? Let's say that it'll be people who claim to be, and Lestat will be left with the dilemma . . . whether it was true. But that particular question is just the tip of the iceberg of what the book's all about. I'm terrifically excited about it, and that's exactly what it's about. It's like David Talbot in that room saying, "The truth about us is in this book Genesis, but it's not what we think. It's in here, though. It's in here." So now I'm going back through all of the Old Testament and the apocryphal books, the books that are not part of the canon, the Holy Book of Enoch and all those different books. I'm going through all that material searching for a truth there, and yet I'm doing it with the absolute freedom of a fiction writer. I'm not doing it like a Jesuit; I'm not trying to find a new philosophy they'll let me publish.

I don't believe the Catholic Church is the one true church established by Christ to give grace and that everyone else is going to Hell. But the fundamental power of the Church's ideas continued for me. The lights continued to burn in the corner of my eye. I continued to see them. They never went out. Now I'm just so wrapped up in all of it that I'm ecstatic. I can't tell you the reading I've done about those early years trying to figure out what happened between the death of Christ and, say, Gregory the Great. I just barely touched on it with Ash, just almost had fun with it, and then backed off from it. The part I love best is when Ash says, "Can you see what suckers we would be with Christianity?"

RILEY: Despite your own break with the Church, in the long run have you turned out, ironically, to be a Catholic writer after all?

RICE: In some respects, because of the concern with good and evil, the concern with how we save our souls. I'm not surprised my books are taught in Catholic schools. I turned out to be of great interest to a Catholic readership, let's put it that way, and they've been very forgiving in reading my works, interested in the overall spiritual themes and forgiving of the strong statements that I'm an atheist or that I'm anti the Church. Also, I think that for many people in the Catholic Church one of the things we all carried away with us is that spiritual urgency, that inability to ever forget about good and evil, and right and wrong, about whether our lives are worthwhile or stupid and shallow, and a kind of suspicion of materialism. My books are all about that, and they're read by people who are concerned with that, both Catholic and non-Catholic.

RILEY: Is New Orleans Catholicism different in some recognizable way from Catholicism elsewhere?

RICE: I think the salient characteristic of my Catholicism was that it was blue-collar Catholicism. I grew up in a workingman's parish, and I went to poor parish schools more than to fine academies. My experience in private schooling was very brief, St. Joseph Academy for one year, and most of the social values that were mixed in with my Catholicism were very distinctly working-class values—the view of women as people to iron shirts and help with Mother and not to go to college, but to seek a husband and to be a good wife—that was much more heavily mixed in with my Catholicism than, say, the Catholicism Jackie Kennedy would have experienced, or Mary McCarthy, or many other people. By the time I ran into Catholics from a different background, where perhaps college education had been the norm and professional life had been more what the family went into, I was out of the Church. I never went to a grand Catholic college. I don't know what it means to take a course in "The Theology of Catholic Thought" in a good Catholic college. I experienced a little bit of it at the University of San Francisco, but not really. I never took any religious classes. I just took a few other kinds of classes and found the kids to be so young, so almost sexually naïve, so biased, so believing in the old clichés—a good girl doesn't let you kiss her, you know—that I couldn't deal with it.

So I just left. I was only going there because they had night classes and you could take one or two if you could pay for them. I would have never gone to a Catholic school otherwise.

"LISTENING TO THE FLESH"

RILEY: Talking about the period in your life when you met Stan, you spoke of your conflict with the Church's insistence on the idea that physical purity is morally superior to the claims of the flesh. Eventually you rejected that as false, as an idea that was basically life-denying. In your novels, too, characters often caution others to beware the idea, the abstraction. The wiser characters, those who in some sense rank higher in the moral structure of the novels, always argue for substance and the wisdom of the flesh. This is obviously a deep conviction of yours, and yet you are yourself fascinated with ideas.

RICE: Yes, but I see the best ideas as those that have come out of listening to the flesh very closely.

RILEY: In your view, then, there is no fundamental wisdom that can be cut loose from, or can exist independent of, the flesh?

RICE: I don't think so, but growing up in the Catholic tradition, you grow up being taught that the flesh is bad. The world, the flesh, and the devil, those are your enemies.

RILEY: Do you believe there's something truer in our feelings about life than in our thinking about life?

RICE: Oh yes. You see that contradiction repeatedly. Most religions have bodies of ideas that condemn the flesh, condemn the carnal, say it's evil and it can't be redeemed. Instead, you must follow a path to get away from it, to deny yourself, to get closer to something of great value that has nothing to do with the flesh. I believe just the opposite.

RILEY: Given your study of the history of religions, why do you think that's been the case?

RICE: I'm baffled. I want to get into it in this new book, but I am truly baffled. Certainly, as you look over the history of religions, you can see it's almost a universal impulse. What other religions believe about the evil of the flesh is in many ways more shocking than what Christianity holds about it.

RILEY: Your wariness about abstractions isn't confined to religious ideas. Do you mistrust the intellectual?

RICE: Totally!

RILEY: Why? In what ways?

RICE: You're asking a vast question. People have written volumes on this very subject. The intellectuals I've known have been rather merciless people. They're really not charitable. They're not kind, and they're very self-deluding. I saw so much of that, particularly in the sixties and seventies, all those ideas. They pick and choose whom they want to sympathize with, and they fall in love with ideas that enable them to do what they want to do. Basically, they are unkind people. The intellectuals I knew in California hated the middle-class American. They didn't have any mercy for such a person. They didn't want to hear anything about the goodness of a family man anywhere in the United States. They had convinced themselves that the underdogs were the ones who were good, and that their time and energy were best spent in the company of black people or Vietnamese or third-world people, as they would put it. They were filled with illusions. Some of them had never worked at a forty-hour-a-week job in their lives. They didn't know anything about the third world; they didn't know anything about the working class. These were all ideas to them—but the ideas gain credence and become popular, and you have people spouting them who have no idea what they're really about. I saw that rampant around me in California. You know, my major when I was a student was political science. I did a lot of reading in that area, and I was appalled at the way people would style themselves Marxists and move through the affluent world of Northern California spending money from their father on expensive vegetables and wine so they could go to a dinner table in Berkeley and have a ferocious argument about the farmworkers. I came to feel that intellectuals can be very dangerous people, that once people become convinced an idea is a good enough excuse to be rude to others, they can move very quickly to being cruel to others, and then even to killing others, all in the name of an idea.

RILEY: But that's not necessarily the case. You're an intellectual. Stan's an intellectual.

RICE: In the broader sense of the word, yes, but I'm using it in a very limited sense. I mean a person who puts ideas before real people. We have to remember that, for example, as Ayn Rand said, Nazism was a body of ideas, and the Nazis believed in self-sacrifice. I've never read Ayn Rand, but I saw her in a couple of television appearances. I was totally unfamiliar with her philosophy that systems that believe in ideas involving self-sacrifice can in many respects be very inhuman and monstrous. She used Nazism as a perfect example. I remember a light going on in my head and understanding exactly what she meant because I was at that time surrounded by what I considered to be fascist liberals who were positively vicious in the way they talked about other people. Feminism took a turn in that direction for a while, where it became a huge stick with which to beat people over the head. Women would attack other women in the most insensitive ways. I remember once mentioning to someone that I was writing to a male convict—for a brief time I had a correspondence with him—and a woman who really didn't know me that well, and yet had known me for years, turned around and said very coldly, "There are women prisoners you should be writing to." Just think for a moment about speaking to another person like that. But ideas give people that kind of license. When people become truly enamored of ideas, when they believe they're absolutely right, they will do the damnedest things. When they stop observing what is really happening right around them with their fellow human beings, they can get swept up in some pretty crazy cruelties.

In an important sense, the founders of America, the writers of the Constitution, were not intellectuals. They had something besides intellectual pursuit. They were people who lived in the real world. That's what I'm talking about. You know, when you're growing up and you first meet friends who read books and who take ideas seriously and care about something besides materialistic values, they seem to you to be the best people in the world because they really care about making the world a better place. But the longer you hang out with those people, it seems to me, the more strident they sometimes become. That doesn't always happen, of course, but the more you meet the strident ones among them, the more you come to realize they can be very inhumane. I suppose Russian Communism is the most outstanding example of a body of ideas that ran out of control. They were hatched out of the brain of Karl Marx, a German middle-class intellectual who really didn't know much about work. He wrote *Das Kapital*, as I understand it, in the British Museum while living in London, and those ideas were taken up by these really angry Russian intellectuals who then were responsible for the deaths of literally millions of people. It's almost on a scale we cannot imagine, the people who died under Lenin and under Stalin. We're just beginning to know now how many there were. That's intellectualism run rampant, and it is death. We always have to guard ourselves against the pure intellectual, the person who's so far from the truths of the flesh that he has no heart, no real conscience. He thinks he's on the right hand of God, and that's very dangerous. I've often said this and I really believe it: For the liberals of Berkeley, their idea of being liberal is to burn at the stake a conservative. I mean, they really think that's liberal! I can't deal with it too well in my fiction. I tend to mention it and go on by it, because I don't write about people I don't like. I write almost entirely about people I believe in and ways of triumphing, rather than trying to skewer people I hate in a book.

Another thing that probably makes me conscious of this is that since I did grow up a Catholic, and then left the Church, and in the sixties and seventies was an atheist and a liberal and a Californian, I saw and heard many intellectuals' condemnation of the Catholic Church. I heard it, I took it for granted, I believed they were right. It took me maybe twenty years to see how little such intellectuals really understood about the principles of goodness and charity that exist in a religion like Catholicism, what charity really means when religious orders feed the sick and give shots to little kids so they won't die of disease. We grew up knowing people did that, that the working Church did that. There were thousands of nuns and thousands of brothers who did only that. They taught, they clothed, they visited the sick. It was routine for members of my family to do that. My father was with the Holy Name men, and they got out every Sunday and visited the poor of the parish and took them things and saw how they were doing. There was a St. Margaret's Daughters, who would make sure all the little girls in the parish had the dresses they needed for First Communion. These women would sew the dresses so the poorest child in the parish would have a pretty white dress on that day like everyone else. All of that was very much a part of life, but I heard religions like Catholicism put down as if they were completely evil. I heard them put down by people who did not have a particle of real charity, not a particle of genuine concern for others. They had an idealized vision of some third-world person or country about which they really knew nothing. I saw these things, and as I came back to appreciating those earlier values, my suspicion of intellectuals and blanket condemnations grew and grew.

I find it easiest to talk about the good in people. I find it very hard to declare that something is totally evil. I'll give you one example. I have, let's just say, what I would call a raving liberal friend in California whom I really love. I speak to her often over the years, and she certainly considers herself in the know. She thinks she's very aware of what goes on. She would run into a black GI in the student union, and he would tell her the only place he'd ever been treated with equality was Saigon. She and I would get into violent arguments when I would try to explain that he was wearing the uniform of the monied and conquering army in Saigon, so that his perception of being treated well in that Asian society was completely warped. It did not mean the Vietnamese people were morally superior to us simply because they had treated this one black American well. I remember at one point this particular woman, who was an intellectual, became extremely taken with the story of a priest she'd heard about who worked in South America and had died on some sort of commune or farm helping poor people. She told me that when she asked about him, they told her very frankly that there were many people like that in the Church. I almost felt like laughing and saying, yes, that's absolutely the truth. And I thought, how strange for this woman to reach the age of about fifty-five and to have lived all her life as a conscientious liberal, supporting this correct cause and that correct cause, and not even realize that a great many people whom we call immoral go from the cradle to the grave helping others every day of their lives. They don't listen to KPFA on the radio, and they don't know anything about the Peace and Freedom Party, and very possibly they had a son who went to Vietnam, but they really make charity and goodness and generosity part of their lives. I've known them, and this person had not. Her idea of a good person was a radical New Yorker or Berkeleyite who basically styled himself or herself a Marxist or even a Stalinist. I found it maddening. I got into pitched battles all over the place. I thought Communism was such a ruthless system and Communists were so guilty of mass murder that I couldn't understand how any American intellectual could justify those things or even think there was anything of value. They could say, "I want to go to Russia to help the Revolution, but I can't. I have to go to Berkeley right now."

"A REFUSAL TO BE DOOMED"

RILEY: Whether we are speaking of your novels in terms of ideas or spiritual themes or of their providing a kind of bridge for those who know they are dying, it seems to me that as a writer you've been engaged in a quest to discover not just a system of belief but a consolation in the face of death. It seems important that your books strive to realize something that will survive the moment of death.

RICE: They're my attempts to find the best thing that can be said about it all. They're attempts to say that basically this world of ours is worth it and it's beautiful. There are times when we have to work hard to remember that. We have to remind ourselves, and we have to find new ways of seeing that. But it's true, and in that truth lie a thousand other truths for us to discover. To paraphrase Keats: That's all you need to know, that a thing of beauty is a joy forever. In a way, that's where you can start, by believing the world is beautiful and it's worth it, and that conviction alone can save you. My novels are always trying to say that somehow or other, no matter what's happened, the world is not meaningless, and it is not absurd. It is not, in itself, horrible, and neither are human beings. No matter what's gone down, there's some capacity to understand that redeems us. There's some capacity to do better, to want to do better—that we're actually inherently good. That's what *Tale of the Body Thief* said: that we're inherently good, and that real evil is almost a fiction. Even if you get in the most evil character's mind, like Lestat's mind, you're going to find he's basically a good guy making certain decisions. In the book he says, "I'm basically a nice guy, or I would have been."

RILEY: Were you redefining evil in that novel?

RICE: No, I don't think so, not really redefining it. Take the works of a man like Jeffrey Burton Russell, his four books on the Devil, Mephistopheles. I read him all the time, and I'm enthralled by his insights. He's really tied together the philosophy of evil, the picture of evil that emerges from Christianity and Judaism. He has very sophisticated ideas. I'm playing with all that in an emotional and perhaps simplistic way. So I wouldn't say redefining evil, but just defining it, over and over again defining it, what it's all about, and maybe trying to redefine salvation.

RILEY: What do you think is truly evil in the world?

RICE: The taking of another life. The deliberate inflicting of suffering on a sentient being. I believe Russell says that: The killing of people, the starving, the beating, the maiming, the neglect, that's where real fire-and-brimstone evil arises, in a war, in famine. I suppose, being a child of this age of war, I'd have to say that for me war is the ultimate evil. Women, men, and children, people of all ages, are murdered and maimed and destroyed, and lose all possibility of ever really having a life, ever seeing this beautiful world and enjoying it, knowing what it's all about. That is really evil.

RILEY: To me, the most terrible moment of evil in all you've ever written is the young girl on the stage at the Theater of the Vampires.

RICE: It's a terribly sadistic scene. I don't know if I could write it today. I don't have many other scenes like it. In the book, of course, it represents an obscenity to Louis too. He knows there's no necessity for powerful predatory killers to do that to their victims. They don't need to suffer. If I remember correctly, there's a moment in the novel—I know it's in the screenplay—when Lestat says something like, "They don't need to suffer, so just get on with it!" So the scene is supposed to make clear the obscenity of this Paris crowd that would do that.

RILEY: One question that drives *Interview*, not just Louis but the novel overall, is the awful possibility that suffering could be meaningless. Have you discovered since writing *Interview* that that's not true? Do you believe suffering can be meaningful?

RICE: It's not that. It's that I've come to terms with the fact that it *might* be meaningless. Even in *Feast of All Saints* there's a scene where Marcel goes to Christophe and says that he's heard of a horrible execution that took place in Saint Domingue. He says, "If something like that can happen, anything can happen." In fact, it's the central image of my work, that if people can gather together and burn another person alive, they can do anything. I keep going back to it. I have to almost stop myself . . . the images of people being burned. When people do that, real evil is afoot. And, of course, it's all through our history, the lynchings in the South, the witchcraft trials in Europe or in Salem. It is an image that recurs throughout history. When people really get worked up against other people, they burn them, whether as a group or as individuals, and it's seen as acceptable. I think when I wrote *Interview* and when I wrote *Feast*, the thought that suffering might be meaningless was excruciating to me. It's not that I don't still find that possibility appalling. I do, but it may just be what is. And in the face of that, what we bring to life, the meaning we give to it and the meaning we take out of it, is to me a wondrous thing. That's where the new optimism comes from, a coming to terms, of saying death is just death, finally everybody does it. But that does not mean we can justify the suffering of a child or cruelty to a person. I don't feel the same kind of almost going-over-the-brink madness I did when I wrote those books. There's been some way for me personally to live and to see beauty in spite of having seen death and suffering.

I think one of the great pitfalls of being my age, and being who I am, is impatience with other people. When you've been through a lot, you have to watch yourself that you don't get impatient. Not long ago I was listening to somebody talk about how they'd lost their faith after a parent died, and I thought to myself, what an absolutely preposterous thing to say, that they lost their faith in God because an old person died. Have we gotten so far from reality that we don't know our father and mother are going to die? Where are we that we would dare to say something like that? That's become a cliché you find all through American life, people of every rank and class saying they lost their faith when Barbara died or Mary died or Leo died, that after watching this person go and that person go, they don't believe in anything, they don't have any faith. I don't feel that way at all. Now, I may be riding high. If something were to happen to me or to those closest to me, I might be pitched right back into the pit of rage and despair. At the moment, though, I don't feel that so much as I feel a kind of optimism and an ability to accept certain things, an ability to look at what is and say, my God, this is beautiful.

RILEY: Do you believe in God?

RICE: Yes, more and more. But I don't know exactly what that belief means. This is of very great concern to me in the novel I'm writing now. I've been immersing myself in the history of religious ideas and the history of religion. I'm particularly engrossed in the work of the anthropologist Mircea Eliade. I've got multiple editions of his books, copies here and in New York, and the New York copies are all marked up. I'm very, very curious as to whether God exists, and the older I get, the more it seems to me to be an absolutely pompous notion to think He doesn't. I'm more curious and serene now. That's how I feel about most things. I'm so enthralled with all aspects of what's happening around me that I'm not very much in touch with any rage. I realize, of course, that it could be circumstantial. After all, I haven't received a phone call telling me I have cancer. But when I hear of somebody losing his faith in God because a parent died, I have a lot of trouble with it. I think something's wrong with us if that's really what we want to focus on emotionally in that instance.

RILEY: It seems to be a need to be assured that nothing bad will ever happen to us, or otherwise we will lose faith.

RICE: This is one of the things I want to get into in the new novel. I don't frankly expect God to be concerned with any particular death anymore, and this is an image I want to explore. When you and I sit in this garden, we are not going to go on our hands and knees through the dirt and make sure every grub and worm that's dying is old and ready for it and has lived its full life, and I don't think God is going to do that either. More and more, I tend toward that perspective in trying to understand things. I'm fascinated by it right now, and my attitude is more one of serenity and curiosity than one of condemnation and rage. That's definitely charted in the novels, although I don't think there could be a novel much more full of rage than *The Tale of the Body Thief*—somebody just coldly enraged. Lestat talks about rage and disappointment and about pushing ahead in spite of them. From one point of view, in choosing to tell only one tale *Body Thief* takes on a lot less, but in a way it takes on more. It's saying that in this one tale it's going to perhaps be more uncompromising about evil than the other books have been. It's going to play fewer games, and when it plays a game with the reader, it's going to admit it. But ironically it's also about playing games. Lestat claims to be good and claims to be sorry he's done all this, but he's not sorry. He really enjoys it, and finally he can't say he wouldn't make Claudia a vampire again. So in his game he's confronting his own evil, the real depths of his own evil, the ruthlessness in himself.

RILEY: So he's ruthlessly honest in this book, but still he is evil?

RICE: I would say so. For all practical purposes, yes, but I think he's a being with a very fine conscience who knows right from wrong, who strives very much not to be evil, but he is.

RILEY: When I've heard people express discomfort or ambivalence about *The Vampire Chronicles*, it's usually had to do with this very issue, the dilemma of evil in these characters. No doubt that's at least partly because Lestat himself so frequently speaks of it. It's not an issue that gets glossed over. If Lestat is evil, is he then doomed?

RICE: I think the novels are about a refusal to be doomed. They're about assuming the guilt for killing, assuming the guilt for having all kinds of advantages that human beings don't have, and bearing that guilt, and refusing to behave as if one is doomed. Lestat insists on moving through life like a good man. That's the dilemma that's discussed over and over again when he says, "I refuse to be bad at being bad. Because this is what I have to do, I have to be good at it." I see it as related to all of us. I've used this example a lot in the last few years because it's really true. As we sit here, people are starving, they are dying of disease, they are suffering such injustices that somebody could come down from another planet and ask, "How can you sit here, how can you sit at this glass table, wearing these clothes, with food and drink all around you in this house, when thousands at this moment are truly starving?" Yet we choose to do this. We choose to do this because we choose to live our lives in spite of the injustices we really don't feel we can rectify. We don't want to lose our lives to try to save a village in India. We don't want to lose the fruits of a lifetime trying to save one impossible situation in South America that will continue after we're dead. We do make that choice. I often think of that when I'm writing from Lestat's point of view. He makes the choice to move through the world and take the sacrifices of human life that are necessary for him, and he doesn't kid himself about it. But basically what he's striving for, I think, is the consolation and comfort and the freedom of a wholesome, good guy. He has a determination, an absolute refusal to give up. That's his argument with Louis: "I'm not going to just beat my chest and act like a penitent. I can't live like that. Everything you say may be true, that we're bad guys, we're damned, this is Hell, this is a nightmare, but I can't keep that in mind all the time. There's just too much music to be listened to, there are too many places to go." That's kind of the way I feel about life itself. Now, that may be the philosophy of someone who feels stricken with guilt from a Catholic childhood. Just to live and enjoy a moment, free of guilt, becomes a big struggle for a person like me.

RILEY: Do you think we—you and I and others who do choose to sit here, as it were—are evil because we don't address the injustices of the world, or are those injustices simply a fact of life that exists on too large a scale for us to respond, short of extraordinary demands for sacrifice?

RICE: I think we are and we aren't. In the purely objective sense, yes, we're certainly evil, and when people look back on our age, they'll ask how could we have done it, just as they will ask how could the French aristocracy have been giving big parties when people were starving in Paris. They will definitely want to know that, and it's very hard to understand. But on the other hand, we're not evil. We can't solve it. As we watch the images on television, I think all of us feel that if there were a number we could dial at that moment to directly help, and we were confident the money would help the people we see starving and not go to some huge bureaucracy or agency or some racket, I think we would do it. What stands between us and action is the absolute impossibility. One of the things I was taught as a child growing up a strict Catholic was a very strong sense that you had to do something about those things, so in a way my answer to you is very Catholic. Yes, we're evil if we fail to do something about those things. It's our concern, mankind is our business. It really is. When I went out to California, and I left the Church, and all of those things happened throughout the sixties and seventies, I ran into many people, many young people, who were not from a Catholic background but who had adopted a revolutionary posture and felt they could not go on with life until they rectified some of the evils. Now, I think they were very misguided in many respects, and there was a pick-and-choose quality to the way they went about living their lives: We're going to fight for this cause and ignore that one. It was sort of absurd, but certainly even in the most naïve, the most rambunctious, the most thoughtless kids there was a real desire to change things. They were saying, we can't just enjoy our middle-class lives if this is going on. That was an inspiring thing. I think people are very concerned with rectifying evil, and I'm optimistic about our times. But objectively I know that there's still an enormous amount of suffering about which we could do something, and our efforts fall far short.

RILEY: Wherein lies salvation—for Lestat or for any of us?

RICE: I think the first rule is to hurt no one, not to consciously bring pain, injustice, deprivation, suffering to another human being. That's the first thing. If you can go through your life obeying that rule, you will avoid almost all evil. The second thing is to try to share what you see and what you have with other people, insofar as it's good. I truly believe that, sentimental as it may sound.

RILEY: Still, suffering persists, and the uncertainty of meaning. There's a point in the *Chronicles* in which one of the characters says, "I knew perfectly well there was an abyss . . . into which I might suddenly and helplessly drop." What is that abyss?

RICE: I remember writing that. The abyss is the possible meaninglessness of it all, the unknown.

RILEY: At the conclusion of *Interview* does Louis achieve at least a measure of what he has sought—the meaning of his existence, whether he understands it or not—by the very act of telling his story?

RICE: He ends as a failure, angry that the boy's response is that he wants to be a vampire, and Louis does not seem to know, or take responsibility for, the fact that the reader's likely response is to want to be a vampire, too. He's definitely right when he says, "I've failed." He's made it seem very glamorous and like a lot of fun, a lot better than ordinary life, and, I think, made nine out of ten readers say, "Well, give me a chance at it and let me see what I can do with it!" Louis doesn't acknowledge that, while at the end of *Tale of the Body Thief* Lestat does. He says, "I have done it again. I have triumphed and made it seem terrific. But it's not terrific, it's horrible, and I have failed to show the horror at the heart of it." I think Lestat's being more honest about it: "I've enjoyed telling you the tale, and enjoyed being the star of the show, and enjoyed making you think for a little while I wasn't evil. But that's what I've done. I've won again." I think it's a far more mature and honest statement than Louis's at the end of *Interview.*

RILEY: Given the pervasiveness of evil, its inescapable place in the vampires' lives, I wonder if that might actually be a dark part of their appeal. Perhaps that's something we all share—the fear that when all is said and done, we are in fact evil. Nevertheless, we desperately seek something that is redemptive, some meaningful basis for going on, some way of giving life value despite the fact of evil.

RICE: I believe Anne Frank's words: "People are really good at heart." They don't want to be evil, but they face all kinds of compromises. I do think most of us are afraid we're evil. We're afraid we've chosen the selfish path. We've never been able to successfully balance our selfish desires with what the world and morality seem to require of us. That's what I meant about ruthlessness: We make these ruthless choices to live our lives. I make the ruthless choice that I'm not going to go to India and help all these people being washed out by floods, and there are many other choices. For that matter, there are injustices right here in this city. One doesn't have to go to India. You just have to go over to the St. Thomas project by the river to see people living in abject poverty and confusion and conditions involving crime and dope that are just unthinkable, and it's just a few blocks from here. But I really do believe we do the best we can, and that's what heroism actually is for most people, doing the very best you can. The uncompromising saint is a rare person, and perhaps not a complete person, in some ways a very partial person.

RILEY: What's the role of what you've called "the savage garden" in all of this?

RICE: By the savage garden, I mean simply that there are no principles of justice in nature, there's no harmony. Things are truly savage if you go out there and look at what's eating what. To this day I'm still amazed by the way people romanticize nature. I really don't understand it, whether we're talking about the Romantic poets or about some lady on television who says that wolves are better than people. Like hell! I don't understand how somebody could say that about animals that surround a caribou and tear it to pieces. I don't know what they're thinking when they say all this about there being harmony and peacefulness because the wolves only kill the old caribou. Would they like to be torn apart by wolves rather than grow old? It's so absurd to me that anybody could believe those things. That's what I mean. Lestat is my character who faces that reality. He says, "There's nothing romantic about this. It's beautiful, but it's purely incidental that it's beautiful. Or is it?" He's asking, but it's never not savage.

RILEY: But savage doesn't equal evil in nature, does it?

RICE: No, that's true. The savage garden isn't the evil garden. The savage garden is truly just the savage garden, and when Lestat says there are no laws but the aesthetic laws, I think there's a big case for saying that's true. If you consider the entire history of the world, laws that pertain to color and shape and harmony and sounds are the most consistent rules we've got.

RILEY: And those are rules we discover rather than rules we have made for our own sake.

RICE: Definitely. They are rules we discover in the savage garden.

RILEY: But one of the ways we seek to escape evil is to make rules for ourselves.

RICE: We try to do better. We try to do better than nature, and we try to do better than the savage garden. We try in our own lives and in our own groups to achieve a kind of peace and charity that does not exist in nature in any form.

6

"A place where Ezra Pound and Mickey Spillane touch"

RILEY: Suffering and serenity, evil and the refusal to be doomed, charity and violence—these are some of the oppositions that suffuse your novels. There's also an appetite for passionate feeling and spectacle. All of this emerges in the fiction from the convergence of your imagination and your experience. I'd like to discuss some of the things that have influenced you, that are reflected in your life as a writer, and that compel your interest. Let me begin with something that puzzles me a bit, which is your attitude toward violence. You've been quoted as saying that you love violence. I think I know what you mean when you say that, but I'm not sure. A love of violence isn't a part of your character as I know you.

RICE: I love it in movies and books. I think it's a powerful metaphor for what's going on in our minds, and I think we're finding out today that most women like violence, that most movies aren't violent enough for the women in the audience. If people object to the violence, it's not the women. Maybe that's because as women we see that violence in a more metaphorical way, more removed, more like an artistic or psychological acting out of what we're feeling. But I do like it. I enjoy watching things that are extremely violent, like *Predator* or *Terminator*. I certainly don't take them literally. For me there's a suspension of disbelief as I get into that world, and I love to see the way the violence is executed and how far it's going to go and what it's going to show me. I thought *Robocop*, for example, which is an incredibly violent movie, was fabulously interesting. I don't know why that is except that it speaks to me. It distracts me and holds my interest, and it seems to be about something important beyond itself. It speaks to me more than ordinary realism. The world of the pedestrian realistic movie and novel basically posits that there is no violence. If people die they're going to die of cancer, they're going to die of old age, or maybe sometimes they're going to die from suicide. Only occasionally is there a reference to violence, like somebody being killed in a robbery, but it's very rare. The pedestrian realistic novel is about the tedium of daily life and the lack of glamour, and the presumption is that this is really the way life is for all of us and that coming to terms with it is about the highest thing human beings can do. They can hope for some small revelation that allows them to accept the fact that their town is really where everything is. Well, I don't see that at all; I've never believed any of that. When I turn on a movie and see a really well-choreographed and well-done violent scene in which two people clash, it speaks to other levels of me that ordinary realism doesn't.

I can give you a good example. There's a scene in the beginning of *Conan the Barbarian* that's one of my favorite scenes in all of the movies. If I remember correctly, this is the way it goes: A marauding tribe has come down and slaughtered everyone, and Conan and his mother are the only survivors. James Earl Jones is the warlord who slaughtered everybody, and there is a point at which he turns his back to Conan's mother and gives her a moment in which to kill him with her sword. But she doesn't do it, and James Earl Jones turns around and chops off her head. It goes flying like a beach ball. [*laughter*] I love that scene; I would put the movie on just to see that. I know what it's about. I know what her hesitation is about. I know what her compassion is about. I know what his ruthlessness is about, and I know what the truth of it is about: that his kind wins. I know how the little boy is seeing it. That scene touches something very profound for me, but someone else might think it's just disgusting. Of course, there are movies I do reject as disgusting. I don't watch the Charles Bronson movies, for example; I find them disgusting. But that scene in *Conan* is an example of exactly the kind of violence I like. You have a metaphorical frame. You have a slight remove from reality; it's ancient times. You have very strong faces—James Earl Jones is a terrific actor—conveying a great deal, and the woman's face is filled with feeling.

RILEY: So the metaphorical frame and distance is a necessary dimension of it?

RICE: It is one dimension, yes, but I also like gritty realism like *GoodFellas* where that frame is supposedly absent, because for me it's not really absent at all. To me

GoodFellas is a very artful movie and very stylized in the way Scorsese presents those gangsters and the way they talk to each other. It's all heavily stylized, and it's very romantic. Stepping into that world is almost like stepping into *Conan*. You say to yourself, I'll take leave of my world and I'm just going to hang around with a bunch of fast-talking Italians in New York and all these horrible things are going to happen. But their speech is going to be so melodious and so quick that it's going to be like a dark symphony and it's all a work of art.

RILEY: Given that the movies have always been such an influence on your imagination, what do you think of the state of movies today?

RICE: I'm too behind. I get things about a year late, and I watch them on laser disc. But I've been knocked out by some of the things I've seen. I thought *Henry and June* was a fabulous movie. I thought *Last Exit to Brooklyn* was amazing. After a long period during which daring films like *Last Tango in Paris* were no longer being made, I think things are being done again that are very daring. I think there's a new freedom. There's a new release to experiment.

RILEY: I'm sometimes dismayed by what seems to dominate movies today. There's been a powerful pull toward the spectacle, not just in the scale of films but in their determination to produce the most intense visceral experience the medium can conjure up. Too often I find that if a film isn't highly charged in its style as well as its action, if it's not extremely electric and violent, audiences are less likely to be engaged by it. It's as if it takes an ever-greater stimulus to provoke a response.

RICE: Well, look at that a little more kindly. I think

everything you say is true, but I also think the production values are higher than they've ever been. The sets and the costumes will be so far superior to anything thirty years ago in getting the atmosphere and the realism and the lighting. Sometimes it can just be horrendous, I know. In general we see a lot of trash today that's packaged so exquisitely that it looks like it has to be something significant. I think *Silence of the Lambs* is a perfect example. I think that is a piece of caca, but it was packaged and labored over and given so much technical and financial support you were convinced you were seeing a work of art. It was no work of art at all. It was a piece of shit; that's basically what I think about it. I think the book wasn't, though, because Tom Harris's writing was good enough that I felt I got a lot from the book. But the movie—the idea of this transsexual-transvestite killing women and taking their bodies for the skin, and this lunatic who eats people's livers—the whole thing was offensive. It didn't speak to anything deep in me—I don't think to anything deep in anybody.

RILEY: I haven't read the Harris novel. Does the film change it significantly?

RICE: No, the film is amazingly faithful to the book, and it's just as preposterous in the novel as it is in the film. I suppose one guy's trash is another guy's profound work, but there's something so dishonest about the film of *Silence of the Lambs*, deeply dishonest.

RILEY: I think it's a film that just pretends to be about something.

RICE: Pretends to be about something, that's it. It pretends to be about that FBI worker and how she's forced to explore herself by this lunatic, but it's really not about that. It's really about seeing dead bodies on tables and people screaming from pits and people chasing other people with guns and your breath being forced out of your body. That's really what it's about, and it sold a big bill of goods to the public that I think was really awful. I had a particularly strong reaction to that movie. I was so blocked by that movie I couldn't write. I felt like if I was writing stuff that was like that, I didn't ever want to write again. I was so nauseated and upset by that movie, and I wasn't by the book although Thomas Harris would push anybody to the threshold who says she likes violence.

But to get back to your question about the state of movies. What I wanted to say is that, at least in terms of what interests me, I think we're in the golden age of the gangster movie. We're getting some of the best movies to do with Italian-Americans and gangsters that we've ever had. Several of our greatest actors, such as Robert De Niro and Al Pacino, are people who play Italian street punks better than they play anything else. It's a very interesting phenomenon. When people look back on this age, they're going to see Scorsese's movies and other similar movies about gangsters as being some of our best. Some of our most coherent and intense movies are in that mold. Perhaps it's pure coincidence, but it is that way. When people come to you and say, what actors do you admire, it's a little unsettling to realize the actors you love are all good at stabbing and shooting people. [*laughter*] Pacino in *Scarface* gave a fabulous performance. You could watch *Scarface*—which of course is not about an Italian gangster but a Cuban gangster—but you can watch that film just for his performance. It's a stronger performance than *Scent of a Woman*, as far as I'm concerned, a more interesting performance. The whole movie is about this crazy, drug addict killer, and it's mesmerizing. The momentum of that performance is terrific. When people look back, they will value those films of ours. Of course, it all started with *The Godfather*. It was *The Godfather* that moved those films away from the James Cagney type of thing to something totally different. It must be very hard for people who don't particularly care for that material, people who are fed up with seeing the Mafia as some sort of symbol of everything and don't want to see it, because some of the best movies are set in that milieu right now.

RILEY: One of the reasons, I think, that *The Godfather* films—particularly Parts I and II, I didn't care much for *Godfather III*—are as powerful and compelling as they are is precisely the characters. In addition to being great action films, they are also great family melodramas.

RICE: I think that's exactly right. That was it from the beginning. They are about families, and people wanted to see that. They are about ties of blood and the struggle of these clans. If they had not been about that, it would have made all the difference in the world. That was the appeal of *The Godfather*, that deep involvement with this very carefully delineated family. I think that was really the most powerful thing, the mixture of that with the violence. Another thing that's happened in movies in the last twenty years that I've found tremendously exciting is the growth of a whole new kind of movie that never existed when I was a child. I would call *Splash* one of those movies, or *Dick Tracy*, or the *Batman* movies. I was really laid waste by *Bat-*

man II. I knew it was reminding me of a great director and a great silent film, but I didn't know which silent film it was. I had to do some rooting around, and then I found out it was Joseph von Sternberg's *The Scarlet Empress* with Marlene Dietrich, which it turns out is not a silent movie after all. But I was swept away by *Batman II* because that's what it looked like to me, like a huge Russian silent movie. I'm not sure the public perceived it that way, but I thought it was a very exciting development. That takes a lot of money, though. Some critics have called it the movement of taking the B movie and doing it with an A budget. Taking B subject matter—like a mermaid comes to New York and falls in love with a guy—and doing that with an A budget. We've seen a lot of that in the last few years, and I'm very excited by those movies. I think to be able to make a movie like *Splash* completely straight like that and keep that tone was quite an achievement. It's a hilarious movie, and I die laughing every time I watch it.

There was another one, *Edward Scissorhands*, that I was watching with Chris, and I remember telling him that when I was a kid there was nothing like this. I don't know what we would have thought if we had gone to the movies and somebody had given us *Edward Scissorhands*. First of all, we would have loved it. The nearest thing we got to it was *The Red Shoes* or *Tales of Hoffman*, and a lot of kids never saw those because they played in art houses. These films today are giving kids big chunks of a special kind of fantasy. I thought the story of *Edward Scissorhands* was drivel, but there was something really compelling about the movie. There was something compelling about the character, and at moments it achieved real beauty.

RILEY: You know, *Edward Scissorhands* and the *Batman* films were all directed by Tim Burton.

RICE: Yes, I know. I met Tim Burton once and talked to him when he was toying with the idea of directing the rewrite of *Frankenstein* that I did for Universal. Nothing ever came of it, but we did meet for a few minutes in New York and talk about it. I very much admire what he's doing a lot of the time. And oh, I have to mention Sam Raimi's *Darkman*, which is the quintessential masterpiece. That's really like a comic strip. That's a movie using those conventions, like *Batman* does, and telling you it's going to play by those rules, and it's dazzling, filled with all kinds of crazy things and originality and flashes of genius.

EARLY INFLUENCES: IMAGES, STORYTELLING, ILLUSION

RILEY: You've said that movies have been a greater influence on you than literature. What is it about the movies that so activated your imagination?

RICE: I'm a very slow reader, especially with prose that's dense with abstraction, so as a child I never read for sheer pleasure as many people do. I never sank into books. I mainly read nonfiction, things that would gain me something. I read very few novels in school, but I did go to the movies from the very beginning. I went to a neighborhood theater sometimes two or three times a week if I could get away with it. I can still remember the first time I went to the movies. I went with my mother to the Loew's State Theater to see *Caesar and Cleopatra*. I remember Vivien

Leigh having herself wrapped in that rug and being taken up to the ship and then dumped in front of Claude Rains. I also remember seeing *A Night in Casablanca* with the Marx Brothers, and I remember later seeing *Casablanca* and being very disappointed that the Marx Brothers weren't in it. I mean, we were in Casablanca, weren't we? [*laughter*] Those are movies I saw with my mother during the war or shortly afterwards, so I must have been very little. After that, it was the neighborhood theater with the other kids, and we just ate up the movies. For some reason, those visual images made an enormous impression on me. Whether that's hereditary or not, I don't know. My mother loved the movies so much, and I knew of that special love. I grew up hearing stories out of the movies. She would tell me whole stories, everything that happened in those movies, every dramatic scene and how it was filmed. She had a great appreciation of them, and I grew up with my mother's enthusiasm and love, and with them also working very well for me—sinking right into the illusion, getting totally swept up in them, loving them, coming out not particularly liking ordinary life. My parents were very permissive about it, too. I do remember their not wanting us to see some movies, though. One was called *I Confess*, and they didn't want us to see it because it was about a Catholic priest.

RILEY: That's the Hitchcock film with Montgomery Clift.

RICE: Yes. I remember that I got to the theater to see it, and my father was very angry when he found out. I think I'd persuaded my mother to let me go, and he said, "I did not want you to see that movie." Another movie we never saw when I was a teenager was *Baby Doll*, because the Archbishop of New Orleans declared it a mortal sin to see it. It was a huge controversy. There were many movies I didn't see at that time because a Catholic girl would no more have gone to see them than she would have gone into a brothel and done a striptease. You just didn't do it. It wasn't until college that we burst out of that and could see really "racy" films. [*laughter*] As I went into my twenties, foreign films—Ingmar Bergman, Fellini, all of those filmmakers—became the toast of the town. The big talk of that period was the foreign directors and how great their movies were. So there was another impetus to take the movies seriously, but in a different way—to look to them for something besides just entertainment, to look for inspiration, to look for insight, and to look for something refreshing from Europe that could teach us something that was more honest and had more integrity than our own films. I went all through that phase. My cousin Allen Daviau, who's a cinematographer, and one of his friends took me to see the first Ingmar Bergman movie I ever saw, and they were certainly the first to take me to see an old Charlie Chaplin film and treat it as art. It seemed that every time I ran into my cousin we'd wind up going to see some foreign film I wouldn't have seen otherwise, and we'd walk out of a film like *Sundays and Cybèle* just dazed by the experience. So I came out of childhood absolutely adoring the movies, and then went into a stage where they could be seriously studied. I believe they're still the primary influence on me.

RILEY: Where does literature come in? Where does your great love for it and a sense of yourself as having a literary identity take shape?

RICE: There's something else I want to mention before we get to that. I know now that one of the most profound influences on me was radio. I had forgotten this until recently when we began to drive to our house in Florida, and we would load up on tapes of old radio shows. When I heard those old broadcasts, I realized the similarity to my writing. I realized I'd spent my early childhood listening to *Lux Radio Theater* and to *Suspense*, to *The Inner Sanctum*, all of those different shows. Writing is in some way, to me, being in one of those radio shows. It's the words making that story and that illusion. Now, there was never any doubt in my mind either as a child or an adult that books, that something like *David Copperfield* or *Oliver Twist* or *Jane Eyre*, were the highest form of all this I loved. So when you ask where did literature come from, I thought of all that as under the umbrella of literature. I didn't see it as divided up. It was storytelling, it was using images and stories about people to talk about life. Whether you're considering *Don Juan* or *Jane Eyre* or *Robin Hood* or *Great Expectations*, the whole impact is of a narrative about characters in motion, and what they're doing. Gradually I became a better reader and read more and more, and loved books as much as movies. But I can't say that as a child I read any novel that swept me off my feet. I didn't read *Great Expectations* and *Jane Eyre* until high school, and when I did I loved them both. They did spellbind me; I was just gripped. But I was not a kid who read Nancy Drew.

RILEY: It occurs to me that your mother's role in this was very influential. With her, you weren't only getting the story. You were actually standing in the room with the storyteller. The telling was itself an action you were made very aware of.

RICE: Oh yes, she would act out these things for us. She wanted us to get the innuendoes and the suggestions and the drama of scenes. Over and over again, she would tell me scenes and use these phrases that implied things or from which you could draw inferences. So there you have the spoken word, you have her weaving this tale. You have this Irish Catholic Southern woman with a great gift for language and a great gift for drama telling you something that's as gripping as *Lux Radio Theater* will be later when she turns on the radio, and a great deal of what she talks about includes the plots of novels and stories about authors. It's all deliciously connected.

LITERARY INFLUENCES: "PEOPLE WHO BREAK ALL THE RULES"

RILEY: In terms of your own imagination, who have been the most important writers to you?

RICE: My memory gets worse as I get older, and each time I'm asked, I give a different group of writers. [*laughter*] But above everyone else Charles Dickens, even from early childhood. I didn't read him all the way through then, but I paged through Dickens reading sections of the books. As a writer I've adopted him as my guardian angel and mentor, and I go to his biographies by Fred Kaplan and by Peter Ackroyd over and over again to see what he did at a certain time or how he coped with something. The Brontë sisters, particularly Charlotte; *Jane Eyre* had a profound influence.

I didn't read Emily Brontë's *Wuthering Heights* until I was about thirty-five. Of the other writers who powerfully influenced me, I guess the most significant was Nabokov—*Speak, Memory*, and *Lolita*—the beauty of the language, the thrilling, almost experimental quality of the prose. Carson McCullers was just an incredible influence, and I go back to her over and over again. I pick up *The Heart Is a Lonely Hunter* and *The Member of the Wedding* to see how she did things. I love her short story "A Tree, a Rock, a Cloud" and also *The Ballad of the Sad Café*. In *The Heart Is a Lonely Hunter* she hit a sort of innocent and loving tone that I constantly strive for in my own work. She loved her characters. She was wonderfully compassionate to them, and she had a really gentle vision. I love that in her. The Russians were a big influence when I finally discovered them in my early thirties. I read *The Brothers Karamazov* and *War and Peace* and *Anna Karenina*, and I was just absolutely swept away.

For me generally it's been a process of discovering people who break all the rules. Kerouac's *On the Road* was a rule-breaking, exuberantly wonderful book to read. I didn't know you could say a character looked like a Modigliani. Everybody was always saying you weren't supposed to do *this* as a writer and you were supposed to do *that*, and here was this guy Kerouac breaking all the rules, and it was great. Hawthorne, the short stories—"Young Goodman Brown," "The Minister's Black Veil," and a few others—were very influential, but not necessarily anything else. I never could get into the novels very deeply. And Mary Renault's *The Last of the Wine* and *The Persian Boy* absolutely. I remember walking around Berkeley in the rain not wanting to finish *The Last of the Wine* for the second time and thinking, someday I can make somebody feel what this book makes me feel. I can make somebody feel in my writing that they are as wrapped up in my characters as I am in hers.

Given some people's view of me, I know this is a risky statement, but Sidney Sheldon was an influence. He was one of the first big, booming bestseller writers I read, and I was impressed by the structure of *The Other Side of Midnight*. I felt there was something to be learned from the way Sheldon structured a book. If I could bring my characters, my concerns, and my language and mix them with the way he moved a plot, the way he cleared everything out of his way, there was really something to be achieved. I'll give you an example of a book I think really did that, *The Executioner's Song* by Mailer. There's a book that's clean and has this fabulous momentum. You know, there's a place where Ezra Pound and Mickey Spillane touch, where the bestsellers with their economical language and their effective storytelling can teach you some very specific things about craft.

RESEARCH: A HUNGER FOR BOOKS, A "MANIA FOR HOTELS"

RILEY: What do you read now? Do you read new fiction, or do you read specifically for purposes of research?

RICE: I'm still a terribly slow reader. I don't read ninety-nine percent of the fiction published. I can't keep up with it. I don't read anything that doesn't feed my own work.

When I flip over a novel like *The River Sutra* by Gita Mehta or Donna Tartt's *The Secret History*, it's because it's giving me something. It's making me want to go to the machine and write. I do pick up things and try them, but nine out of ten times I never finish. They just don't move me enough for me to make the colossal effort to put everything aside and read them.

RILEY: In that case, what moved you to read *The Secret History*, for example, in the first place?

RICE: I read an article on Donna Tartt in a magazine in the doctor's office, and it sounded interesting. Then I saw the book in a store and remembered it, so I bought it and was swept off my feet and fell in love with it. That's all there was to it. It was published by Knopf, but nobody there sent it or anything like that. In fact, my editor is not the one at Knopf who published it, so I didn't hear about it through any regular channel. Although I don't read much fiction now, I do read an enormous amount of nonfiction—history, archaeology, religious theory, and the philosophy of religion. Not so much works that are abstract, though; more those rooted in history and biography. I read very little abstract philosophy or abstract historical analysis. Barbara Tuchman was absolutely wonderful with the fourteenth century in *A Distant Mirror*. Robin Fox, who writes about pagans and Christians, is an author I love. Also Mircea Eliade, and that wonderful scholar who wrote the history of Christianity and homosexuality, John Boswell. Their books are well researched, and I devour that stuff. I read it very rapidly. I can take several biographies of Akhenaton the pharaoh and pretty much in a week's time go through them with my highlighter and absorb all I want to use of that character. I enjoy that tremendously.

RILEY: Have the psychological theories of Carl Jung been an influence on your thinking?

RICE: I hear of him all the time, of course, and I have the kind of thirdhand knowledge you get of Freud or Marx or Darwin in our culture because their ideas have been so influential, but I've never read Jung.

RILEY: Your notion of the continuous intelligence or continuous consciousness has a strong resemblance to some of Jung's ideas.

RICE: So I'm told. Katherine Ramsland has written essays on the books for Jungian journals, I know, but I don't know his work directly. I'm always meaning to read him. I just haven't gotten to it, but I will. I've never read enough of Freud either. I consider that a real gap in my education, not to have read enough of Freud or Jung or Darwin. That hits right at the weakness in my kind of research, that I tend to read the collator who will quote Jung rather than Jung himself.

RILEY: The kinds of research you do are really quite varied. There's what you've just been describing—biography and social and intellectual history—but there are other kinds as well. For example, you must have read widely on medicine and medical technology for *The Witching Hour*.

RICE: More than was ever required in a million years. I just did it and did it. I read every book like *MD*, or books about what it's like to be an intern, or "my first year in medicine," or memoirs of a neurosurgeon, or women in medicine. Every single thing is documented, although finally in the novel it gets just a few sentences. If Rowan goes into the room and there's a mention of a microscope and tools, they're exact. If I said she had them made in Switzerland by a watchmaker, that comes out of a book on medical instruments. Rowan's statements about prejudice against women doctors, all those came out of well-researched books written by both male and female doctors. Even the concept of neurosurgeons as chatterboxes who smoke heavily is thoroughly documented, and apparently very true.

RILEY: There's a kind of informal research, too, isn't there, where you consciously explore and study the world of daily experience, the popular, the familiar, the ordinary world around us. That's very much part of the texture of the novels.

RICE: I can get almost speechless and overwhelmed in a Long's drugstore in San Francisco or in one of those great all-night markets in Dallas. I have to restrain that part of my writing, actually. I've never been able to make successful the experience of Lestat walking through a market and looking at all the things you see—just think of all the colors of shampoo, for example. [*laughter*] Those sections get pushed down into one paragraph, and I go through them fairly fast. But I've actually done research like that, walking at two o'clock in the morning through a great big market looking at the enormous number of things that are there and seeing it all as an eighteenth-century man perhaps would see it. It's just overwhelming.

I especially remember the hotels I've loved and the way I tried to write about them. I don't know if you noticed, but there's one scene in *Belinda* where they go to three hotels in one day. It's positively outrageous. It's my mania for hotels. I think they go to the Clift, where Alex Clementine has some beautiful hustler lying on a couch, and then they go to the Hyatt, where Bonnie is. And Jeremy winds up at the St. Francis reading Bonnie's biography. I thought, Anne, you're really pushing it. But I have this big romance with hotels. I did roam around them as a child, and I'd go into their coffee shops. When I first lived in Dallas, I went to all the big hotels downtown, and I would go in and order a fifteen-cent half-a-grapefruit for breakfast and drink coffee. I hung around the Sheraton and the Hilton in downtown Dallas a great deal. I have an absolute obsession with hotels. Here in New Orleans it was the Monteleone, the St. Charles, and the Roosevelt, and I had to rediscover them in my writing. It took me a long time to get to it. Darting in and out of fancy hotels—their dazzling quality and what it meant to a character to see people moving in that milieu totally acquainted with it—somehow that's always been very important to me. It still is and it's all over my novels to this day. But nobody notices it. Nobody ever says, there are three hotels in one day in this book!

I also love the Ponchartrain Hotel here. A friend down here told me that the first time in his life he'd ever gone to eat in a restaurant was at the Ponchartrain. He went to the Caribbean Room. So in *The Witching Hour* I gave Michael an experience where he was taken to eat at the Caribbean Room in the Ponchartrain. As a child I used to pass it, and I absolutely love it. It's a symbol of elegance and luxury to me. People come to town and call the Ponchartrain and ask to stay there because of *The Witching Hour*. They say they want to stay in the suite that Michael and Rowan stayed in, and the Ponchartrain has let me know that they are very pleased with that. [*laughter*] And reporters have been known to come here to do an interview, and they'll call the Ponchartrain and the Ponchartrain says, "Well, you must stay in the Mary Martin Suite if you're going to interview Anne."

This gets thicker and thicker and thicker, you know. I had such a regard for the Ponchartrain that when Aaron Lightner was killed I moved him down the street half a block. I didn't want to kill him dead center in front of the Ponchartrain. It had been haunting me for two years that Aaron was hit by a car right in front of the Ponchartrain. I kept seeing it. No matter what I would write, I would see Aaron hit by this car. So finally, I had to yield to it and have Aaron hit by the car. But I moved it. I'm very aware of all this, and I don't know what it all means. I just wanted to mention that because it's the kind of thing that very seldom gets explored by anybody.

But I'll tell you, there was a long period when we were living in San Francisco when I was rather reclusive and withdrawn. In our own way we were depressed, clinically depressed. You remember that; it was a time when you were there. I went almost nowhere. It seemed that the effort of getting out and experiencing anything firsthand was almost impossible. Do you remember going to the Symphony with Stan? I didn't want to go; you went by yourselves. I did not want to be there. I had become enclosed, just holed up in there, and at that time I would have to force myself to go out and look at things in order to write about them. I was very bitter about it and angry at myself, at the circumstances in life that had put me in that position, and at my inability to overcome it. But that isn't the way my life is anymore. I have so many experiences now, and there's so much stimulus. In the course of a year I'll travel and see so many things that I don't have to go out consciously and look.

I went to England at the beginning of the year [1993], and I went and stood on Wearyall Hill in Glastonbury. I walked into the George and Pilgrims Hotel, and I didn't know I was going to use those things in *Taltos*. That's a wonderful feeling, to have your life a little bit ahead of your research, for once. I didn't know I was going to use that town; I didn't know what I was going to do. Our guide was this flaky hippie who kept talking about Joseph of Arimathea, who according to legend rested on that hill when he landed in England, and King Arthur, whose bones were supposedly found in Glastonbury Abbey. We were freezing to death, and he kept going on and on. Actually, he was a sweet guy. He owns a great bookstore in that town. In fact, he's one of my New Age contacts. If I want to get a certain New Age book, especially if it's an English book, I can call him in Glastonbury and he'll ship it. So that's the answer to your question: It's more that way now. It's almost like tumbling through a variety of experiences of all sorts, and when I start to write, they're all there. In the beginning of *Taltos*, for example, I was actually writing about our apartment in New York. That's the view from our apartment except that we have a building in the way, but I moved it. [*laughter*] There is a swimming pool on the top of the

Parker Meridien Hotel, and there really was a man swimming in it and the snow was falling on the dome. I don't have to go out looking for these things. I don't have to do research to find them. They're all there right now, and I love that.

RILEY: Are you more interested in the contemporary world now, rather than the eighteenth or nineteenth century?

RICE: Much more, very much more, and yet enthralled with certain ages. Like, I didn't get to Gregory the Great in *Taltos*, and I wanted to. But I'm saving him for another novel. I'm fascinated by the character of this early Pope and what Rome was like around 600 A.D. It was all ruined and pigs were walking around in the ruins of the Forum, and Gregory the Great became Pope and united all of the Roman Church and evangelized the English and really whipped the Celtic Church. Just stomped on it and practically did away with it. That's a fascinating period to me, and there are a couple of characters that I want to deal with directly—Cassiodorus, the great librarian and scholar, and Gregory the Great, and some others. It's fabulous to me that I can now write novels in which in the same book I can deal with things like a man swimming in the pool on the roof of the Parker Meridien and also Saint Columba.

DRINKING: "A DISASTROUS MISTAKE"

RILEY: Your comments about the range of experience in your life now and its positive influence on your work lead me to ask you about another, quite different and potentially destructive kind of experience in your past. You have spoken very frankly about drinking. Beginning with Michele's illness and continuing for several years after her death, you drank a great deal. You quit drinking when you were pregnant with Chris, and then both you and Stan quit completely not long after Chris was born. What was the impact of that experience, not just socially but specifically as a writer?

RICE: As a writer, I've so used that experience. I've mined it for gold, so I can't imagine life without it. I don't know what it would have been like. Any experience for a writer, anything that involves pain, suffering, joy, anything, you can use. Being that much of a drunk over that long a period of time was an intense, even a rich experience for me. It was a rich social experience in that I participated in a lot of late-night dinners where people bared their souls and liquor often functioned to remove inhibitions and good judgment, at least verbally. In its own way all of that was very rich, very interesting. I still remember big dinners in bars and big talk-fests with friends who weren't as drunk as I was, by the way, but who were part of my life as a drunk whether they drank or not. And it's hard to regret it. It really is. But I passed out at a lot of parties, and of course I have to say thank God we weren't killed on the freeway or wonder how could I have encouraged Stan to go out that many times to buy more beer when he was drunk already. How could I have been so crazy as to send somebody out to drive in that state when he could have been killed or have killed someone else. But I also got a lot out of it in its own way. It moved me into groups where I might not have gone and to meet people and listen and talk to them. I think that very early on, though, it began to be a disastrous mistake. I had many blackouts right from the beginning, from the very first time I ever got drunk. I blacked out and didn't remember what happened.

RILEY: What about drugs, which became a widespread experience at that time in San Francisco and Berkeley, and, for that matter, increasingly throughout American society?

RICE: I was very cut out of the dope world. I didn't take LSD. I smoked very little pot, and I was never part of the psychedelic flower children thing. The closest I came to it was through drinking, so I largely missed that experience of people getting together and all taking LSD.

RILEY: Why did you miss it? Did you want to try it?

RICE: I was afraid to take dope. I was absolutely convinced that LSD would unhinge me mentally, and I'm very possessive of my brain. I want to be smart. I like being smart. I like thinking. I don't really want to see things and not know if they're real. As one of my friends said, "If you don't know whether the stove is turned off or if the door is locked, don't take LSD." She said, "I know those things but you don't, so don't ever take those drugs." I was very afraid of them. There were some occasions when I was with friends when they took LSD. Not in big groups, but one to one. It seemed to have an incredible effect on them, and not always a good one. With pot, I just didn't like it enough to smoke it. My fears would overcome me. I'd get too upset. I'd have almost a psychedelic experience on pot, so I used it very seldom. It just wasn't any fun. It was pretty scary, so I shied away from all that. Alcohol turned out to be my drug of choice, mainly for the social lubrication—the intense experience of feeling really good, of being able to enjoy the sunset, of being able to sing with everybody, of being able to really get down and discuss things in a heated way. But as I said, it was a mistake, really, right from the beginning.

CRITICAL REPUTATION: "MY READERS TOOK ME OUT OF THAT WORLD"

RILEY: Let me ask you about a very different matter. You have overcome many personal obstacles in your life and taken on the biases of commercial publishing to build a career that's true to your own vision. But there are those who would look askance at your popular success and sometimes without even reading the novels dismiss the possibility of serious literary achievement, as if popularity and seriousness were mutually exclusive. You've spoken of the frustration that comes from reviews that simply dismiss a book about vampires on the assumption that the subject would be of no interest to an intelligent writer or reader. And yet your novels not only reflect a wide range of research in various intellectual disciplines, but they are now being taught in schools. Students frequently tell me that they first read one of your books—usually *Interview*—in a class. How would you assess your literary reputation? Do you know if there's much academic criticism, for instance—studies in literary journals, that sort of thing—beginning to emerge around *Interview*, *The Vampire Chronicles* overall, and the *Mayfair* novels?

RICE: Actually, I haven't gone to look. I knew how to do that in the old days. I knew just where to go in the library, what to look for, and could have done it on any other author. I remember doing it on Mary Renault, reading everything that was published on her. I just haven't done it, though. In the last three years I haven't stopped for breath long enough to even check that out. I know there's a recent book on my work by an academic critic [Bette B. Roberts] that was published by Twayne. Other than that I did get a general impression a few years ago when there was a story done for *The New York Times Magazine*. I don't know if you saw that story. I thought it had a rather nasty tone, but I know why it did. The woman who wrote it came here, and it was a very big story for her and a very big story for me, too, because it was the cover story of the Sunday *Times Magazine*. It was a huge break. Basically the whole view of her story was that I was very popular but I didn't have real literary acceptance yet. I think she looked up all that stuff at the time, but I'm not sure. Katherine Ramsland would have done it for her biography, too. Essentially what the writer of the *Times* story said was that anybody who talks to me can see that's a sore point. Since that time I've been more detached from it, whereas in the old days I was so angry about it that I would bring it up. If somebody said, are you a popular writer? I would say, no, my books are taught in classes.

RILEY: I remember you once talking about seeing yourself compared to the historical novelist Frank Yerby and chafing at the implications of that comparison.

RICE: I was very upset. I was compared to him in a quote on *Feast of All Saints*, and I had higher aspirations. I wanted to be perceived as a more serious writer than Frank Yerby, but one of my friends said, "Don't feel that way. He was a very solidly respected book club writer."

RILEY: How do you account for the change in your attitude?

RICE: Well, I am not an elitist. I think that runs through everything I'm saying. I hate elitism in some very deep way, and I don't know why because I think the vast majority of people from my background are elitist. They have found what they sought among an elite of some kind, either an intellectual elite or an academic elite or perhaps just an elite in the community. What enchants me, on the other hand, is the thing that can be given to thousands. I was able to express that with Ash's character in *Taltos*. It wasn't really the subject of the novel, but I was able to create a character who was a powerful man who had a vision within the novel that I thought was very realistic for a powerful man: that the Industrial Revolution had made it possible to bring beauty to millions and that was a true revolution under the sun. I really believe that, and I'm very fired by that. I'm glad the readers of my novels include people who aren't necessarily highly sophisticated. That thrills me. So I've changed. I'll never again bristle because I'm called a popular writer. I'm even called a pulp writer routinely by people who really are mistaken. They just don't realize what they're saying. Like someone will call me for an interview, and he'll tell me how much he loves the books, and then he'll publish the interview in a magazine and say, "Rice takes ghosts and witches and turns them into her own brand of pulp fiction." They will send me that and think they've paid me a compliment. I would have cried five years ago, but now it doesn't matter. I've gotten the readers I want, and they will decide whether I'm mediocre, good, excellent, outstanding, great, or whatever. I got there, and I got there in the American marketing machinery.

RILEY: What brought about the change? What freed you from being hurt or disappointed by that kind of judgment?

RICE: My readers. The numbers alone freed me, and also actually seeing my readers and meeting them. You see, I'm an author who does go out on tour regularly. I see my readers, and this has been going on for years. I went with *Queen of the Damned*. I went with *The Tale of the Body Thief* and *The Witching Hour*. Before that I'd gone with the publication of the paperback editions, largely because it wasn't economically feasible for a hardcover house to send an author on tour. It's too expensive. But when you have a book like *Queen of the Damned* that sells 300,000 copies in hardcover, it's feasible. So I'm very acquainted with my readers, and I have the visceral experience of seeing hundreds of them show up at the bookstore, pushing and shoving and saying, "We love your books." I am so blessed by that, so fortunate, and that gave me the armor against any perception drawn from reviews and periodicals and even chitchat at parties about what my image was. My readers took me out of that world. I live in a world now where I never have social contact with anyone who would be called part of the intellectual community. I don't even know who they are. Now, most of the interviewers who come to this house are clearly intellectuals, and they place a high value on my books, and sometimes they're a little puzzled by my view. They'll say,

"Surely you see yourself as an intellectual writer, don't you? You see your books as literature." I remember Digby Diehl said that to me at one point in the *Playboy* interview: "Surely you see them as worthwhile." I said, "Yes I do, but it's just that for so long I tried to prove that and I screamed that until I was hoarse. Now I no longer do it, so if you want to bring it up, we can talk about it, but I don't have to."

RILEY: It's not a hunger for you anymore.

RICE: No, not at all. That's why I wanted to give you that *New York Times Magazine* story, because the way that writer described it is not the way it is. What you're getting in that story is that writer's own insecurity. I'm not sitting here waiting for recognition. And Stan was so deeply betrayed by that story. I'm used to people telling absolute lies about me, but he isn't. She described him as doing a "nightmarish doodle." She had actually asked for that drawing, and it wasn't a nightmarish doodle at all. It had nothing to do with that. The way she had set up that scene and the way she portrayed us was such a lie. I don't think he ever quite got over it. I remember my father reading that story. Of course, everyone in New York was going, "You're on the cover of *The New York Times Magazine*!" but my father read it and he said, "I wouldn't trust this woman if I were you, and I wouldn't let her in my house again." Right you are. But it proved to be one of those ironic situations. To be the cover story of the Sunday *Times Magazine* was such good publicity, and it was such an enormous literary popular victory that it really didn't make any difference what she said. I'd guess that nine out of ten people who read it didn't pick up on the snideness. They didn't pick up on the negative tone and twists.

RILEY: What do you think explains her tone? Was she insecure about the fact that she actually liked the books?

RICE: I think she was desperate that she not seem to be writing a puff piece, that she appear critical rather than appear to like the books.

RELATIONS WITH OTHER WRITERS

RILEY: Living in New Orleans, you have the luxury of being removed from the pettiness that can sometimes characterize the New York scene, or the competition that writers can feel with each other. Over the course of your career have you had much contact with other writers?

RICE: Not at all. The richest period of my life with other writers was my unpublished years in Berkeley when we would get together and talk about our manuscripts. It's interesting that most of the people I knew then got published. I had writer friends like Carole Malkin, Carolyn Doty, and Cleo Jones, just friends I knew in Berkeley who belonged to different writing groups. I didn't really belong to any of those groups, but I knew them. We were all working to get published, and we all took ourselves very seriously, some more than others. After that there was never any community of which I was a part. Publication virtually destroyed that. You know, writers are really very competitive, and they're very paranoid. They work alone, and I don't think they make easy alliances in groups. I've heard of one well-known writer in San Francisco who actually goes to the public library every week and meets with a writers' group and reads her manuscripts to them and gets feedback. But it's rare to have even that degree of community.

RILEY: When you were still living in San Francisco, did you find that once you became a commercially successful published writer it changed your relationships with people because they now viewed you differently or perhaps even saw you as having sold out?

RICE: Oh absolutely, with no question. I think the competitiveness and the resentment were enormous, and I was very hurt by it in the beginning. I wanted to be taken seriously. I was outraged anyone would think I was merely a commercial success. I wanted this dark, strange novel written in this cluttered, book-filled apartment, with beer cans and pot smoke, to be taken utterly seriously. The idea that someone would personally despise me because the advance on *Interview with the Vampire* was $12,000 was a shock. I don't feel that way now. I'm a little kinder. I understand how hurt people can be if they work for years and can't get published and then they hear that some lunatic, who they've always felt was an obnoxious drunk at best, has just sold a book for $12,000. I'm kind about it, but I don't want to hear it. I don't want to be around them. But a lot of people moaned and groaned, and acted very nasty about it, and were very unpleasant. For instance, I had some friends in Berkeley that I saw for years. Right up until about a year before we left San Francisco, I still saw them for dinner, and we occasionally went out together. I can remember telling them about the pornographic novels and selling the first one, *The Claiming of Sleeping Beauty*, for $10,000, and I remember looking into the face of one of my friends and seeing absolute glaze-eyed hatred. I mean, the dinner was over! So I learned not to tell them those things, not to call them with enthusiasm and say, "Oh, guess what, this book has been accepted as a featured alternate by the book club." It finally reaches the point where people you know very well want to say, "Who wants to hear it? Okay, your third novel's a book club featured alternate. I can't even get these people to return my manuscript." So I drew away from people. Even with those friends who did get published, it was a similar problem because there would be a small printing and few sales, and small, elegant signings—a completely different kind of publication. If anything, proximity to me tended to spoil it for them. I'm not talking about dozens of cases, of course. I'm just talking about four or five friends, but basically I grew away from everyone, and I don't much associate with other writers.

If I meet a writer I deeply admire, it's very nice, but I don't think I could handle it if I were to see Donna Tartt and Scott Turow and Amy Tan every week. I'd be too scared and threatened by things they were saying. I need to work alone. I need not to hear what they're doing. I need to develop my ideas without fearing that I'm taking someone else's idea or maybe they're going to take mine. I can get very mixed up on that level because I'm so afraid of committing a mortal sin or afraid that what I have is not deserved, so I don't make a very easy companion. I like to see people like that for ten minutes in a lobby and to shake their hand. You know, I met Scott Turow recently at the

American Booksellers Association convention, and it was a nice moment. He introduced himself, and he was very nice. I really admire him. I thought his first novel showed tremendous talent. There was a piece in *Newsweek* on him recently, and I think it was very well deserved.

RILEY: George Will, of all people, did a column on Turow.

RICE: That's right. It was at the end of *Newsweek*, and it was about this fascination with crime and how Turow's books are really better than all that. That was kind of the theme of my review of his first book in *The New York Times*: This is really a good book; whatever you think about this genre, this is good writing. Even though I don't believe the ending, the book is powerful. But anyway, no, I don't see other writers and I don't know them. I don't seek them out and I don't write them letters. As far as I know, I don't think they seek out each other either, and I can tell you that the book industry keeps us apart. It's very conscious of the insecurities of its authors, and it doesn't want its middle authors to be hurt by parties thrown for its big authors. It takes a lot of effort to see that doesn't happen. About three years ago, they gave a party for Stephen King at the American Booksellers Association, and they wouldn't let me come. I teased the hell out of Dutton NAL because they publish my pornography and it sells a lot and they wouldn't let me come to their party for Stephen King. [*laughter*] But they just had a rule: No other authors at the party. And I know why they had it. They wanted whoever was there to be focused on Stephen King, and maybe they didn't know how he would react, so they didn't let any other author come to the party. They go to great lengths to keep you apart and see that you don't tread on each other and don't hurt each other, and they never try to bring you all together to talk because they know better.

I went to one dinner in San Francisco in the eighties that was given by Knopf, by Sonny Mehta and Jane Friedman, sort of the heads of Knopf by then, for all their West Coast writers, and it was the grimmest, saddest affair. I heard later that some people cried, that they went home upset because they weren't positioned close enough to Sonny at the table. I mean, writers really took their treatment at the dinner as a measure of their current stock and success, and of course nothing could have been farther from the truth. Sonny is a very quiet man who simply sat there with all these people who were at the table, and I don't think he gave any more thought to who was to his right or his left than to who was at the end of the table. I think writers are famous for that. They take it all personally, and they go home and they cry, "I'm not important to Knopf. They put me at the end of the table." I've learned enough not to do it, just to relax, and yet I can still fall into it. If they had given that dinner and failed to call me, I could have been crushed for months, and yet it could have been nothing more than that they failed to call because they had the wrong number. They're that disorganized. That's how little these things mean. The biggest example was a huge party in the sixties given for Günter Grass on this huge houseboat, and they neglected to invite Kay Boyle, who had just interviewed him. Maybe for *The Paris Review*, I can't remember. But nobody thought of her. The people giving the party just didn't know Kay Boyle. When I heard people gossiping about her being left out, I remember thinking at the time, nobody meant that to happen. Why in hell didn't you just tell them to call Kay Boyle yourself? But no, writers don't talk to each other. I don't want to know them, and they don't want to know me. Writers need to work alone.

PART THREE

7

"Nobody's going to make this movie"

RILEY: The journey from novel to film was long and torturous for *Interview with the Vampire*, but at last the film has been made. What's more, it's been a great success not only in this country but overseas as well. That's been very gratifying to you, I know, especially since it sometimes seemed the film might never get made, or if it did, that it might end up betraying your own faith in the novel. It's unusual for film rights to have passed through so many hands over such a long time and to have survived so many aborted efforts, so before discussing the film itself, I'd like to trace its background. You originally sold the screen rights to Paramount in late 1975?

RICE: I think it was early 1976, and the book was scheduled to come out in May. The agent called from New York and said, "Paramount wants it" and told me all the points of the deal. Of course, it sounded fabulous to me. It was basically $100,000 and then a matching $50,000 if it showed up on the bestseller list in either form—and it did, so it was eventually $150,000, which seemed a fortune. The rest of the contract was something of a mystery. I basically left it up to them, but I remember asking the agent, "Will it revert back to me? Will there be a clause that says it reverts back if they don't make it?" He said, "No, they wouldn't do that." So to this day I don't know why there did end up being such a clause, but certainly the whole history of my career was influenced by there in fact being a clause that said, "If purchaser fails to commence principal photography within ten years from the date of this agreement, all rights revert to the author."

RILEY: The reversion of those rights was to become a crucial issue later.

RICE: Yes, ten years later it actually happened. While some TV people were trying desperately to make it, it reverted, and the producer called and said, "You won. Congratulations. It's yours." Now, I had to pay back the $150,000, but the next purchaser of *Interview*, which was Lorimar Pictures, actually paid that.

RILEY: As I remember, Richard Sylbert, who was then head of production at Paramount, was originally the prime mover.

RICE: Yes, and I think Bob Evans, they were the heads. The contract took several months to prepare, and wasn't signed until the end of summer. By then the book had not become a hardcover bestseller, and also things had happened at Paramount. Bob Evans was gone and so was Richard Sylbert, so it was like one minute we were in and we were hot, and the next minute we were a back-burner property of the old regime. I didn't quite grasp all that at the time. It took me years to see that's what happened. Richard Sylbert stayed on as a producer at Paramount for about a year and a half, and he developed one script with me. We had a very good time working on it, but basically when he tried to get the movie into production again, he was told that it was going to become part of a package for John Travolta. Because Sylbert had no turnaround rights, no rights to control it, that was the end of his involvement. It then languished for years in limbo at Paramount with some question of its being available to Travolta if he wanted it. Apparently, Travolta personally didn't want to make it. It was his manager's idea that he ought to. Actually all I know is hearsay, but scripts were done in which the role of the boy interviewer, whom Travolta would have played, was greatly expanded. After that, it passed through many hands, and I don't know the whole history. Every now and then I'd call down from San Francisco and ask, "What's happening with it?" I remember at one point they told me somebody named Ara Gallant—I'm not sure I have that name right—was writing the script. I heard later that this was a New York hairdresser. You see, I was never able to get reliable information. People would get interested and they'd call, and we'd refer them to Paramount, where they were just told it wasn't going to get made. I remember at one point there was a woman involved with it—I think her name was Dawn Steel—and I heard that she said this is totally politically impossible to make right now. It's got incest in it; it's got child molestation. Nobody's going to make this movie.

In the meantime I went on writing books, and by the time *The Vampire Lestat* came out, I had the right to sell that to anybody. There was a clause in the contract that my lawyer, Christine Cuddy, had advised me to get. She said, "Get your sequel rights." In other words, get your right to sell your sequel to somebody other than the owner of the original movie if they don't want it. They do get first crack at it, though. I'd gotten that because of Christine's mentioning it. It's called a holdback, five to eight years, something like that. Anyway, eight years had passed, and they had not shot a movie, so if they did not want *Lestat*, I had the right to sell that book elsewhere. By that point, I'd made communication with Julia Phillips. The moment *Vampire Lestat* went into manuscript and was going to be published as my fourth novel, Julia was interested. She had apparently always been interested. She writes about it in her book *You'll Never Eat Lunch in This Town Again*, how she had been interested in *Interview* all that time and been trying to get it from Paramount, but she couldn't. So she went after *The Vampire Lestat*, and she and I set it up at CBS Theatricals. This is after Paramount passed on it. The clock was still ticking on *Interview* at Paramount, yet we were able to sell *Vampire Lestat* to CBS Theatricals. Then CBS Theatricals went out of business. As I recall, Julia then tried to set it up at Taft Barish. While that was happening, *Interview* reverted back and we celebrated. Julia called and said, "Free again, free again, God Almighty, free again." And she sent flowers. So we had both properties. At that point, we set them up with Lorimar. ICM was the agent all the way through, so when I say we set it up, what I mean is that Julia did the pitching. She would do the incredible, enthusiastic talking about what kind of movie this could be. I joined her in the Lorimar part of that. She had done it alone with CBS Theatricals and with Taft Barish, but when it came time to set it up with Lorimar, I did go down there and we went together to Peter Chernin, who was the president, and Eileen Mazell. We told them how we envisioned the whole project, and we signed a contract for three books—*Interview with the Vampire*, *The Vampire Lestat*, and *The Queen of the Damned*, which was not even written yet. They would get all of them as a single property, and Julia would produce with her partner, Mike Levy. What eventually happened was that I wrote a script for Julia, but by the time my script was written, Lorimar had collapsed. Although Eileen Mazell and Peter Chernin liked the script and were ready to hire me to refine it, they suddenly didn't exist anymore as a studio. Flowers came with the note saying, "We're sorry." At that point, Warner Bros. took over the property from Lorimar, and apparently David Geffen got involved with it. I still to this day don't understand who exactly owns what, but it became a Warner Bros./Geffen Pictures property at that point. They decided they didn't like my script, and they abandoned it almost immediately.

RILEY: This script, then, was an amalgam of the first three novels of *The Vampire Chronicles*?

RICE: It was a long script "bible" based on all three, and in it Louis was a woman. Absolutely the only way I could get Lorimar to keep the story of Claudia and Louis was if I made Louis a woman. I actually had a lot of fun with that script, making Louis this extremely strong transvestite woman who just refuses to accept the limitations a woman would face. You know, legally at that point in Louisiana a woman couldn't own property, so I had this woman land in Louisiana after a voyage, with her dead husband and child, and simply take her husband's clothes and say, "This is my plantation." She just legally functioned as a man, and that's how it opens. Louis is this very independent person, and the men in the colony want very much to get her and get the property, but there's no way anybody can because they can't prove she's a woman. They can't get her to admit it, or they can't discover it. She's a very good shot and very good with a sword, so that's the person with whom Lestat falls in love, and I had envisioned this played by Cher. Other than that, it was utterly the same. Every philosophical question, every major scene was the same. It was just going to be Cher dressed as a man playing those scenes. It was very exciting, but of course it wasn't really *Interview with the Vampire*. It was something different.

RILEY: I suspect you couldn't have done that later because the devotion to the novel had become so intense.

RICE: I even got a lot of negative feedback at the time. I heard within just a few months of letting people know about it that my readers didn't want that. So I was very conflicted about it and willing to drop it. It truly had been a last-ditch stand to get the story of Louis and Claudia into the movie. At that point, Julia Phillips, Lorimar, and whoever was interested in the movie wanted to make *The Vampire Lestat*. They were no longer interested in *Interview*, so that was my attempt to get that story in. And it's true that I also got very excited about the idea. As you know, I've always had a passionate interest in transvestites and gender-bending and transcending—and I was enamored of the idea of this eighteenth-century woman who refused to capitulate to the legal status of a woman and insisted she was a man. There are stories of such people in Casanova's memoirs. It's a common theme in the eighteenth century. At one point Moll Flanders in Defoe's novel goes around as a man. To dress as a man meant to be a totally different legal entity, and I got enchanted with that idea. I also felt that Louis was me, and because of that the whole thing made better sense when it was a woman. I didn't see it as in any way betraying the material, but my readers let me know right away they didn't like it. So I was happy to drop it, and very glad to hear that the film people didn't pursue it.

In any event, when David Geffen took over the property, at first he said he liked this script and wanted to work with me, but within a few days of the deal being consummated, he said that he didn't. I told Julia, "Let it go. Get somebody else. Don't let me be the cause of contention here." She apparently at that point recommended the writer Michael Cristofer. David hired him to do a script just of *Interview*, and it took years and years for the Cristofer script.

In the meantime I wrote more books. *The Queen of the Damned* became the number one bestseller. I went on to *The Witching Hour*, and when it came out, it was a huge bestseller, too. All that happened, and all the time—I think three years—Michael Cristofer was writing away on the script. They picked up the option when it came time. They could have just renewed their option for $100,000, but instead they bought the property. We got a call one day saying, "Warners and Geffen are picking up their option for $500,000, and you'll be getting the check." This was an option for the three books, *Interview*, *Vampire Lestat*, and *Queen of the Damned*, that Lorimar had owned as a single property. There was a $200,000 option for a year and a half that got extended because of the writers' strike. According to the contract, at the end of that period Geffen could have picked up another year for $100,000, but either he didn't know it or nobody told him. In any case he bought the entire property outright for $500,000, and what he bought with that was five years of time. If he had taken the additional year option, he would have had six years to make the movie, but he didn't. So suddenly I had $500,000 in my hand and *Interview* belonged to David Geffen. Meanwhile, all I heard was that Michael Cristofer was writing the script. That was the only word. It wasn't until after *Witching Hour* was published and after I had really stopped being friends with Julia Phillips that I actually met David Geffen and he asked me to read the Cristofer script and give him an opinion. I read it and my opinion was, don't make it. I asked him not to. I said, "It's really a story of its own. It has nothing to do with the book. It's an original work by Michael Cristofer, and there's no point in doing this. You might as well throw the book away if you're going to do this." The characters did entirely different things; different things happened to them. It bore very little resemblance to anything in the novel other than the names. David then abandoned the Cristofer script and asked me if I would write the script. I didn't want to do it, and we argued and argued. Finally Lynn Nesbit, my agent, said, "I think you should do it, because if you don't, they're going to keep bringing scripts to you until the end of time." So I said okay, and then I got excited about writing it. You remember, I sent you that script. And David, when he got it, was eager to move ahead. He was very enthusiastic. But then as we presented it to director after director, they turned it down, or they wanted to change it dramatically, or they were afraid of *Dracula*. We heard that a lot—Francis Ford Coppola was making *Dracula*. We got turndowns from every major director, saying "not for me" or "not with *Dracula* in the works." The list is like David Cronenberg, Oliver Stone—everybody passed on it. I was not at any of those meetings with directors, and I never heard what was said. I just know that the meetings didn't lead to any director wanting to do it. David, I think, was pretty loyal to the script. He didn't want to sign somebody who was going to radically change it into a different movie.

Then he hit upon the idea of Neil Jordan. He called and said, "What do you think of Neil Jordan?" I didn't recognize the name. I didn't realize he was the director of a movie I loved called *The Company of Wolves*, which I'd actually mentioned in *Tale of the Body Thief*. David said, "You've got to see his new film, *The Crying Game*," so I did. I liked *The Crying Game*, and David proposed the whole thing to Neil Jordan, and Neil wanted to do it. At that point, though, the contract was running out, and I insisted that it be officially and legally renewed. There was no way they could have actually started a Neil Jordan movie in the time left before the rights came back to me again, so rather than extend or let the contract simply lapse and let everything go into legal limbo, I wanted an extension. And I got it. He paid me and extended it for a year, and during that year, Neil Jordan made *Interview with the Vampire*. So that's it, the real fast version. [*laughter*]

SCRIPTS OLD AND NEW

RILEY: When Richard Sylbert first had it, didn't he commission Frank De Felitta, who wrote the novel *Audrey Rose*, to do a screenplay? I seem to remember reading a screenplay by him years ago and thinking it was not very good.

RICE: All I remember is that it was faithful. I don't remember much else about it now except that it did go event by event through the book. I don't even remember exactly how it ended.

RILEY: That's when you did the script for Sylbert that you mentioned?

RICE: Legally I was hired only to do a polish of De Felitta's script, but I actually did my own. Richard Sylbert flew up to San Francisco a couple of times to see me, and it was a lot of fun. I learned a lot about scriptwriting from him, and I did that script, which languished at Paramount for ten years. I don't even have a copy of it now.

RILEY: Years later when you wrote the script for Geffen, did you refer back to that original script you had written?

RICE: I couldn't. It's what's called a "sterile script." It belongs to Paramount. I went back to my book, and if I remembered anything specifically original to my earlier script, I couldn't use it. But years had passed, and I had a totally different take, so I had no problem whatsoever writing. By this time not only had there been *Queen of the Damned*, but *Tale of the Body Thief* had also been done, so Lestat was very developed for me. The whole material had taken a different path. I wasn't the same person I was in 1977 when I wrote that first script. I knew the rules. I couldn't use that, and I didn't have any desire to do so anyway. It still belongs to

Paramount, and I guess all the others do, too. For a while there, I thought David had bought all the scripts, but apparently he hadn't. I did what you called my "reinvention" of the book and went from there.

RILEY: When you finally sat down to do the script for David Geffen, how did you approach adapting it? What were the most important considerations to you? What seemed critical?

RICE: I'd already finished *The Tale of the Body Thief*, as I said. I don't think it had been published yet, but I'd finished it. I didn't like the Cristofer script; I didn't care for the changes. So when David asked me to do it, the most significant difference was that I said, "Okay, I'll do it, but only one way. I will do exactly what I want with it. Everything else I've done, the one I did in 1977 for Paramount, the one I did with Julia, there were concessions to what the production people said had to happen. If I'm going to write this for you, I'm going to write only what I want to see on the screen." And he said, "Okay, do it." I think he's almost the only man in Hollywood who really can say something like that with any credibility. He also said, "Now, you are going to be working for me, aren't you?" I said, "Yes, but I'm not going to do anything I don't want to do." So I went to the beach, to our place in Destin, and to tell you the truth, at first I didn't have a clue as to how to make it into a movie. [*laughter*] I sat there and thought, God, I don't know how to adapt this. Then I just sat down and started writing, and I wrote the script in a weekend. But this is my method of working, long fifteen-hour days. The way I write a script is that I type very fast and I'm actually seeing it like a movie. Everything is moving in it. I literally just went through it, and at the end felt an absolutely wonderful elation that I'd really done it, that I had made a movie of it—a movie that I understood.

The main focus for me, the main thing I wanted to do was bring in the warmth and the depth of Lestat which had developed in the later novels so that he would be a more rounded character. In the other scripts, he had been more or less a flat villain, and I was concerned that that not be the case. I had also told David in earlier discussions that if we were going to focus on *Interview*, the only appropriate climax for the film was Claudia's death. That would be the way I would do it. I'd focus on the love of Claudia, and when she dies that would be the end of the film. There's really no story after that. That was the only incident in the material that made for a dramatic ending. So that was important to me, that architecture, and that remained in the finished movie. I eliminated various things—Lestat's father, for example, and Louis's family. As you know, in the final film those changes were maintained. Jordan also left those things out and focused on the rise of Claudia, the creation of Claudia and her death, and the failure of Louis's quest, dramatized in the murder of Claudia. That's basically what happens, and so, to me, it worked very well. I had to make it work dramatically, just beat by beat. I have to do the same thing now with *The Witching Hour*. When I sit there and do it, I'll actually see it. All kinds of possibilities will come up.

It's wonderful fun to do these scripts, and I have no hesitation about redramatizing something, like removing Louis's brother. I said Louis was a widower. That was an idea I had used in the "bible" script, and I took that idea of a widow arriving with a dead child, and I made Louis a widower. I meant to thereby establish that he was bisexual, that there wasn't any question of his not being capable of being heterosexual, that this movie was not about gender. The other stuff I didn't want in because I wasn't interested in it anymore. I wanted to get right to the story. I couldn't have everything, so I just went for it. Those were my main concerns, that we focus on the love among those three characters, and how they were outsiders, and how they sought to make some kind of tolerable life for themselves within this terrible state.

I did put in my script, as you know, a number of flashbacks in which Lestat told Louis about his life. In fact, the very coherence of my script depended on the fact that in the middle Lestat explained to Louis why he couldn't answer his questions—that he didn't know the answers, that all he had found in Paris was Armand. I implied that Lestat couldn't tell him about what the readers would already know about Marius because Marius had forbidden him ever to tell anybody. So I did a whole section where Lestat said, "Look, by not answering you, I was trying to protect you. There's nothing there!" That was all removed from the final shooting script. Jordan conformed more to the book in that there's no explanation of why Lestat won't answer their questions and there's no explanation of why he wants to keep them in New Orleans. I think, frankly, that my script worked better [*laughter*], but that's what happened. Jordan basically omitted things from my script. He didn't actually alter it.

RILEY: The flashbacks you're referring to essentially dramatized part of Lestat's earlier story that comes at the beginning of *The Vampire Lestat*.

RICE: Yes, there was a point right before Claudia is made a vampire where Lestat tells Louis that story. It's when he goes and finds Louis that night and the rain is falling, and Lestat says, "All right, I'll tell you how I was made a vampire. And I don't know anything!" He proceeds to tell Louis exactly what happened with Armand and how there were no answers. What he'd found was just a superstitious band under Les Innocents, and they didn't know anything. Then Lestat says, "I'm trying to protect you. I don't have any big secret." At that point Louis goes out and blunders into Claudia, and it proceeds from there. So I felt I had been able to bring in book two and book three in a way that made the first book more coherent. But they eliminated all that.

RILEY: The risk in that, I suppose, would be seen as suspending the story of the three by going outside of it.

RICE: It was also too long. I think my script was too long for a movie. But obviously in that part of the movie Jordan chose to use the time on humorous scenes, like the killing of the piano teacher, the killing of the dressmaker, things that I would have never done, comic relief scenes. I would have used that time to more fully develop Lestat as having a past. Now, some of that development was left in the script. Some key remarks were left in. There were things like Lestat saying, "In Paris a vampire has to be clever for many reasons." That was not in the book. Lestat never indicated where he was from. He never said a word, so that line about Paris was left in. Also, the very important concept that Lestat himself had been given no choice in being made a vampire, and that he was practically orphaned by the vampire who made him. That was tremendously important, and that was left in the movie. I love the scene where Tom Cruise is striding back and forth across the room, talking about how the person who made him didn't teach him anything. All that remained in the movie and, I thought, gave depth to Lestat, even though the detailed flashbacks about what had happened were taken out. That was one of the reasons I was just overwhelmed, because I thought it was terribly important that Lestat say, "I wasn't given the choice, and I want you to have the choice." That was the key change that I'd made in my script, and that was retained. Not only was it retained, it was repeated at the end of the film in a scene that Jordan created. So I was delighted. I thought Jordan had done a wonderfully generous thing, just building on the scaffolding I'd created. I had no idea that he thought he had completely rewritten it and that he was going to be furious when he didn't get writing credit.

RILEY: One of the things that play a big role in the novel is at the very beginning before Louis has met Lestat, and that's Louis's intense guilt over his brother's death. Why did you decide to omit the brother and make Louis a man grieving for the death of a wife and child?

RICE: I felt the wife and dead child would prefigure Claudia better, that it was a tightening up of things, and that the grief and the loss would be the same. I didn't see it as terribly significant. Whatever I was playing with in the book about the brother was no longer of interest to me. It was only important that Louis be in that state of grief, that he feel completely alone, and that he be living in a self-destructive way. But I've since realized that some people see this as much more significant than I did. I've had a number of phone calls from people who've said that the guilt was terrifically important and that the theme of the lost brother was key to the whole book. I didn't see it that way. I just saw it as somebody in a self-destructive state of grief who was victimized by a vampire. The scenes I wrote were in the film practically verbatim, I believe, the scene in the tavern and all of that. I had developed this whole idea. The scene where Lestat sees Louis in the tavern was strictly something I'd developed in the script. It wasn't in the book. There is no tavern scene in the book any more than there's a ballroom scene. These were all things that were in my script. To me, that was what was important. All that discussion in the book about whether the brother had been a saint and whether one accepts the belief in saints or vampires was no longer of interest. I thought *The Vampire Chronicles* had traveled a long way from all that. That was something that interested me in the days when I had no idea what was going to be on page 45, so I simply eliminated it. I told that to Jordan. I said I had dropped the brother because I wasn't that interested, and he said, "Neither am I." I dropped Babette Freniere for the same reason. I wrote those sections of the book when I didn't know what was going to happen next. I felt the book hit its stride when Claudia was born. So when I went back, I just went right to Claudia. I was determined to get the fact that these characters loved each other. They really loved each other, but they were in deep conflict. I felt Tom Cruise got that in the film. He really loved Louis. "In the old world, they called it the Dark Gift and I gave it to you": that's a line from the script that I love him for.

When we turned it over to Neil Jordan to proceed with the movie, I had finished my work contractually, and I didn't collaborate with him. He didn't ask me. We talked here in this living room, and I said, "My main concern is, please don't make Lestat a flat character. Please understand that in the *Chronicles* he is really the hero, and if you bring his warmth and his wit and his charm into this piece, it will work better. The darkness of Claudia and Louis will work." That had been the theory of my script, and to my amazement he left quite a bit of that in. In the final shooting script of *Interview*, Lestat is not a flat character. Also Tom Cruise injected it with a great deal of passion and charm. So in a way, oddly enough, I won on that one. In my discussions with David, he always focused on Louis as the star of the movie and felt that he was too passive. And I would say, "David, Louis is the witness. Let Lestat be the hero. Let him be in the limelight, and it will work. Don't worry about the passivity of Louis."

Well, as you know, when the finished movie came out, Louis was, if anything, even more passive than he was in either the book or my script, and Lestat was in fact the star, Tom Cruise. I won the battle of shifting the focus to Lestat, and I don't know how I won it. I don't know whether it was deliberate on Jordan's part or what, but as you know, a lot of very unpleasant interview material has been published discussing this very thing. There are magazine articles in which people connected with the production have accused me of not knowing one book from another, and not knowing who my own character was. I don't need to dwell on it, but it got quite nasty.

A BROADWAY OPERA

RILEY: Let's backtrack a little here. Over the years, as *Interview* passed through the various hands, you were courted by and met many times with people in Hollywood who expressed interest in it. At one stage, if I remember correctly, wasn't there some consideration of making it into a musical? Or was this *Interview* and *Vampire Lestat* together?

RICE: It was right after it had reverted back from Paramount. I already had a deal with Julia Phillips to do *The Vampire Lestat* as a movie, and Julia had become completely interested in the second book. She was no longer really interested in making the first book. She felt the second book had rendered the first obsolete. She thought it would be a good idea to develop *Interview* as a musical on Broadway while doing the film of *The Vampire Lestat*. Julia tried very hard to set that up at Taft Barish. It all fell through, finally. There was some small payoff, and it collapsed. By the time the whole property—that is, *Interview*, *Vampire Lestat*, and *Queen of the Damned*—went to Lorimar and then to David Geffen, we didn't have any iron in the fire about the musical. We hadn't developed that any further. We just made a deal for the movie. Now, sometime after I wrote my "bible" script that combined the novels, Elton John contacted us and told us he was interested in doing a musical of *Interview*, that it was very important to him. We'd heard this years before. It had been in newspaper columns that Elton John and Bernie Taupin had said they wanted to do something with it. So Julia and I met with them to hear what they had in mind, still with the idea that they could do their musical of *Interview* and that we would do the movie of *The Vampire Lestat*. But eventually, Julia and David rejected that idea.

I liked Elton John. I had a wonderful time talking to him. I thought it was a good idea for him to do what he called a Broadway opera, a serious work. I responded very much to him and to Bernie Taupin and was perfectly happy to go ahead, but it wasn't my decision. The dramatic rights were under the umbrella of the contract. David was already involved at that point, and David and Julia decided not to do it. She writes about it in her book, but I don't remember the details. I think she says it was his decision. She told me she didn't want to do it. I remember being kind of put out because I hadn't wanted to fly out to California in the first place. But she had flown me out there to meet them, and we had a wonderful time. I'd gotten very excited about this being a musical starting in the West End of London and then going on to New York, but then she changed her mind. She just said that after thinking it over, she didn't want to go this path. She wanted to focus on the movie. So we went back to focusing on the movie, and within a short time I was out of the picture altogether because David Geffen wanted another scriptwriter. I don't think it was something he felt about me. It was just, "I read her script, but I'd like to do something else." Michael Cristofer was an award-winning playwright, so I don't think it was anything personal. David didn't know me then. We'd never met.

EARLY CASTING POSSIBILITIES

RILEY: I remember our conversations about different casting possibilities for *Interview*, but obviously this was also going on formally at the same time as part of the development of the project. By 1992 or 1993, when the film was verging on becoming a reality, some of the people who'd seemed appropriate ten or fifteen years earlier were now older and less likely. Who were some of the people you thought of or who were proposed to you?

RICE: The only person I felt strongly about was Rutger Hauer. I felt the young Rutger Hauer in *Blade Runner* and *Ladyhawke* really looked like Lestat, and that character, particularly the character in *Blade Runner* of this replicant who was angry and violent and wanting more life, as he puts it in the movie, that was very much the way I wanted Lestat to be portrayed. Many other names were mentioned. One very meaningful visit I had was with the actor Brad Davis, who later died of AIDS. He wanted to do it very much, and he came to San Francisco to ask me if it was possible for him to get involved. He said he wanted it so badly that he almost didn't even want to reach for it, but he wanted to play Louis. I mentioned his name in the Lorimar meetings, but nothing came of it. I was never able to further his cause. I didn't have the power to do it. We remained friends, and Brad went on to do other things. But I had no power to see that Brad Davis or any other particular actor got the part. That's really all there was to it. Other names were mentioned too, of course. At one point, Julia had Richard Gere on to be Lestat, and I met with Richard Gere and Julia, and also with Oliver Stone. She wanted Oliver

Stone to direct it. He was an almost unknown director then who had a movie coming out called *Platoon* that nobody had seen yet, and his first movie as a director had been *Salvador*. When people heard that Julia wanted Oliver Stone, it was really, "Oliver who? Are you kidding?" She said, "No, I see something in this guy. I think he's going to be good. I want him to do it." And she wanted Richard Gere to be Lestat, which was a stretch for me, but Richard Gere had an enormous amount of energy and talent. I'd loved him in a film called *Breathless* and in *King David*, and I thought he could do a version of Lestat. It wasn't my highest choice, you understand. It was not who I would have picked, but I thought he could do it, and that he would do something wonderful with it. Oliver Stone ended up passing on the film. He just said he didn't want to do it, and as we know, within a year *Platoon* had won the Academy Award and he was launched. He was world famous, and Julia was, if anything, upheld that this had been a brilliant guy whom she had seen early on. With Richard Gere they never cut the deal. They never got to a contractual agreement, so the property went on without him. They couldn't negotiate what he wanted in terms of money, so he became detached from the project. I did have an enjoyable meeting with both of them, though.

RILEY: Early on, as I remember, you were interested in Richard Chamberlain. Was that for Louis rather than Lestat?

RICE: I had been interested in Richard Chamberlain for Lestat in the very beginning, but I had no contact with him. At the very end of the original contract period when they were trying at Paramount to mount a TV production of *Interview with the Vampire*, they said they would get Chamberlain if I would extend their contract. I could extend it contingent on their getting Chamberlain. I was so tempted, but once I saw the script they had in mind, I felt it was a completely shallow rendering of the novel. You remember that script; you read it. I just decided I didn't want to do it. I made the choice that I would let things play out with Paramount and then cooperate with Julia. I was very taken with Julia. I was very good friends with her, and I think she did an enormous amount to try to get this movie done. I don't know what really happened between her and David Geffen, but it was my understanding that she brought it to David's attention, and that she's the one who got him involved in it. He has a different take on that, but that was the way I heard it. Julia liked David Geffen. She thought he was a good person to be involved with this and to take care of it at Warner Bros.

CONFLICT AND ESTRANGEMENT

RILEY: As you say, a great deal has been written about your relationship to the film, including quite hostile personal comments about you by Neil Jordan and others. When I went back over much of this material—clippings, articles, and the like—I was surprised by how many of them seemed to be simply repeating each other rather than looking into matters on their own.

RICE: What happened was that I renewed the contract for David Geffen, and at that point communication with David ceased. I didn't know it then, but he was very angry about having to pay for the renewal. Then Neil Jordan was hired, and I visited with Neil several times, still not realizing that at that point David was really alienated from me and from any further cooperation with me. I had nice meetings with Neil. He seemed to like the book. He wanted to do it, and everything was on go. The extension had been signed, I got my money, and then virtually all communication stopped. We would call and ask, "How are things going?" and they'd give us a report, but there was no real communication because David was still angry with me for having demanded the legal extension, and for having demanded money for it. The next thing I heard was that Jeremy Irons had been cast. It was in the pages of *Variety*, so with great enthusiasm I called Geffen's assistant and said, "This is wonderful!" And I spoke with Jeremy Irons's agent and said, "If there's anything I can do to be supportive, I really want to do it," and the agent told me frankly that they hadn't heard anything from Geffen. This item was in the paper, but they had not yet been contacted. Well, within a few days, it appeared that Tom Cruise was cast, and we called and said, "Is this true?" At first they wouldn't give us an answer, and then they said, "Yes, it's true. Tom Cruise is going to be Lestat."

At that point, it had been made very plain to me that David felt intense animosity toward me personally. We clearly weren't speaking to each other. That was the situation. I read about the casting in the paper, and I didn't understand it. I didn't know what the thinking was behind it, and I got very upset. I tried to live with it for about three weeks. I watched everything Tom Cruise had done, and I liked him enormously. I thought he was tremendously talented, but I could not imagine him as Lestat. In the meantime, Neil Jordan called and he said, "I hear you're upset, Anne," in that lovely Irish way he has of putting a question at the end: "You're upset, are you?" And I said, "I don't understand how this is going to work." Neil assured me that he felt it could work, that he very much believed in Tom doing the part. He thought there were things in Tom as an actor that had yet to be tapped, and I said, "Okay, if you really believe it."

As the weeks passed, though, more and more phone calls came in. More and more attacks appeared in the press, more and more letters. People were calling here five and six times a night to say, "How could you let this happen?" They were just outraged. And there was a very vicious article in a Hollywood periodical. In fact there were several vicious articles attacking the casting and attacking Tom Cruise. Finally the way my name got into it was that a woman from the *Los Angeles Times* called and asked me what I thought. She just hit me at a moment when I told her absolutely what I thought [*laughter*], and to my utter amazement that made the wire services—that I thought it was a ridiculous casting choice, that I didn't know how he could do it, that combined with Brad Pitt they were like Huck Finn and Tom Sawyer, that I couldn't imagine what was going on.

All this happened in an atmosphere of being completely cut off from David Geffen and feeling kind of helpless. And you know the rest. The outcry continued. I really didn't start the outcry, and I never successfully stopped it either. It was something that came from all over. Many people thought it was a crazy idea and said so. We continued to have no contact. They would issue statements that were ferocious and negative, and I would issue statements that just held the line: I didn't see how this was going to work. As far as I know, the fans inundated them with letters and phone calls. I was told by a good source that Warner Bros. had never seen anything like it. They had been totally unprepared for it. They'd never expected this to happen, and they were overwhelmed. Now, what actually happened in the development of the movie from the time I spoke to Neil about Tom, I don't know, because I never had any official, or even informal, contact with any of them afterwards. As Neil revised and rewrote the script, as they cast the rest of the roles, as they shot the film, as they edited the film, I had no contact. I still don't know the story of how the film was made. I meanwhile went on and wrote another novel, *Memnoch the Devil*, and just prepared for the worst: that the movie would come out and it might be something that would be so bad that it would block me and hurt me.

PERSONAL IMPORTANCE OF THE FILM: "I WAS PASSIONATELY INVOLVED"

RILEY: It seems to me that nobody has ever really understood the nature of your connection to a film of *Interview*. In all of the things I've read—quite apart from some of them being negative or just taking shots at you, which there was a fair amount of—repeatedly the line would be some variation on, "She wrote the book; she sold it; she made a lot of money on it; she has no further claim on this whatsoever. She should at least be discreet enough to keep her opinions to herself." For some people in Hollywood that seems a persuasive argument, but I'd say it's irrelevant when it comes to you and a film of *Interview*. From the very beginning, from the moment the rights were originally sold to Sylbert at Paramount, this was never for you just a matter of a movie being made and hoping it was going to be a big success and make a lot of money. No doubt most authors feel that way when their book is sold, and I'm not suggesting that you were on a lofty plane above such mundane concerns. Of course you wanted that, but there's always been something more intensely personal to you about a film of *Interview*. By contrast, for example, you had nothing like the same possessive feeling about the recent film based on *Exit to Eden*.

RICE: Absolutely nothing, right. First of all, *Interview* stayed completely alive for me. I was invited to write the script twice, and when I write something, I give everything to it. When I wrote the script for Richard Sylbert in 1977, I reentered the novel and became completely enamored of the idea that I could have an influence and be involved in making the movie. The same thing happened with David Geffen. When he invited me to write the script and suddenly I was doing it again, I became totally swept up with the idea that I could have an influence, so I gave my entire commitment to it. When I sat down to write the script, I wasn't just doing a job for hire. I was really trying to make a movie of this novel work, and by that time I had written three other novels with that character, so it wasn't just *Interview*. It was part of *The Vampire Chronicles*, this ongoing work that I had been developing over the years, and there wasn't any question that I was passionately involved. I mean, anyone who thinks that you just take the money and go home is a fool. You shouldn't do that, and to my knowledge nobody ever really has. Authors suffer a lot about what happens to their books. But in this instance, I was not only suffering over *Interview with the Vampire*. I was suffering over the fate of a character who had appeared in four different books, and suffering over the fate of two scripts that I'd written in the heat of passion. So I was very deeply involved, and it will be the same when I do *The Witching Hour*. I'll be very deeply involved. I'll do my best to create the best script I can of it, and I will be passionately committed to it and ready to talk about it. When Neil Jordan came, I welcomed him into my home. I had three meetings with Neil. I was ready to give everything to this movie. I would have been happy to meet any actor connected with it, but I was never approached. I never received a phone call, a postcard, or a line. My phone was listed. I could have been reached at any time. All someone needed to do was pick up the phone and say, "I'm going to be in your movie, and I just wanted to say hello." But nobody ever did.

In retrospect, I can see why they didn't. It had to do with how angry David was with me, and I think he discouraged any contact. So one has to realize that by the time I spoke out, that was the backdrop. It was silence, and it was animosity. If there is any protocol or simple courtesy to these things, nothing was followed in this situation. I was not even told by phone that it was going to be Tom Cruise. I saw it in the papers. I would have been completely willing to cooperate at any point, as I did with Neil. I called Neil myself in Ireland, and he called me. He came here, and we talked all about it. You see, I thought we were all going along rather happily until I suddenly discovered that we weren't, that David was really very angry, that Tom Cruise had been cast, and that I was out of the picture as far as communication was concerned. And, of course, once I made a public statement, it was completely beyond hope. That was apparently interpreted as danger on their part, and they battened down the hatches. Eventually, I think, everyone who worked on the movie had to sign papers that they wouldn't talk to anybody about it. All kinds of things happened, but I know nothing about what really occurred. The way I feel about it now, though, is that I don't see how it could have turned out any better. To me the movie is so good that I can't go back and regret any part of it. All I ever said was that I didn't think Tom Cruise was right for the role; but he proved me wrong. I think he did a magnificent job. Whether our phone calls and letters and interviews influenced him to play the role faithfully to the book, I don't know, but when something turns out as well as this turned out, it's hard to have regrets.

8

"The things I loved . . . the things I didn't"

RILEY: You and Tom Cruise have talked since the film was finished, haven't you?

RICE: Yes, we have. It must have been in August. I'd finished *Memnoch*, and I was here at the house recovering from some minor surgery. I got a call and was asked if I wanted to see a tape of the movie. I couldn't believe that David would really send me a tape of *Interview*. They had even invited me to a screening. They were trying to make peace. They were saying, "Come see a screening, you're going to like the film." Well, I couldn't go to the screening for health reasons, and I wouldn't have gone because of things that had been said in the press at that point. Then David offered to send the tape. I heard that he'd taped an interview with Barbara Walters which was going to run later in the fall, and that even Barbara Walters wanted to know why Anne Rice hated this film, and that had motivated him to say, "She hasn't seen it. Let me try to send her a tape." And he did, and I loved the film! I was astonished at its fidelity to the book and to whole chunks of the script I wrote. I loved what Tom Cruise did. He made me believe he was Lestat. It's all in the public statements I've made since then. I totally loved it. David put his home phone number on that tape, which is something that most people who call me don't do. They'll call me at home at any hour and then say, "Call my agent in order to reach me." But David has always given me his home phone. His note said, "Call me at home after you've seen the film." And I did. I picked up the phone and said, "I love it. It's really wonderful. It's terrific. The kid who plays Claudia is great. Everything is great. Tom looks beautiful." I was just swept off my feet, so I decided to make a public statement about it, and took out two pages in *Variety* to do that. I wouldn't tell David the contents until I'd already done it. At that point I did talk to Tom. He called and he was very charming. He said, "This is Tom Cruise," and I started to tell him how much I loved the film. I said, "I really loved it, Tom. You did a wonderful job." And he was completely charming. He said, "That means a lot to me, hearing it from you."

RILEY: Did you discuss the controversy about the casting?

RICE: He didn't mention anything about the controversy, and he's never mentioned it to me. He simply behaved as if that never happened. Beyond that, I don't think it's fair to quote what he said in a private conversation. In interviews, though, he has said that people asked him, "Tom, why are you doing this? Why are you putting yourself through it?" I think he said that on the Oprah Winfrey show. I believe it was on that show that he said his wife Nicole would ask, "Why go through this?" and he'd say he really wanted to do it. He wanted to play this part. But I would prefer not to quote anything directly from his conversations, except to say that they were very agreeable, and there was nothing particularly earth-shattering said. It was really just me telling him how much I liked his performance and him telling me how much he appreciated it. My impression was that he is an extremely nice guy. I still believe, based on what I know, that he had no idea what he was getting into when he signed on. I don't think he knew that there was a whole series of books here, and a huge readership that had very possessive feelings about the books, or that the books fell in this strange category of sort of being cult favorites and yet having huge mainstream success. I don't think he was aware of all that. When the outcry began, I suspect he was hurt and confused by it, but for whatever reasons, he wanted to play the role, and he hung in there, and I think he did a great job. He did the crucial job. I don't think the film would have worked if he had failed. The others were wonderful, but I don't think the film could have been saved if he hadn't succeeded. I think he saved everybody on board by doing a fabulous job. He really made himself that character. He seemed to feel compassion for the character of Lestat that apparently wasn't felt by Neil Jordan or Stephen Woolley or David Geffen, because their statements never reflected anything except that they thought Lestat was a nasty character. But Tom seemed to believe that the character had depths, and he played him that way.

CASTING AND ADAPTATION

RILEY: The film director Frank Capra once said, "Casting is instant meaning." He was referring principally to a star's persona, the on-screen personality that accumulates as an actor moves from film to film, but there's an implicit acknowledgment of old-fashioned "star power," too. And as Katharine Hepburn once said, "I don't know what it is, but thank heavens I've got it." That's certainly an aspect of the casting in *Interview*. Quite apart from talent, the actors all have a compelling screen presence. When I think of the impact of scenes such as the one when Lestat looks through the shutters at the rain, which you've mentioned elsewhere, I'd say the audience's response is partly because of the dramatic context, that moment in the story, and the assumptions about the character we bring to the scene, but a big part of what makes that simple moment work the way it does is just Tom Cruise. If that's especially evident in particular scenes, it's no less true throughout the film.

RICE: The guy is absolutely the embodiment of what you're saying. He is a star. In every scene in *Born on the Fourth of July* and in *The Firm* and *Far and Away*, he takes over the whole screen. Whenever he's on, pity anybody else who's sharing the frame with him, because he takes possession of it. I think you see him do it very clearly in *Interview with the Vampire* against terrific odds. He totally takes over. He can take over when you can hardly see him in the chair in his last scene. He's running the scene! I mean, he's really running it, and in a half-light! [*laughter*] I think something very interesting happened there. The chemistry, really: How do you explain this? Okay, you have Brad Pitt, who's famous for doing this, taking over a scene or a whole movie, in *A River Runs Through It* and *Kalifornia* and *Thelma and Louise*, and suddenly Brad Pitt, for one reason or another, totally underplays in this movie. So what you get is the tremendous vigor of this star posed against the exquisite beauty of this other actor who has that potential but never really displays it here. Physically it makes for some enchanting chemistry that reached a lot of men and women. And it does have something to do with men and women. Brad Pitt's really a woman in that part. He said afterward, "Now I know how women feel." I joke about it: His problem is he's playing a girl. [*laughter*] But that's really what happens, because he does not show any of that power he has in those other films, but he's so exquisite. It's as though you take all that, you bottle it up, you put it inside the character, and you have a moment like the one where he goes down to the street and looks around and he hears a noise. It's the only time he's fully lighted in the whole movie, and he's just so beautiful it's almost beyond belief. Then Lestat grabs him, and he runs up the steps. Who can forget that scene? He's so gorgeous. It's like looking at an enormous bouquet of gorgeous flowers or a whole handful of jewels. Somehow or other they used that very well. They used Brad's exterior beautifully to express guilt and passivity, and they let Tom go like an explosion, and he propels the whole movie. With Antonio Banderas, it's the same; that power is coming from the screen. I have no idea whether anyone is consciously responsible for that in the making of the film. I know David Geffen is responsible for choosing them, but whether Neil Jordan's direction is what made that chemistry work so well, I don't know. But it sure worked for a lot of people.

RILEY: For all the film's fidelity to the novel, there is one omission I find puzzling. Your script, and the final shooting script, both include the confrontation scene with Lestat in Paris for a kind of trial at the Theater of the Vampires. I gather that scene was actually shot but cut from the final version of the film.

RICE: I wish they hadn't omitted it. I think the film suffered on two counts because of that. Number one, you have no real explanation of how Lestat survived all during the second half of the film. You see him on fire at one point, and then the next time you see him, it's a century later and he's sitting in a chair in New Orleans. There's no explanation of what happened during that period, and that's a real hole in the plot.

RILEY: Do you have any idea why it was cut?

RICE: No, Neil Jordan is the person to ask. It was his decision apparently. The other reason I think it was bad to cut it was that Tom's performance was so powerful that the audience really wanted to see him again and find out what was going on. They missed him, so I think it was a real flaw in filmmaking that Lestat disappeared and he didn't show up in Paris. What the thinking was behind that decision, I don't know. I really know nothing from Neil Jordan as to why they cut it. I think David indicated—I'm sure he wouldn't mind being quoted—that they shot it but it didn't work. But I'm not sure what that means. It was confusing to me. I also don't think they got in the movie any good reason why Brad Pitt would hate Tom. Tom was so charming that it was rather difficult to understand why Brad Pitt becomes such a kvetsch, so I thought that was a flaw. I mentioned that in my statement after the film came out: When you have Tom playing Lestat with such dimension and power, and showing the conflict and the rage and the loneliness, it's hard to understand why the Brad Pitt figure is so sour on him, just totally turning away from him, particularly in their last scene. In my script, there was a lot more attention to the conflict and the mixture of feelings—"I love you, I don't love you"; "I love you but I can't be what you want"; "Yes, I know I shouldn't have done it, but I had to do it." I had already written in *The Tale of the Body Thief* about whether Lestat, if he had it to do over again, would make Claudia a vampire. So my script was written by a person who'd been through those experiences in the books, and I was very concerned with that. I feared, more than anything else, a flattening of the characters, and there was in fact some flattening in Jordan's shooting script. There was certainly a flattening of the character of Armand. The viewers and the readers seemed to respond very strongly to Armand, and the actor, Antonio Banderas, is so beautiful and compelling that that section of the film works very well. It's not the Armand of my script or the book, though, because my Armand was attractive. I can't see in the film why Louis would want to be with this Armand. Banderas plays it so heavy, with the black wig and the hissing voice, that I think he's not a terribly attractive character, and yet obviously the viewers feel differently. They love him.

RILEY: I would explain his attraction as a kind of unacknowledged sexual magnetism rather than any promise of answers or meaning that he holds out for Louis. But certainly in the novel one of the things that make Armand so compellingly attractive to Louis is the promise that seems embodied in him. It's as if this is what Louis has been looking for from the beginning.

RICE: But, you see, they keep that line in the movie. There's a shot where Louis leaves the Theater of the Vampires—it's an overhead shot of Brad Pitt—and he says, "I knew that Armand was what I was searching for. He would never withhold knowledge the way Lestat had." But if you go back and look at the scenes with Armand, there's no reason for Louis to say that, because Armand really is kind of unpleasant.

RILEY: A scene that I think is not nearly as powerful in the film as it is in the book—and not so indirectly this has to do with the way Armand is characterized—is when Louis makes a vampire of Madeleine. It lacks the resonance of the same scene in the novel. When Louis says, "What died in there was the last vestige of humanness in me," that's really the horror of that moment for him. He has taken an irreversible step that had been unthinkable to him before.

RICE: Which he'll never do again in any of the books.

RILEY: And he does it with terribly divided feelings. He does it only because Claudia demands it.

RICE: Yes, her rage is so enormous in everything she says. A good part of that gets into the movie, but not all of it. Claudia says, "You have to do it, Louis. You have to do this because you're going to leave me."

RILEY: I believe that despite having virtually the same action as the novel, the principal reason why that scene doesn't resonate the same way is that the film has not made us feel how powerfully compelled Louis is by Armand at that point. Because that's the fatal convergence. On the one hand you have Claudia's demand, which, given Louis's character as we know it, he might otherwise have said no to. But when that intersects with his attraction to Armand and the promise he seems to embody, then it's almost inevitable that Louis will not fail to do it.

RICE: I totally agree with you. I think that's lost because Antonio Banderas played such a heavy that you don't know why in the world Louis would be charmed by Armand. The way Louis dismisses Armand in the museum is a more appropriate response to Antonio's portrayal. The thing that impelled Louis, that tore him up so much, was the conflict between his love for Claudia and his desire for Armand. He really wanted to leave Claudia for Armand. That's lost in the film because they don't let Antonio shine enough in our eyes and Louis's eyes. They make him too sinister. He's powerful and there's a great presence, and the actor's wonderful. But I don't think the character is someone you'd fall in love with and want to stay with. Women come out of the theater and say they want to sleep in Antonio's coffin [*laughter*], but I didn't feel that. You don't get the power of those moments between Louis and Armand. You don't understand the terrible conflict. What I did think was terribly important was where Claudia asks, "What was it like making love?" and Louis says, "It was a pale shadow of killing." But they didn't include that in the movie. The main thing was to have Armand taking Louis away and the terrible dilemma for Louis of this helpless person that he loved and that he was going to have to give up.

RILEY: One of the things that bother me about the film—not as I watch it, but as I reflect upon it afterwards—is that Armand is not in it enough. He needs to be foregrounded more if the attraction and conflict are to have the force they're meant to.

RICE: There's no great romance. There's no scene where they go to the tower and climb together, for instance. It's pretty much confined to them down there in the basement of the Theater, and I don't think they're even alone together very much.

RILEY: Armand is perhaps an underdeveloped role in the film, but even so, I'd suggest that's partly offset by something that's unique to the medium: the utterly unpredictable, highly charged energy that can pass back and forth between an audience and particular actors on the screen. Some actors simply seem to have an ineffable quality that compels audiences' attention. Certainly that's always been at the heart of the star system, and it's not the same thing as acting ability.

RICE: I think of the scene when Lestat rides into the fire and then turns on the horse. Tom is so overwhelming that I really believe that's a great scene. And the scene where he's looking through the shutters at the rain is another great moment. Also the scene by the bed in Louis's room. There are three or four absolutely perfect examples. But Antonio never has a scene like that. He's never lighted well enough or on the screen long enough or seen closely enough except when Brad Pitt dismisses him, and then the focus is really on Brad. There's the one place where Brad Pitt's voice is beautiful.

RILEY: You're right, of course, that Antonio Banderas never has a scene like any of those you mentioned with Tom Cruise or those that highlight Brad Pitt's physical beauty. Yet the reaction he's provoked in this film suggests he has that same star quality, whatever it is, that they do. I think this is almost the only way to account for why audiences have been so affected by the relationship between Louis and Armand, because the skeleton of the relationship is there but not a great deal more.

RICE: The person who cast the film was really David Geffen, and I think he looks exactly for that. That's what he's telling me now about *The Witching Hour*, that it has to be cast in the same way. Every single person he casts has that kind of power. There's nobody in *Interview* who doesn't just leap out at you [*laughter*], and I think that was David Geffen's intuition, just his visceral response: If this person doesn't move me, I'm not going to cast him. He could tell you more interestingly than I could, but I think that's what he did. From the beginning, with his original concept of Daniel Day-Lewis and Brad Pitt, he had a great idea. And I didn't know Tom was going to live up to that, but he did. I think David picked them all on that instinct. I think Antonio certainly has that, and it comes through really under a handicap in the movie. He's handicapped with the wig, he's handicapped with lines and settings that give him less opportunity to be attractive than the other characters, but somehow he overcomes that.

DISTURBING SCENES, QUESTIONABLE CHOICES

RILEY: Although you love the film and have very publicly embraced it, there are also some aspects that have disturbed you.

RICE: There was a viciousness toward women that I think marred the film. I think the scene in the Theater of the Vampires was unforgivable. In the book the girl was entranced and confused, but she was not tormented to that degree. Nobody pushed her or shoved her. The scene was horrible in the book, but she was entranced. Armand completely enchanted her. She died in his thrall. She suffered no pain at all. But in the film, to show those guys pushing and shoving that girl on the stage like a bunch of punks in an alley was, to me, disgusting. It was almost an unwatchable scene. It wasn't sophisticated enough for the audience *within* the film who were supposed to be watching it at the Theater of the Vampires. I mean, what do these Parisians think is going on? At least in the book, it looked like a pageant up there on the stage. You have this beautiful girl and the audience thought she was part of the whole play. But who could think that while watching what was shown in the movie? It was crude and it was filled with hatred for women—filled with, I think, almost an Irish hatred of women. I felt the scene with the whore was, too. I don't know why we had to see her with her legs sprawled apart and the blood gushing down her dress. I don't understand what motivated Jordan to go to those lengths. That's not something Lestat would particularly care to see either. The scene is vicious in the book, and he kills the whore. There's no question about it. He torments her, but it's not the same. There's something that crept into the movie. It's very hard for people to do my work because I have almost no concept of sex being dirty, and it's almost impossible for them to translate my work without getting in the idea that sex is dirty. It happens over and over again, and it happened in those scenes. When she's sitting there with her legs sprawled apart and her dress sagging and blood gushing down, the suggestion is that sex is inherently vulgar and dirty, and whores are slobs, and women who live like this are distasteful. It's quite different from the type of scene I described.

RILEY: Implicitly it becomes a rape scene.

RICE: Yes, and I've done rape scenes, but even when I do them, there's no idea that sex is dirty. It's more that sex is a mystery and that aggression and sex can combine in a mysterious way. There's a scene in *The Tale of the Body Thief* where Lestat realizes he's raped this mortal girl, that he's really done something that was terrible to her and he barely noticed it. I was trying very hard there to fathom how a male mind works. I was totally identifying with him and talking about something which I think is very human—the ability to hurt someone else without even realizing how that person feels violated. But I don't in general see sex as repulsive, and I think that crept into Jordan's film. It crept in in those scenes. Unfortunately, there wasn't anything sufficient to balance them, so they tended to give a jarring feeling sometimes, which I believe put some people off. I don't think they were necessary. I think he could have made a great movie without going to those extremes. But the last time I saw the movie, what I discovered was that the things I loved, I loved more than ever, and the things I didn't like were making me really unhappy. I was really building up a head of steam. Like *Tequila Sunrise* on the marquee: No! I was going *Boo! Hiss!* in the theater for nobody at all, just me being dramatic.

RILEY: I liked the idea of Louis going to the movies in

the modern age and seeing the sunlit world that has been forbidden to him for so long, and I think the use of Murnau's silent film *Sunrise* is an interesting touch. One might consider that merely clever, but it's more resonant than that. Murnau's is a very great film, and its title is nicely apt and even witty—a kind of visual pun. I have to say, though, that I think it's a sheer lapse in taste to use *Gone with the Wind* and *Superman* and, worst of all, the title *Tequila Sunrise* on the theater marquee. The associations are shallow and facile.

RICE: Absolute vulgarity. That's what I said in my statement: It was an unforgivably shallow thing to do.

RILEY: There are things that one may or may not like, or as you say, there are moments for you that are gratuitous in their violence toward women. But they're not shallow in the way that is.

RICE: No, as a matter of fact the scene is actually in *The Vampire Lestat* where he says he went to the Happy Hour Theater and he glimpsed the sun and then he ran home and never went out again. I used it in the script to have Lestat tell Louis—if you remember the scene, it's totally different in the end—he says, "Louis, I have been to the theater and I have seen this wondrous thing," and Louis says, "There are even greater wonders, Lestat." That was a very important thing, what it would mean to the old ones to see the sun, and I thought it was trivialized in that scene by not giving it to Tom but instead giving it to Brad Pitt and having him sit there and underreact the way he did to everything else. Switching it around like that—I thought was terrible. And that shot from *Gone with the Wind* is a sunset, so that was simply stupid, to take the most famous sunset in film history and talk about it as if it were a sunrise! [*laughter*] There are so many other wonderful things they could have done. Think of that scene in the desolate world of *Soylent Green* when Edward G. Robinson is dying and the beautiful pictures come on the screen before him. He sees scenes of the sunlight and flowers because the authorities will let you see those images as you die, and Charlton Heston asks, "Was it really like this?" and he says, "Yes, it was." Think of what could have been done with that kind of magic in those few minutes. And they have all of film history to choose from! They could have chosen something absolutely mesmerizing, but at that point, they're slipping. Louis has been played as almost paralytic all the way through, and nothing was going to make him jump for joy. [*laughter*] So they just blew that. The same mentality that blew that scene also blew the comedy in the beginning with the piano teacher hitting the keyboard and the dressmaker being killed. I didn't mind the scenes. They didn't make me want to get up and leave the theater, but they were very trivial. I think Neil Jordan has that ability to just suddenly trivialize and blow a moment. I think the end of *The Crying Game* is somewhat trivialized with the story about the scorpion. There was something great happening in *The Crying Game*, but I didn't really like the way they talked at the end. That story about the scorpion's nature didn't have anything to do with the Stephen Rea character as we've seen him.

RILEY: I very much like *The Crying Game*, but that film's final moment strikes me as too self-consciously enigmatic. It leaves me wondering if the filmmaker has come to a point where he doesn't know how to get out.

RICE: Yes, it does.

RILEY: What do you think of the humor in the film?

RICE: I'm not against there being humor in *Interview*. In my script the humorous scene was where Claudia cut her hair, dressed as a boy, and ran off to the church, and they found themselves trapped in the church. So I certainly believe in humor. I wanted the humor, and I thought that was a very funny moment when Lestat says, "Now everybody just scream and run out of the church," and suddenly they burst out. That's actually in *The Vampire Lestat*. He and Gabrielle do that, and I loved writing that scene. So I was not in any way opposed to humor, but the idea of that piano teacher hitting the deck . . .

RILEY: It doesn't rise above slapstick.

RICE: No, it's farcical and surprising, and it threw a lot of the audience. They didn't know how to react to it. They didn't know if it was okay to laugh. They weren't sure what was happening, but they sensed that it was off a little bit. Actually, I defended it. I got used to it. When my sister Karen and I go, we laugh at all those scenes. I think it's very funny when he comes up to Claudia and says, "Not in the house." That was perfect. I really did think they pulled it off there. And when he slapped her hand. Those scenes were funny. But Jordan really pushes it when we get to that scene with the family. They're all sitting there with the family, and Lestat says, "Play *A Little Night Music*." We're really almost to the edge of failure there, don't you think? Then in the next scene they're carrying out all those coffins. I think those were moments when Neil Jordan didn't have a sure feeling for what he was doing, but I'll never know because you can't know what was intended to balance what. I know there was a big scene where Brad Pitt killed the priest at the foot of the altar. It was shot from above, through the arms of the cross, but I've never seen it. It was cut. So I don't know how all this played in the director's cut, which I think was shown in New Zealand. It would be interesting; I'd love to know.

THE FILM'S POINT OF VIEW

RILEY: You mentioned earlier that Louis is if anything more passive in the film than in your script or the novel. Why do you think that's the case?

RICE: As I look at the screen, I see the camera frequently cutting away from a young actor, Brad Pitt, who is very good at showing guilt but does not have a great range of emotions to give to that character. I see the camera moving more toward people who have a greater range, like Kirsten Dunst and Tom Cruise. The camera cuts away many times from Louis's face at crucial moments. As I said in my statement, one of the big puzzles to me, which nobody has responded to in any form, is the point of view in the movie, which I find very interesting. Not a single person has addressed this in any phone call or letter, but I'm intrigued why we are being told it's Louis's point of view, when in fact the movie doesn't really show us Louis's point of view. You and I talked about this recently when we were discussing

The Innocents, the movie based on Henry James's *The Turn of the Screw*. That *is* Deborah Kerr's point of view. You don't see anything Deborah Kerr doesn't see, or in a way that she doesn't see it. But in the film of *Interview* you are not seeing what Louis sees. I don't know why that decision was made. It's as I've said: It was a "footlights" approach. It's as though a camera is at the footlights of a play, and people enter from left and right, and they act, and they move out. I don't really know the answer. But I would have to say that Brad Pitt's been overwhelmingly successful for the readers of my books. They like him very much. They all think he's exquisitely beautiful. He suffered magnificently for them. But why the filmmakers made the choice they did with point of view, I don't know. Perhaps there could really be mundane practical reasons.

RILEY: In literary first-person narration, you simply use the pronoun "I" and point of view is established. On the other hand, narrative film, even with a voice-over, can never quite sustain that to the same degree, or at least in the same way.

RICE: I think the film of *Wuthering Heights* would be a good example. The old woman starts to tell the traveler the tale, but then what you see is just the story without really feeling that it's through her eyes.

RILEY: Do you feel that *Interview*'s first-person viewpoint essentially recedes from the film, leaving the interview itself as only a convention rather than the embodiment of Louis's experience and outlook?

RICE: It doesn't work at all. You hear Louis's voice saying things about Lestat that don't correspond to the way

Tom Cruise is playing the role. Repeatedly, the emotional impact of the scene that the camera is giving you is not the same as what Louis is reporting to the boy interviewer. For example, in the graveyard we see Lestat behind Louis before Louis does. What's the point of that? How can that be conveyed in an interview? Are we to assume that he said, "Unbeknownst to me, Lestat was hovering over my shoulder"? In the book Louis conveys his emotional reaction to everything he reports. The movie isn't doing that at all. The movie just takes the interview frame and then shows us all these characters together, and the whole emotional impact is for us. It's not *through* Louis. The *audience* is supposed to be startled by Lestat in that scene, not Louis. Or take the scene where Lestat comes around the bed in Louis's room. That scene is shot for *us* to think Lestat is beautiful and seductive as he walks through the mosquito netting and talks, not for the guy lying in bed with his face covered. It's not really shot that way. It would be very simple to make it more Louis's point of view without going as far, as you said, as to place the camera where his eyes are all the time. But we don't get a shot of Lestat up through the netting. We don't see him slip in and out of lucidity as Louis tries to focus on him, nothing like that. In fact, we never get inside the head of any of those characters except for that one moment when they're being carried through the passage. We never get the swoon. We never get how it feels. We're always watching as if it were a conventional play. It was a very interesting path to go, and I'm not sure why Jordan did it. The scene where I missed it the most, where it really left me unsatisfied, was the scene with Claudia when Louis first finds her. I didn't get from that scene any sense of the seductiveness of Claudia to Louis. The scene is too brief. We see Claudia, we see how helpless she is, we know Louis is suffering, but we don't really see the juiciness and the humanity of Claudia. We don't get a sense of his being engulfed in this sensuous drinking of blood. What we see—the camera draws back—we see him trying to bite her neck and we see Lestat come through the window. And suddenly Lestat takes over the scene, so the swoon, the conflict, the whole agony in the book—"I heard her little heart beating and beating and I just . . ."—that's just gone. The camera made that choice for us. It's not shot from the point of view of the conflicted character of Brad Pitt. It's shot from the footlights; we're watching it as a play. Not only that, but Louis doesn't even hold her long enough to have the effect that's basically so important.

RILEY: I agree, but I would suggest that in the later scene when Claudia is actually made a vampire the emotional temperature or tone is far more compelling than in the scene of the first encounter.

RICE: Oh yes, I think that's a great scene.

RILEY: In the earlier scene when Louis first happens on Claudia, the main point seems to be Lestat's appearing and catching Louis and laughing at him.

RICE: Right. You don't get any view of Louis tunneling through the dark and then seeing this shining child. You're seeing things from her point of view. The camera's behind her head. It's a curious choice, a very curious choice. It's behind Claudia most of the time, isn't it? I believe it is. But the other scene, you're right. The other scene is so beautiful where Lestat leans over and strokes her face and says, "I'm going to give you what you need to live," and Brad Pitt backs away. We do see that, I think, the way those two are seeing it as it happens. It's very intimate, and you do feel it's Louis's point of view: "Oh my God, what's going to happen to this child?" Then you see this incredible transformation. But in general I think the film is not from Brad Pitt's point of view. Often what you're seeing in the film isn't even what the Brad Pitt character is capable of describing.

RILEY: Can you give an example of what you mean by that?

RICE: When Louis takes Claudia back to the room and tries to describe to her why he victimized her. That's one of the most flowery passages in the book, so it's easy to criticize, where Louis makes a speech that says something like "You had a heart like no other heart and you smelled of salt and dust as children do." None of that is in the movie, so he doesn't in any way give Claudia the explanation of why he fed on her. It's not there. He just takes her to this place, he shows it to her, and he stands there and she says, "You fed on me," and she freaks out. Then he says, "I took your life and he gave it back to you." But you have no sense of the terrible conflict and the terrible love. He tells us in the voice-over narration that sometimes he would look at her and he would think, "I have taken this person's life, and I fed on her as a human," but there's no resonance to that because you don't really see that. In fact you see hardly anything from Brad Pitt's point of view that I can remember. The beauty of Lestat is for us; the beauty of Claudia is for us; the beauty of Armand is for us. Everything is playing to us across the footlights as if we were sitting a few feet away.

RILEY: I was once talking with Joan Didion about the

film that the director Frank Perry made from her novel *Play It as It Lays*, and she characterized that film's point of view as being what she called "close third." In other words, strictly speaking it was a third-person point of view, not the central character's eye, but nonetheless it was a kind of analogous sensibility, as if the third-person narration had moved in very close so that the view the audience got was not exactly the character's but was anchored in her sensibility and experience of the world. When I see the world of the film of *Interview*, aren't I "in" the world that Louis is living in?

RICE: I understand what you're saying, but I'd say that the narration of the film of *Interview* is not a close third. We're ostensibly being told the story in the first person by Louis, but the point of view is strictly that of the viewer of the movie—or maybe, in a sense, of someone who's read the book. But it really is removed from Louis's point of view, so it does create the potential problem of how you sympathize with him. It's true that it didn't create a problem for me because it's captured visually. Everything is captured there for us.

RILEY: Well, that's what I'm getting at. There's a way in which the film's narration captures that intensity for us, the viewer, so that we in turn project it onto that character. I do think, for example, that Brad Pitt's performance is excessively passive, but I think a major reason why that doesn't undercut the effectiveness as much as it would have is that the film is so visually intense for the viewer, its atmosphere so enveloping. In other words we "read in" the intensity of our response for his. It was partly with this in mind that, after seeing the film several times and rereading your screenplay, I reread the novel recently. I wanted to compare Louis as the storyteller in the two works, and I was reminded that for all of his passivity Louis is still a passionate character in the novel. Even in his grief and guilt, his is not just a mournful sensibility. His sensibility as the narrator is quite passionate. I think what Pitt's performance runs the risk of—although apparently for viewers this hasn't typically been the case—is Louis seeming to be overwhelmed by a kind of ennui.

RICE: Oh, yes, he's almost a paralyzed character. Significant things like the fistfights with Lestat are left out. His anger at Claudia after the killing of Lestat doesn't happen. Her blood-tears scene, where she cries, is not there. When they cut back to Louis in the room with Christian Slater, his reactions do not seem equal to what we've just seen. To see one tear fall on the tape recorder and have him say, "A vampire can cry once in a century"—if I wrote that in the book, and I hope I didn't, I don't think I did—to me that is a paltry description of the tragedy we've just seen. After Lestat's death, when the interviewer asks, "Did you miss him?" and Louis says, "He was all I knew," that doesn't live up to what we've just seen, this dazzling, impish, charming, wonderful, powerful guy. There's no admission in the film of the way in which Lestat really made life worth living for them. It's not there. It's in the book, and I thought it was in the script, but it's not in the film. And I think that's the film's central flaw. If I were just a viewer walking in off the street, that would strike me: Why does this guy not realize how incredibly beautiful and magnetic this other guy is, and why doesn't he stay with him? Why doesn't he try to make some kind of peace with him? Isn't there any back-and-forth at all?

RILEY: Do you think, then, that Louis's love for Lestat is lost in the film?

RICE: Totally. In the book there was a very important paragraph when Louis said, "I sold my soul. What would God have had to do to get me to follow him like Matthew or Peter? Dress well, to begin with, and have a luxuriant head of yellow hair." I remember Vicky Wilson saying at the time, "I think you're way over-romanticizing the character of Lestat at that point." And I said, "Oh no, he's very compelling to Louis. I have to have in there that Louis knows he was swept off his feet by the beauty of Lestat." That's one of the few things I remember from our editorial discussions, that I didn't want to change it. He had just met Armand, and he was sitting on the steps of the Theater of the Vampires, thinking, "I killed him for all the wrong reasons." No, I'm mistaken. When he thinks that about the hair, he's in the carriage with Madeleine, but he's beginning to realize how much we sell our souls for style, for beauty, for dazzle. He loved all that about Lestat, and he's admitting it. That to me shows some growth from the beginning, where he's just denying it the whole time. It's a problem in the book. It's not well worked out. I tried to make it better in the screenplay. I tried to make him admit how much he loved Lestat, but the filmmakers went to the opposite extreme.

RILEY: Do you think the film strikes essentially the same pitch on the theme of homoeroticism as the novel?

RICE: It goes further than the novel. The farewell scene

between Brad Pitt and Antonio Banderas goes further than anything in the novel. The only scene in the novel that goes that far is when Louis goes down into the Theater of the Vampires ballroom and he meets the young boy, the mortal boy that Armand is keeping. I mention the fact that the boy had an erection when he bit his neck. That's the only statement in the novel where I go that far, and frankly I would take it out now, because I don't know why I wrote it at the time. It doesn't seem necessary. But other than that, I never had a scene with Louis or Lestat or Claudia or any of them as intimate as that final scene between Brad Pitt and Antonio Banderas. That did disturb quite a few viewers who called and said they were afraid they were going to kiss at that moment and they were very glad they didn't. Many gay people called and mentioned that they loved it. Many young people mentioned that they loved it and wished they *had* kissed each other. So there's a whole spectrum of reactions.

It's my experience that many fans of *The Vampire Chronicles* love the homoerotic nature of all this, and they see it very much the way I do, as equals. They see it as very romantic, and this includes straight people and gay people both. There's no separation. Many women love books about men, and men loving men, and they love to see men making love to each other. I think they responded very strongly to that aspect of *Interview with the Vampire*. From teenagers who said, "If Tom Cruise is going to bite Brad Pitt, I'm gonna be there," all the way to women who just said, "I loved them. I went to see it eleven times, and I just loved it when Brad took Antonio's face in his hands." These people are not making any political statement; this is just something they liked. There are, of course, people who are more conscious of questions of gay and straight, and they do respond to the film as a potential gay allegory or a story with meaning for gay people. They have various feelings about whether it's successful or not. To them it's an interesting controversy: Did it go far enough? Then, obviously, there were a few straight people who did see it as a gay allegory and were offended by it, but they were just a tiny minority. That's exactly the way it shakes down with the books. The response to the movie was very much like the response to the books.

RILEY: You know, whatever one thinks of the various public statements Neil Jordan has made about you and your script, particularly during his attempt to get writing credit, I do think one of his principal strengths was that he wasn't afraid of the material. The eroticism, or the homoeroticism, or the relationship with the child, all of those things that time and again you watched various screenwriters trying to find a way around, didn't inhibit him.

RICE: No, they didn't. I think his films *Mona Lisa*, *The Crying Game*, and *The Miracle* show an obsession with gender and the confusion created by gender, and how love tends to seek the marriage of true minds regardless of any gender impediment. I think those films were very much about that: The people you love are the people you love, and it may break every rule you know, but that's what happens. I think Neil Jordan was perfect for this. He went into it fearlessly, and it fit in with his own obsessions as an artist. He was not in any way afraid of the transgressive side of it. I also think that, being an Irish Catholic, he understood the kind of guilt the story was talking about—the sense of being damned, the sense of futility, the sense of loneliness, the struggling—but, beyond that, why he made it so faithful to the book I really don't know. I don't know to this day who did the final cut of this movie. I know that a great deal was cut, that many scenes he shot were cut, but I don't know the story.

9

"From teenagers to housewives to brain surgeons to manicurists to truck drivers"

RILEY: I'd like to discuss the critical response to the film and the personal statement you published after its release. Let's start with the critical response—not just whether critics have liked or disliked it, but the extent to which they seem to have understood it. Have the critics responded in terms which make sense to you?

RICE: The response to the film has been like the response to the books. There's no consensus. Some people think it's brilliant, and some people think it's junk. I've watched the film go through what the books have gone through for years. You have one review calling them a work of genius and another saying they're just garbage. I've seen the same split. It's interesting to me that the film was that controversial—that someone like Caryn James or Janet Maslin would write eloquently about the meaning of it in *The New York Times*, and yet *Newsweek* and *Time* brushed it off as hardly worth their time. And other people attacked it, too. I was also surprised to see my own name mentioned in most reviews. I had expected to be eclipsed by the film, so I was amazed the author and the book were subjects that reviewers dealt with even if they were panning the movie. But frankly I think the criticism of this film so far has been of no value. The valuable criticism has yet to come. It's too early. It's just like book criticism. There's little there to be studied or learned. Most of it reveals a shallow, haphazard kind of thinking, and I think there's no better example than this film, which obviously deeply moved audiences, which caused a great deal of controversy and was very big at the box office because of an enormous number of people going back to see it over and over again. Yet the reviews, some of them, don't even seem to be aware of what the film was about. It's very much the experience I've had with the books.

RILEY: I haven't read all the reviews by any means, but I've found some of them interesting—the two pieces in *The New York Times* that you mentioned, for example. In some other instances, though, I've been struck by a failure to understand not just the film, but the myth that underlies it. And here I'm not focusing on whether the reviewers liked the film or not. Let me give you an example. In a popular weekly magazine a reviewer wrote: "A vampire story needs a human victim to lead the audience into the vortex and help them escape it." As a general proposition about the genre, that may be the case. What this claim misses, though, is the extent to which in your version of the myth viewers and readers perceive these characters, the vampires themselves, as human. So the audience doesn't experience an absence of a human victim. However paradoxically, the vampires *are* the human victims in *Interview*.

RICE: They're metaphors for us, and obviously that reviewer completely missed that point. If that person had done the simple homework you'd expect of a graduate student looking up data on the underlying material, he or she would have discovered that was not the focus of this work and never has been. A review like that is almost not worth an answer because the movie is so obviously about us, and the vampires are us, and you do identify with Louis and Claudia and with Lestat himself. A review like that is completely irrelevant in my judgment. That would be like reviewing *Philadelphia* and saying, "We don't care about the characters because they're gay." At this point reviewing is so bad, so irresponsible, that frequently it simply has nothing to do with a movie. I don't know how to say it any more strongly than I did in my statement. But I've gotten many reviews like this over the years, because there's no real tradition right now in America for writing good reviews of movies or books. Anyone can review anything and say anything. But we don't have that in the world of opera or ballet. You have to know something about those art forms if you're going to review them. If you say to *The New York Times*, "I can't stand a bunch of Italians screaming, so I hated this opera," they'll fire you. But because, as you once said, everybody feels they know about movies and that movies belong to them, there is no standard of informed and responsible reviewing. You can say virtually anything, and as a consequence they have no substance. In fact I'd say the bigger a movie is at the box office, the greater its success, the more likely it is that a reviewer will write something shallow about it. I've watched it happen in publishing, not just with my work but with other authors', too. You don't find intelligent, thoughtful reviews of Stephen King, for example. They aren't there. There are many things that can be said about Stephen King's work and the way people respond to it and what it means about our times, but reviewers don't bother. So none of the reviewing of the movie was particularly shocking. It was just what I'm used to with the books—the same babble of voices, people that didn't do their homework.

To me, there's no question that it's a great movie, and it affected the public consciousness, and will have a tremendous journey in the public mind. I think no one will even remember the reviews. The Romantic idea of the man of sensibility talking about his own personal responses has reached its zenith in the reviewer, to where absolute fools come out and say, "I just didn't like it." Well, fine, but are we supposed to take time to listen to this? This whole system, as you know, has been created by the fact that people who make books and make movies and make Broadway plays have relied heavily on quotes from reviews to sell them. They've created this power structure, and now they're stuck with it because they've trotted out the quotes of these people and used them in ads. But it's a very poor system. So, unfortunately, there's nothing really meaty or wonderful to be discovered in the reviews of *Interview with the Vampire*.

Now as the journals come out, as film people write about it, and as books are written about the evolution of the horror film, we will get some serious scholarship. We'll get some thoughtful articles and real analysis. Maybe in a few years we'll even have a really intelligent book on how the film was made, the choices it made and how people responded. Right now in the popular press? No, there's not a ghost of a chance of that happening in this field. It might happen in opera, it might happen in ballet, it might even happen in restaurant reviewing. [*laughter*] After all, you can't just say "I don't like Chinese food" and expect to keep your job and be taken seriously. But at this point, book and movie reviewing is total license. You rarely learn a thing from it. It's just luck if somebody like Janet Maslin likes it and writes a thoughtful piece. As Stan says, "You're lucky. You got through that minefield without being blown up."

THE SECOND *VARIETY* STATEMENT

RILEY: Why did you decide to write and publish the long second statement that appeared in *Variety*?

RICE: I just wanted to talk about the film and what I thought about it. I'd wanted to do that from the very beginning. I said that even if I hated it I would wait a few months until it had finished its run and then I would write what I thought about it, so I had a desire to do it out of pure enthusiasm. I had no idea anyone would think it was abnormal. I wanted to point out all the things I loved about it and the things I didn't. I chose the ad because I didn't want anybody to edit what I said. I offered the piece to the *New York Times* "Arts and Leisure" section, but they said it was too long. So I took out the ad space.

One of the reasons I chose *Variety* is because it's inexpensive, and *Variety* is also what I call a seminal publication. Many people pick it up and talk about it. As far as I know, all of the big computer services downloaded the entire statement, so it went on-line on CompuServe, America Online, and Prodigy. We also mailed out 2,000 copies I signed to members of the fan club. So that was the best we could do to make it public. To run that ad in *USA Today* would have cost hundreds of thousands of dollars. We tried them, but that was the answer: $300,000. That was absolutely out of the question, whereas it was just a modest amount to run it in *Variety*. Also, *Variety* is very cooperative. They worked with us on my first statement just before the film was released, and I like them as a magazine. I don't consider them vicious, or just the company magazine for filmmakers, so that was all part of it. My idea was to get it to the maximum number of people in the best way, and we have a second edition here that we'll send now to anybody that sends us their address. I have a phone line that I've set up and I tell people, "If you want the statement, send me your address." My desire was just to praise this film for all the things I thought were wonderful in it that had not been mentioned in reviews. I wanted to make my own enthusiastic statement about what I liked, just as if I were sitting with a group of people who asked, "What did you like about the film?" That was all I had in mind. I also mentioned the things I didn't like, and I answered a few people, like the columnist Liz Smith. So I was quite surprised that anybody would even ask why I was doing it. I thought it was obvious. But everybody did ask. Christine, my lawyer, said, "Why are you doing this?" Lynn Nesbit, my agent, said the same thing. David Geffen said, "I beg you not to do this!" I think it all blew over real fast. I don't think it had that much impact.

THE FILM AS HER READERS SEE IT: "A GREAT GIFT, A GREAT JUICY THING"

RILEY: Whatever the impact of the statement, you've been getting a lot of responses to the film from your readers in letters and phone calls. How have they felt, by and large?

RICE: The readers have overwhelmingly loved it. I had a phone line listed almost from the first week after the film opened, and we've gotten nonstop calls. We have stacks of tapes I'm listening to of recorded messages of people calling in. I haven't done an analysis, but I've listened to many of them, and I would say, in general, that for every twenty-five calls saying, "I loved it," there may be one that says, "No, I did not care for it." There are a few random calls saying, "We don't like you, and we don't know your books, and who the hell are you to run an ad?" But that's to be expected. Those people have nothing to do with anything because they didn't see the movie or read the book. They just responded to the idea that an author would take out this space in a magazine.

RILEY: Of those who've had complaints or caveats, is there any pattern to them?

RICE: The overwhelming response is that they perceive this film as a great gift, a great juicy thing for them to chew on for a long time. They say they went to see it seven and eight, ten and eleven times, and they enjoy talking with other people about the pros and cons of every aspect of it. That they see it pretty much the way sci-fi buffs see a sci-fi film. When a good one comes along, they feel like, ah, we have a hunk of stuff to play with now. That's what I've found. People were lovingly satisfied by this film. I haven't seen any overall pattern of complaint. Basically, the people calling me say they also didn't think Tom could do it and were happily surprised that he did it very, very well. They go out of the way to say how much they loved Brad Pitt and how beautiful he is and how he got the guilt of Louis. They have nothing but praise for Kirsten Dunst, who was Claudia. That's the one character who has total consensus. Everyone thinks she was fabulous. And they mention the sexiness of Antonio Banderas. The other things they talk about range too widely for me to make an analysis. One person will call and say, for example, that it was a mistake to take out the brother, that the whole question of brotherhood was key to the story. But they're often simple comments, just interesting and thoughtful comments about the content of the film. Very few people called to say, "I hated it. I was disappointed. I hate you. I think you sold out." But again, until I sit down and listen to everything, I can't tell you any more. I did receive one call from somebody who was very young and I didn't know the machine was on. I don't listen to the calls at the time they come in unless I'm going to answer the phone. I was in my room packing to go to New York, and this person said, "You sold out. Geffen bought you, and this is why you made this statement in the paper." He left his name and number, and I ran to the machine and picked up the phone and called back his machine in a rage. I said, "How dare you say that to me!" I just read his machine the riot act. About a week ago, I looked him up in the tapes and called him and said, "Look, I want to tell you, whoever you are, that I'm sorry I screamed at you. But I was really upset when you said those things. I'd like to talk to you, and if you'll call again, let's talk about it." But I've never heard from him. I gave him the house number, because I felt this was somebody very young and that perhaps I'd frightened him. I mean, the vehemence . . . I surprised myself. I grabbed the phone, and he must have been right there by his machine because I called him like three minutes after he called me. I tried to get there before he hung up, and I just boiled over. I said, "I wouldn't change one comma for David Geffen." He also said the movie was "*Top Gun* in New Orleans," and I said, "That is not what it is. The movie was great. There were great things in the movie, and if you don't see that, that's your misfortune." I just laid in to him, and there was no sound on the other line. He never called back, but I did try to make amends by contacting him and saying, "Look, I'm sorry I blew up at you that way, and here's my unlisted phone number if you want to call."

Several people have called many times. I hear a lot from Louise in Denver, Emily in Canada, Brian in Florida. And people call back just to hear the update and to talk about various things. I update the message on my machine. I'll say, "This is January third. The movie has made its $100 million, and that's good news for all of us who love movies of this kind. Hollywood will now make more. Thank you for your messages. We're listening to everything you say. Please send us a postcard with your address so we can start a newsletter." People frequently call to get the update. I get calls from all kinds of people. I got a call from a couple of truck drivers in Illinois. They told me they love *The Vampire Chronicles* and listen to the audiotapes on the road. They loved the movie. I'd say there are far more men than women calling. I don't know what that means.

RILEY: Do you find any particular difference in the responses from men and women?

RICE: No, I would say that there's a very large proportion of straight males who see this movie who have no idea that anyone would ever think it was a gay allegory, and they notice nothing in it that makes them think of gay life. They think of these guys strictly as swashbucklers, heroes, outsiders, you know, guys on an adventure. They are utterly unthreatened, utterly undisturbed by any question of there being a gay aspect to the film. I get those responses to my books, too. I would say seventy-five percent of my audience doesn't perceive these books as gay allegory.

There was nothing I hadn't seen before in my own career. I don't know what it was like for Tom or David or Brad, but I had seen and heard it all. What that reinforced for me was the fact that the movie is so wonderfully true to the book that it's had the same fate. It's been immensely popular, just as the *Chronicles* have been, and yet there are people who have utterly dismissed it. But it's been a wonderful, exciting thing, and it's just beginning. I'm waiting to hear how people perceive it as time passes, because that's the way it was with the novel of *Interview* in the beginning. It made a bundle of money for me. Everybody knew about it, and yet critically it was totally controversial and actually didn't succeed the way this movie did. This movie really succeeded at the box office the way my first book didn't but my books now do. *The Tale of the Body Thief*, which is about Lestat being in love with a seventy-four-year-old man, was number one for a month on the *New York Times* list, and you can't have that kind of success in America unless you have all kinds of people buying your books, from teenagers to housewives to brain surgeons to manicurists to truck drivers to boys to girls. So it was thrilling to see the movie go right in there and have the same kind of response. I think if it had been a very literary film, or a cult film, it would have had a completely different impact. I think if it had been a bad film it would have sunk like a stone, so this popular success is a great tribute to everyone involved. I mean, it's so easy to make a bad vampire movie that survives for about five seconds. Something like *Buffy, the Vampire Slayer* didn't make it. As far as I'm concerned, *Dracula* didn't really do it either. *Dracula* was successful for other reasons that had to do with Winona Ryder, and dance, and color, and blood, and music, and MTV.

HOLLYWOOD AND VAMPIRE FILMS

RILEY: Leaving aside *Dracula*, it seems to me that if you look back at vampire films in recent years—such as *Buffy, the Vampire Slayer* or *Love at First Bite*—the general assumption in Hollywood has been that the only way you can deal with such material is camp.

RICE: It's almost impossible to do a successful vampire movie. Pauline Kael once said that vampire movies were all so bad she simply didn't review them. There was one with Nicolas Cage where he ate a bug. I don't know if you've seen that one. Julian Sands has made a couple that are very limited and awful. No, they're not even awful. They're just small, limited movies with a couple of ideas. Just think back to how many there are on TV. Obviously *Interview* was much better than anybody expected. Nobody was able simply to make fun of it. Even the most dismissive reviewers generally had to admit that the damn thing was mysterious and substantial. But one of the great curiosities is that, for those who don't know anything about this world, the opinions they have and the mistakes they've made often are quite remarkable. I don't think Warner Bros. had any idea what this world was. I'd be willing to say that nobody on the production end of this picture had ever simply looked at books like Katherine Ramsland's *The Vampire Companion* and *The Witches' Companion*. I don't think they had any idea what the fan club was. I don't think they had any idea of the yearly coven parties where two thousand people come together from all over the world. I don't think they had even the slightest idea of what the other books were in the series. I think there were people working on the film who hadn't even read *The Vampire Lestat* or *The Queen of the Damned* or *The Tale of the Body Thief*. They simply weren't aware. They were totally caught off guard by the enormous outcry about Tom Cruise, and to some extent I believe they were also caught off guard by the popular success of the film. I heard that the people at Warners were flabbergasted. They had no idea this was going to make $38 million in one weekend. I don't know what they were hoping for, but they were knocked out. I know that some people connected with the production went out and drove past Grauman's Chinese Theater in Hollywood, and they saw people in vampire costumes. They spoke of it to me in amazement. [*laughter*] Now, I have known that for years. You see, in the world I live in, people come two-thousand strong to a signing and they're dressed in all kinds of costumes. I've done wonderful signings in places like Change of Hobbit in L.A., The Tattered Cover in Denver, Bookland in Maine. It's common in big cities for that to happen, and it happens more and more in the suburbs. In Long Island, kids come in costumes, and in Phoenix, costumes from all the books, so I was always aware of this. But to these people in Hollywood I apparently sounded like a pathetic author saying, "Hey, we really have a lot of readers out here. Maybe it's worth your while to pay attention to what this is all about, because if you make it faithful and you make these people happy, maybe there's enough of them." I'll never know if the letters and the phone calls and the outcry did put some pressure on them to be faithful, because I wasn't connected with the film once it went into production, and Neil Jordan will never tell me and David Geffen will never, either. But I do know that they were taken totally by surprise by both things—the phenomenal success and the phenomenal outcry at the beginning. I like to believe that somewhere in between those two things, they at least realized there were enough people making noise that they'd better get this film right. I remember when the director Dick Donner came down here and was going to do *The Witching Hour*, which he never did. He said that people were cornering him and taking him by the lapels and saying, "Do it right." He said, "If we don't do your books right, these people are going to jump on us. I've never seen so many people saying, 'You've got to get Anne Rice's *Witching*

Hour right.' " Well, I think that's what happened with *Interview with the Vampire*, but I think the people in control of making the movie were completely unaware of that.

RILEY: I suppose they just thought they had a bestseller on their hands and, after all, that's the stock-in-trade in Hollywood.

RICE: A freaky, unmakable bestseller that had been batting around for fifteen years, that was controversial and had weird elements. I really do think that the magic that got it done was the immense power of David Geffen, and the fact that he was personally obsessed with it. That's something that only he can explain.

RILEY: The most ironic—although certainly not the most uncharacteristic—trait of the Hollywood responses to the novel over the years has been, on the one hand, to have paid a large sum of money to buy a popular novel in order to make a film that will capitalize on its popularity, and then, on the other hand, to be scared to death of it. When I think back on some of the scripts I've read, they often seemed in a sense to be running from the novel.

RICE: There was a period when Hollywood was definitely afraid of the book. That was the feeling. Those who did know about its popular success didn't want to mess with it. And those who didn't care about its popular success . . . how do I explain it? . . . they didn't want to risk something so crazy. They didn't know why it would work. I think they wisely backed off, the directors who just said, "I don't know how to do this. I don't even know what this is." But finally David got it made. He's the magician who pulled it off, and it sure worked for a lot of people. And it's going to keep working. When it goes onto videocassette, it's going to be an entirely new adventure for this film. It's going to have a whole following in videocassette. I'm saying this in awe; I'm not saying it in bravado. There are going to be parties where people show it and talk about it and stop it and fast-forward it, and parties where they dress up as all the characters just like they do now with the books. It's going to be great fun. If the film had fallen short, none of that would have happened, but the film was good enough that it played to this enormous number of people who want to do this with it. Including me. I want to see it again. I want to watch it five or six times. I want to fast-forward and see various scenes. I want to talk about it. Like somebody called the other night and said, "When Brad is lying on the ground in the graveyard scene, there's blood on his shirt, and then when he wakes up, there isn't." Now I want to go back and see if that's really true. This woman also said that when they pull the curtain in the Theater of the Vampires, they blow out all the footlights, and then in the next scene, they're all lighted. She'd like to know who lit them. Well, you know, you only do this with films you love. You may do it a little bit with the worst films, but there's a limit to how fascinated you can get with the art of badness. But when a film is good, those kinds of things are great fun. I want to go back and check out all kinds of things that I didn't see clearly enough the first time.

I wish somebody would write a book about the making of it. I've heard the remarks of Stan Winston and Stephen Woolley and Neil Jordan that were quoted in various fanzines like *Imagifilm*, or whatever it is, and *Fangoria* and *Cinefantastique*, but those have been so saturated with negative comments about me that it's difficult to extract any real information about how the film was made. I remember Stan Winston or somebody talking about how they put that wig on Antonio and everyone went, "Ah! That's it!" I'd love to know more of that. I'd love to know all of these things, and having been cut off, I'm left curious.

RILEY: So those may remain unanswered questions for you?

RICE: Yes, I was suffering exquisitely during the whole thing. It was terribly painful for me. I would never want to fight like that again over anything, to tell you the truth. If they cast Kermit the Frog, I'm just leaving. [*laughter*] People have joked that Jim Carrey will be cast as the vampire Lestat and Anne Rice will move to Madagascar. [*laughter*] I'm never going to get into a battle like that again, but I wouldn't have missed it for the world. It was a great battle. It was exquisitely painful, but it's conceivable that, separated as I was from them, I had a greater impact on what they did than I ever would have if I'd been part of the team. I don't know. They know.

RILEY: Although you objected to the casting at the outset, you went out of your way to speak warmly about Neil Jordan. I remember especially an interview you did on the *Charlie Rose Show* on PBS shortly after Tom Cruise was announced. And yet, as you say, Jordan and some others have been quite hostile in their public remarks about you since the film was completed. Perhaps in Jordan's case that was because of his unsuccessful effort to get screenwriting credit. You've certainly never denied that he made changes. In fact, you've spoken quite openly about that in these conversations, and in any event, the screen credit was decided by the Writers Guild after they compared your script with the shooting script.

RICE: Those have been almost savage attacks on me. One wonders why they were done, actually. It's curious that so late in the game they made those kinds of attacks. It's hard to figure out what was going on in their minds. Later, David's attitude was, "Oh just forget it. It was before the truce." But it's not that simple. Those interviews were given after the Writers Guild ruling giving me sole screenplay credit, so perhaps that explains it. But it's kind of interesting, the degree to which they went. I wouldn't do it any other way than I did it, though. It worked out too well, and I think if I'd been involved, it might never have worked out. When something works that well, you can't finally regret it.

RILEY: It's often said that writers come to a point where their characters take on a life of their own, as if they live independent of the writer. Talking to you now, I wonder if something like that has happened for you with the film of *Interview*. No doubt the first time you saw the tape David sent you, there was an inevitable checking to see how they'd handled your characters, but it's gone past that now. The characters as they exist in the film have acquired a life of their own for you, almost as if they weren't your characters at all anymore, as if they were in somebody else's movie, even.

RICE: It's true. And it would have been very easy to offend me to the point where I would have just backed off. They almost did it with the whore and the young woman in the Theater of the Vampires. I don't look at them when

I watch. But overall I found it fabulously entertaining. They swept me off my feet, and I think that's a tribute to the quality of the film.

A NEW AUDIENCE

RILEY: In likening the popular response to the film to that of the novel, you attributed that to how well the filmmakers captured the book. There is also a secondary effect that I find remarkable. Not only is the novel of *Interview* back on the paperback bestseller list, which is not surprising with the release of the film, but so are all the other *Vampire Chronicles*. *The Vampire Lestat*, *The Queen of the Damned*, and *The Tale of the Body Thief* are simultaneously on the list, too. That means there's a large audience that had not been exposed to the *Chronicles* before but that now, having seen the film of *Interview*, has gone on to read the original novel, and as a result has begun reading the other books as well. Now it's on to *The Vampire Lestat*, which is going to have to be a different kind of film, isn't it?

RICE: I think so. I'm hoping that it will. You see, I really do believe—I have this vision, almost like a Dickensian vision—that you can make something wonderful and deep and it can be available to people from eight years old or even younger. I remember seeing *The Red Shoes* and *Tales of Hoffman* when I was pretty young. I loved those movies, and I respected them. I think one of the mysteries of *The Vampire Lestat* is that you can do everything that's in that novel, and you can still show it to a child. It's a movie that can be understood by any age because there is no vulgar or direct confrontation with eroticism or gender-bending. The novel is not talking about those things. It's talking about being alone, being a hero, wanting to be a success in the world, being cast out of that world and still trying to find some way to be a success, to be significant, to be great, to be heroic. That's something you can make for an eight-year-old—or if you want, you can make it so that it has to be R-rated. There's a choice. *Interview with the Vampire* was harder. It went closer to the transgressive with things like the love between Claudia and Louis, but I think the movie got it exactly right. For whatever reasons, they were faithful to the very things that mattered to me.

10

"A quest for meaning"

RILEY: While the film of *Interview* was being made, you were writing *Memnoch the Devil*, which has had a complex history. Now that it's finished, tell me about its development, the changes in its title, and how it took its final shape for you.

RICE: I can tell you that the idea for the novel was born in Miami. We were in our apartment there, and Stan was reading *Lasher*. That was a very tense time, because when you're in one room and somebody else is reading your manuscript in another, it's not very comfortable. And I remember thinking of this enormous novel, *A Dark and Secret Grace*, that would involve an almost unredeemable man—like a hit man—visited, the way Scrooge had been, by ghosts who transform him morally. That was what I started with. I began to do a great deal of reading with that in mind, and thinking of such things as who were the ghosts going to be, what were they going to say, and so on. I concentrated on reading an enormous amount in biblical history and scripture and the apocryphal texts. During all of this I began to see that I wanted to focus on making a direct confrontation with the Devil and God, and I soon realized that I couldn't do this with the mortal hero. Obviously, a man being visited by ghosts was a very different thing from someone confronting God and the Devil, and every time I'd start the novel with the chapter of how the hit man first saw the character who would later be Memnoch, I couldn't make it work. I couldn't know the mortal character well enough to understand him and put him in as an opponent of God and the Devil, so I went back to the idea of letting it be Lestat. I'd always had the idea that there would be one novel where I would pick up the idea from the Paris café scene in *Tale of the Body Thief* about God and the Devil, and what if Lestat met them. But it wasn't really much more than an idea, and then suddenly I realized, this is Lestat's novel! He's the one who can do this. He can go to heaven and hell. It's the perfect thing to have happen, and I'll tie it in with what he said to David Talbot. I'll use that, and I'll go back and bring it all together. When that happened, it all began to work. I just began to write, and Lestat was right on, and there was David, and there was a whole context for it. But the main thing was I had my powerful hero.

RILEY: Since in some respects Lestat's journey has always been your own, what did you discover in the material that made you realize the story belonged to him?

RICE: There were two things working: There was my desire to talk about religion itself, the history of religion, what religion teaches us, and my own mystification in the face of it all. And there was also the idea of taking Lestat farther along the very journey that *The Vampire Chronicles* have been about all the way from Louis's first saying "I don't know what I am" to finally Lestat with Memnoch at the end. It really was a quest for meaning, and *Memnoch* is a very important book to me. It was much more exciting to write than *Taltos*, although that was great fun. I loved the idea of doing Ash, that gentle giant, and trying to do just really outrageous things in *Taltos* that were hard to pull off, but that was a different type of thing altogether. *Memnoch* to me is really significant. If at any point someone had come up and said, well, you know, you're going to die, you have exactly six or seven more days, I would have kept writing *Memnoch*. With *Taltos* I might have said, well, no, I think I want to do something just a little more . . . if I have to choose, I don't want this to be the last one.

RILEY: I remember writing you a letter when I finished reading the manuscript of *Memnoch* and saying that there was something about it that seemed inevitable, that this book is almost a necessary outgrowth of the themes and questions that have been at the heart of *The Vampire Chronicles* all the way back to *Interview*.

RICE: That's how it felt. It felt wonderful.

RILEY: Why did you decide to change the title again, this time from *Of Hell and Heaven* to *Memnoch the Devil?*

RICE: Oh, just wanting that name. Loving the phrase ". . . the Devil." There's a famous story by Sheridan Le Fanu. I think it's called "Dickon the Devil," and I loved the title. I kept hearing it in my head, and I just needed the name. First the character was named Maxim throughout the whole manuscript, but that wasn't enough. It wasn't a strong enough name. I wanted " '*Da-da*' the Devil." It was strictly words haunting me. *Of Hell and Heaven* was a fine subtitle for it, but it had to be *Memnoch the Devil.* As soon as I got the name, I knew that was absolutely what it had to be. The original title, *A Dark and Secret Grace*, stemmed from the response of the mortal to the revelations he'd received but couldn't speak of to anyone else. He would say at the end, "I have received a dark and secret grace." That was not appropriate for Lestat at the end of *Memnoch* because of what had happened.

RILEY: *Memnoch* emerged as such a different book from the ideas it originated in. What became of your interest in ghosts appearing to a mortal?

RICE: I didn't actually abandon the idea of wanting to do these various novels with ghosts about moral transformation. So after *Memnoch* I focused on the novel I've just finished, *Servant of the Bones*, which is really about one ghost and one man. Finally, though, the focus is on the ghost. You know, as is typical with me, it shifted from the mortal. I never get too far with mortals. [*laughter*] It shifted from the mortal man who's visited by the ghost to the ghost himself. So the whole thing I've done with this, the career and development and psychology of *Servant of the Bones*, is the ghost and what the ghost wants to do. *Servant of the Bones* again goes into these very themes: God and the Devil, and what are the implications of the religious stories that we say we believe? What do they *really* say to us? What *is* a moral transformation? What *is* a human soul? What *is* a hero? All of that, I'm obsessed with it. And *Servant of the Bones* feels wonderful to me, but it's a very dark novel and the protagonist is this angry ghost. But it started simply with the idea of the three figures who would visit this hit man because of a relic he stumbled on. The idea was that he stole the relic, and the relic produced these apparitions, and they transformed his life. I ended up concentrating on the relic and the apparition, but it's the apparition I care about. So it's wonderfully exciting. I've gone deeper into the Kabbalah and reading Jewish history. It's a novel drenched in Jewish history and persecution, and the ghost is a Jewish ghost. It's Hebrew magic that created him. This all came out of the *Memnoch* reading and the enormous amount of research in all those texts that had to do with God and the Devil. For two years I was immersed in reading Mircea Eliade and Jeffrey Burton Russell, all these different books on religion—Karen Armstrong's *A History of God*, anything I could find that dealt with the history of the concept of heaven, the history of purgatory, Carlo Ginzburg's books on night battles and witchcraft, and the whole evolution of our religious ideas. I plunged into it, and I got as many texts as I could of apocryphal gospels and read them, the Gospel of Enoch and the Gospel of Mary and the Gospel of Thomas. I went through all that material and became totally enchanted with it. By the time I finished, I was left with Lestat going to heaven and hell, and also with the prospect of these other books, *Servant of the Bones* and perhaps some others. But I don't want them to be connected. I don't want another series. I want them to be great supernatural novels, and I want them to involve ghosts, but I want them to be unconnected. So that's where I am now, and I'm eager to go in that direction.

RILEY: From the standpoint of storytelling, what's been most important in this change of direction?

RICE: It all comes out of wanting to shift my moral quest from the concept of monsters to the concept of spirits. I want to get away from the monster to the ghost. I started it with Julien in *The Witching Hour*. I already knew I was going in that direction when Julien appears to Michael. That was my first foray. I didn't go as far with that as I wanted to because I was going to do it later in these other novels, but an idea I had at one point was for Julien to take Michael to Storyville, the famous turn-of-the-century red-light district in New Orleans. I wanted Julien to be able to create an entire world and bring Michael into it and take him out of it. I still want to get into that in future novels, the idea that a ghost can do that, that he can transform the setting around you. In fact, in one very early version of *The Vampire Lestat*, that happened. That version started with a rock singer walking up Prytania Street in New Orleans and suddenly everything around her changes to the nineteenth century, and it's Lestat in that house throwing out the spell, trying to lure her into it. I've always been infatuated with that idea. I've seen it done a couple of times in movies, and I saw a wonderful thing on *Night Gallery*, I think it was, a show with Geraldine Page in any case, where a young girl went to visit her aging aunt and uncle, and the house looked beautiful, and then she'd blink her eyes and see it was all falling into ruin, and then it would look beautiful again. I love that idea of creating illusions. So, in a roundabout way, that's the answer to your question. It started with the idea of ghosts.

RILEY: And Scrooge.

RICE: Yes, and Scrooge. As you know I've always been obsessed with Dickens's *A Christmas Carol*, absolutely obsessed with the idea that three spirits would come to Scrooge and transform him. I mean, I'm overly obsessed with *A Christmas Carol.* I've watched the English film version of it probably more than anyone in history has ever watched it, and read and reread the story, trying to think how to redo a modern version, wanting very much for there to be a new film version, and being furious with the one they did for TV with George C. Scott. Did you see that? It was awful. And *Scrooge*, the one with Albert Finney, which at least was better than nothing. I'll sit and watch that rather than have nothing, but anyway that's where it came from.

I had dealt with vampires; I had dealt even with the mummy; and I wanted to go into a supernatural persona that didn't necessarily have a body. I got it with Julien. I got it with Lasher somewhat, and then, to my utter amazement, Lasher got a body! And I was left with a science fiction dilemma. I really was. At the end of *The Witching Hour* I'd thought I was finished. I thought it was a wonderful ending, but when everybody said, "Well, where did they go? Where did they go?" I realized I had to go into science fiction with this mutant from hell. Somehow, I had to find a way to do it so that I kept the Gothic elements that I wanted, the poetry that I wanted, and the magic that I wanted. That was a real dilemma, because *Lasher* was really just a science fiction plot: Another species comes down and threatens to take over the world. But I had this desire to talk in a more liberated way. I saw it as a progression on the ladder of my heroes, that I would now deal with a ghost, a ghost like Julien, who could tell you a story with a wisdom that was even greater than the wisdom of Marius in *The*

Vampire Chronicles. That's still a novel I want to do, the idea that you can have a revelation that transforms you morally but it's really too awful to tell anyone. I guess that's what I've been playing with all along. Marius tells Lestat, "I'm going to tell you the answers, but they'll be too awful to pass them on to anyone." In *Lasher* it works out a little differently, and it goes a step further in *Taltos*. I really tried to say, yes, the species did exist and this is what they were. I loved the happy ending of *Taltos*, when Ash and Morrigan join hands and run away.

RILEY: Now that *Taltos* has been published in hardcover, what's been your readers' response?

RICE: To me that has yet to be judged as a work. The book is just beginning its journey. When a book is out in hardcover and it's still on the bestseller list, I don't know how my readers have responded yet. They don't really tell me how they've received a book until the paperback comes out. They may buy the hardcover in huge numbers, but it takes a little time for the letters and the phone calls and for the response to catch up. Even now, *Lasher* has yet to be in mass-market paperback, and the paperback of *Taltos* is still some months away, so I'm a little bit behind. The hardcover numbers are fine on *Taltos*. The sales are huge, but I have a lot of readers out there who haven't caught up with *Lasher* yet, and they haven't caught up with *Taltos*. I'll be very excited to see how they feel, because in a way I'd like to leave the Taltos story there. I feel that's the end of it. It's like the journey of that gene, or whatever it was, that giant helix, made its way through the family to create Morrigan, and Ash, and we have to trust that Ash is not going to let anything catastrophic happen when he goes off with Morrigan.

I have worked out this other book that would continue the story, but again it gets so much into the realm of science fiction that I'd rather not do it. I'd rather go to Mona and do a book all about Mona and Mary Jane in which we know that the Taltos have survived, but in secret, with no particular repercussions for the family or the world. But when I was planning the sequel, which would be called *Morrigan*, it was going to be very much an "us against the world" story. I was really thinking big, but I backed off from it, just as I did after *The Queen of the Damned.* It got too big, too much comic book grandeur, you know, Morrigan taking over the world with Ash's fortune. Then I thought, wait a minute! [*laughter*] I was getting too far away from what I really care about. But that was quite a challenge. I'd done an enormous amount of research for *Morrigan.* I did research on an island called Saint Kilda in the Outer Hebrides, where Ash and Morrigan are supposed to go. I sent to England for books on Saint Kilda, and the stories of the Hebrides are just incredible. Did you go to them? Did you go to Skye? Kathie Ramsland did when she was researching *The Witches' Companion.* She went to Iona. But I haven't been there. I've read everything I can read on those islands. I know how they get their electricity and everything. I had this whole novel planned. That's where the plane would take Ash and Morrigan, and the conflicts would begin with the family. I may still do it. I don't know. In any event, it had its moment and it burst for me. I wrote a few chapters and it was fun, but I really wanted to do this darker book, this ghost and *Servant of the Bones*. I wanted to get back to those images that came to me even before *Memnoch*, images of particular things I wanted to deal with, moments in history. I'm obsessed with certain moments. There's a moment during the Black Death, you know, when all over Europe Jews were burned alive! They were walled up in the ghettos of their cities, and they were burned alive. I've been obsessed with that vision, and I deal with that in *Servant of the Bones*, that historical event, how these things happened.

I read history all the time, and in the last few years it's been not only religious history but a tremendous amount of military history as well. I've been captivated by the idea of what happened in 500 A.D.—how Cassiodorus and Boethius were really the last two educated Roman gentlemen, and how when they died Italy went dark for something like two hundred years. Nobody even knows what was going on in Italy, but we know Cassiodorus had this beautiful monastery called the Vivarium. Well, I'll get to that. That was going to be in *Morrigan*, and Cassiodorus and Boethius were going to have to do with the origins of the Talamasca. And I'll get there eventually. It's amazing how much of this material is already out there for me, and it's very developed in my imagination. But this is the way I do it. I consider three or four things at once. They're like people at the door sort of shuffling around trying to get in, and finally somebody goes through the door. Now it's been *Servant of the Bones*. But I might well go back to Cassiodorus and the Vivarium and do a novel on the Talamasca and its origins.

RILEY: You've been reading a great deal in science, too.

RICE: I read all the time in science, trying to figure out

how to use what we know about evolution and about anatomy as inspirations for these things. It's wonderfully interesting. I was reading *The Scars of Evolution* last night, all about how the savanna theory doesn't work, and I was just amazed. Novels were coming to me already about Morrigan and the Taltos. My brain was just racing. That's become my world. And people are hungry for that. They're hungry for a world in which they can lose themselves, and again and again they ask entertainment to give them that. They go all out. Look at the response to *Twin Peaks*, for example. They just rolled out the red carpet and said, "Give us a whole world." People went around New York every day discussing it. But *Twin Peaks* stopped with *Twin Peaks*. That was the choice. The same thing has been done with *Star Trek*, but in a sense that material can yield a lot more complexity and depth than the *Star Trek* people have given audiences. My readers are very similar. It's a whole world to them. They love moving around in it, arguing about it, talking about it. Katherine Ramsland's books, *The Vampire Companion* and *The Witches' Companion*, reflect that. It's a wonderful world for me to live in. I know I'm very lucky that anybody wants to read any of it. To be able to do that and make a living at it is just incredible.

RILEY: Since you completed *Memnoch* there has been a very surprising development—at least it surprised me and I suspect it will many of your readers. You've said, "Lestat walked off on me . . . it was just like the wind. I felt it. It happened. I couldn't control it." Can you tell me more about this? When did it happen, and how would you explain its significance?

RICE: The night I finished the final page proof corrections of *Memnoch*—of which there were very few—I felt that the character of Lestat left me. It was as if he left my imagination, my creative world, as if the person of Lestat waved good-bye and walked away. He seemed to be saying, "I have no more tales to tell you. Whatever you write must be about new things." Yet I'm hesitant to talk about new directions in my work. Frequently I've planned and described whole novels that I've ended up not writing. People still ask me about them at book signings, and I have to confess that though I spoke of that planned novel at length in an interview, the novel itself was never born. But this is certain: After finishing those last notes on *Memnoch* I turned to an entirely new character, Azriel, a ghost, and I began and finished *Servant of the Bones*. This new novel was very emotional for me. I felt very close to Azriel, loving him very much, and the novel was finally the realization of a very elaborate plot. I succeeded in putting down on paper what I saw in my dreams. This isn't always the case, you know. As I was saying earlier, it wasn't the case with *Feast of All Saints* or even *Interview with the Vampire*. But Azriel and *Servant of the Bones* has turned out just the way I wanted it to be. I'm proud of it, and have a feeling of satisfaction when I think of it. It involved a whole new period of history for me: 600 B.C. and our Hebrew heritage. It's the heritage of all of us in the West, and the completion of this book, the full creation of it, was a challenge. At this point Lestat as a character, hero, inspiration, teller of tales is still absent. There are two novels I very much want to do now, and they will not involve Lestat. At least not directly.

The period I'm enjoying now—before a finished novel

is published and before I've begun a new novel—is always very fertile. All influences are a joy. For instance, I just saw *Immortal Beloved*, the film about Beethoven starring Gary Oldman, and this was very inspiring because it reminded me of what the heart of Romantic art really is: a commitment to describe how you feel. This film seemed to state the case for Romanticism better than any I've seen. It spurred me to return to something filled with feeling, no matter how dark, and perhaps turn away from the large theological conversations that dominate my latest two books, *Memnoch* and *Servant*.

RILEY: Did you have any hint of Lestat's departure before it happened?

RICE: Before he left I had no hint that he would, except that I didn't have another story with him to tell. I usually have stories with Lestat in my head. I don't now.

RILEY: Why do you think he left?

RICE: I feel it's time to move on. Lestat has made it easy for me to say and do many things in writing. But I have other things I want to do. I feel quite unfinished as a writer and a person. I feel as though I'm only just beginning to see what is important, and I look forward to complex novels that are greater challenges to me than those I've done. Perhaps Lestat closes a phase of my creative search. I don't know. I know that as long as I don't have Lestat with me novels will be a great challenge. Creating Azriel was more difficult. I knew and loved him, but I had to find a way to also make him vivid and utterly familiar to the reader.

RILEY: Listening to you talk about the *Chronicles*, I've sometimes thought that while Lestat is a character you created, a child of your imagination, he gradually became more than that to you. It's almost as if he became your collaborator.

RICE: He did become more than a character. He was a voice, a way of looking at the world, a person who I could automatically become. There was no work to sliding into Lestat. I just became him at will and went around the world as him. Having written so much about him and from his point of view, I found it easy to begin Lestat's last two novels, *Memnoch* and *Tale of the Body Thief*. Both the reader and I knew so much, I could get right to the story. Lestat was a "me." He was a frame of mind I could put on with ease. In some ways he was the dream figure of a strong male me, a doer rather than a watcher, an actor rather than a victim. He greatly expanded my literary work, because *Cry to Heaven*, *Feast of All Saints*, and *Interview with the Vampire* were much more about people who are smothered or trapped. When Lestat made his mother Gabrielle a vampire in *The Vampire Lestat*, I broke free as a writer from the more personal, "I am suffering" point of view and started talking about large issues that concerned me.

RILEY: How do you feel about this change now that it's come about?

RICE: Lestat's leaving isn't sad. It means yet another phase. It means I've taken that phase as far as I can and now I must go on to other things. What a writer writes about is always a mystery. Evidence of expanding creativity means writing books about all the different periods of your life as you live them. Your early work may be about adolescence, loss, being trapped, hurt, disappointed. But then you must go on to the experience of being an adult, knowing some creative success, choosing a definite way to live your life—among family or alone, married or alone, or whatever. The phases continue. I don't want to analyze too carefully, but I dread being a writer who only writes about the first phase of growing up or knowing. In *Servant of the Bones*, through Azriel I feel I'm talking about the sheer loneliness of being a mature adult, the moral pressure of each decision on a moral person, but a person who has no teacher or church or family to uphold him.

Of course, that's only one way of looking at the novel. It's also about the refusal to be bad, and so are *The Vampire Chronicles*. In the West we grow up with the concept of original sin, which means in all creeds, it seems, that we are flawed, we have fallen, we are bad and must be redeemed. That's the basis of Catholicism as well as Protestantism, and I venture to say the basis of Judaism too. Now I'm looking for a new way to see us. I'm looking for a new neutrality or secularism from which to start to make a moral world, a good world. In other words, forget an inherited sin or flaw. Say we are simply here and we are not inherently bad or inherently innocent either. We are simply human. But the obligation to be good remains. In fact, it becomes even more pressing because in a secular world we are both child and parent. All this concerns me as much as any issue in my family life or my personal life. I see any good novel as having a scope beyond the personal. So perhaps Lestat had taken me as far as we could go together with these larger questions that obsess me now in middle life.

RILEY: We were speaking about *Memnoch* as an outgrowth of the themes at the heart of *The Vampire Chronicles* ever since *Interview*. Does Lestat's departure mark not only the closure of those themes, but of the *Chronicles* overall? Here I'm thinking of what you said earlier when you mentioned the freedom you felt to write novels about other characters in the world of the *Chronicles*. You've mentioned Gabrielle, for example, several times during these conversations. Might the *Chronicles* go on without Lestat?

RICE: I believe there'll be at least one more, although not about Lestat or from his point of view. It will be almost an emotional or romantic epilogue to the *Chronicles*. I thought of it while I was watching *Immortal Beloved*. At present I see it as a short novel or novella, but then for me that means three hundred to four hundred pages in manuscript, which for many other people is a full novel. I see this Epilogue novel as rather irrational but moving. Extreme, eccentric, darkly colored, and very emotional. But then it may never get written.

RILEY: Are there themes in the *Chronicles* that aren't completed for you yet? And if so, do they claim a place in *Servant of the Bones* or other novels you envision?

RICE: There really aren't themes in the *Chronicles* that I feel are incomplete. In the Epilogue novel I want to write something that is dedicated to my readers and to the response to me they've shown, a kind of song. Now I think I need new novels to talk about new themes. If we talk purely about the pleasure of writing, I'm eager to do a great ghost story like Henry James's *Turn of the Screw*. *The Witching Hour* started out that way—a house holds a ghost and a mystery—but it mutated into something else entirely. I want to return to the ghost story. I think we've only scratched the surface of what the ghost story can do, and its theme is absolutely eternal. People see ghosts all the time!

The reports never really stop. All you have to do is gather some friends and ask, and someone will be able to describe a fairly chilling ghost story of some sort. It may involve only a voice or a presence rather than an apparition. But to know "ghosts" is fairly common, and our literature really hasn't had that much fun with the idea. So I see ghost novels and stories ahead. I see perhaps another novel involving ancient Egypt. I want to write about the origins of the Talamasca, the fictional psychic detective order that appears in my novels.

Naturally, I write obsessively about what concerns me, and the big danger is repetition. I want each novel to involve fresh ideas, fresh solutions, and, above all, fresh characters and new and beautiful ways to discuss love. History enthralls me because it continues to make me think about one thing: Who are we and what are we? Why can we be kind to one another when animals seem to know nothing about the concept? The older I get, the more love and kindness matter to me more than anything else.

RILEY: And with the publication of this new book, *Memnoch the Devil*, the whole phenomenon, the intense absorption of your readers in this fictional world, is beginning all over again.

RICE: This is the mystery of my life. I can't explain it. I have my own world with my readers, and it's a gigantic world. If people don't know anything about it, it's very hard to describe to them what it is. But once they read the books, they either turn away very early and say, "This is just not for me, I don't like this," or they become part of this world, and they like all of the books. Over and over again, they call and say it's like entering into a whole world. The word "franchise" keeps coming up. They've come up with this word for *Star Trek*, and that's what it's like. It's like a great creative franchise. It's like a universe—"The World of Anne Rice"—and I didn't know I was doing it. What it is is the result of my inability to conform to anybody else's idea of what a book should be. They all came out highly individualistic and yet they had things in common. They were sort of outrageous and didn't fit in anywhere, but there are now thirteen or fourteen of them, and they do make an entire world. And people are buying into that world. They come and say, "We've heard of you and, yes, now we get it, and we love these characters. And what's going to happen next?" The books have a tremendous impact for them. Somehow they create a universe in which the readers can lose themselves, and I love it. I absolutely love it.

About the Author

Michael Riley is professor of film and literature at Claremont McKenna College. A contributing editor of *Literature/Film Quarterly*, he has published numerous critical essays and interviews and is the coauthor of *The Films of Joseph Losey*. He lives in Pasadena, California.